Monks and Markets

MONKS AND MARKETS

Durham Cathedral Priory 1460–1520

MIRANDA THRELFALL-HOLMES

OXFORD
UNIVERSITY PRESS

OXFORD

UNIVERSITY PRESS

Great Clarendon Street, Oxford OX2 6DP

Oxford University Press is a department of the University of Oxford.
It furthers the University's objective of excellence in research, scholarship,
and education by publishing worldwide in

Oxford New York

Auckland Bangkok Buenos Aires Cape Town Chennai
Dar es Salaam Delhi Hong Kong Istanbul Karachi Kolkata
Kuala Lumpur Madrid Melbourne Mexico City Mumbai Nairobi
São Paulo Shanghai Taipei Tokyo Toronto

Oxford is a registered trade mark of Oxford University Press
in the UK and in certain other countries

Published in the United States
by Oxford University Press Inc., New York

© Miranda Threlfall-Holmes 2005

The moral rights of the author have been asserted
Database right Oxford University Press (maker)

First published 2005

All rights reserved. No part of this publication may be reproduced,
stored in a retrieval system, or transmitted, in any form or by any means,
without the prior permission in writing of Oxford University Press,
or as expressly permitted by law, or under terms agreed with the appropriate
reprographics rights organization. Enquiries concerning reproduction
outside the scope of the above should be sent to the Rights Department,
Oxford University Press, at the address above

You must not circulate this book in any other binding or cover
and you must impose this same condition on any acquirer

British Library Cataloguing in Publication Data
Data available

Library of Congress Cataloging in Publication Data
Data available

ISBN 0-19-925381-1

1 3 5 7 9 10 8 6 4 2

Typeset in 10/12pt Sabon by Graphicraft Limited, Hong Kong
Printed in Great Britain
on acid-free paper by
Biddles Ltd
King's Lynn, Norfolk

Acknowledgements

It is a pleasure to be able to acknowledge all the help that I have been given by so many people in the course of my research. Grants from the Humanities Research Board of the British Academy funded the MA and Ph.D. on which this book is based, and the History Department of the University of Durham gave me both grants and encouragement to attend and present papers at a number of conferences. I am grateful to the Chapter of Durham Cathedral for permission to use their extensive archives, and to all the archive staff, especially Mr Alan Piper, for their assistance. I also thank all those who were working on the Durham archives alongside me for their friendship and help in sharing information and ideas, and I owe special thanks to Dr Christine Newman and Dr Lynda Rollason for allowing me access to their databases for the comparison of our findings.

Going further back, Professor Barrie Dobson and Professor Peter Spufford both encouraged and inspired me to pursue historical research when I was an undergraduate, and later helped me to focus on an area for research, and showed a continued interest in my work. Dr Beth Hartland and Dr Kathryn Rix also gave me invaluable friendship, support, constructive comments, and the encouragement of fellow historians at the same stage of research.

My husband Phil has given me a great deal of support over the eight years that this book has been in the making. I am very grateful to him for encouraging me to do the research, for believing in my abilities, and for supporting me emotionally and financially throughout. My parents, and my parents-in-law, have also given me encouragement and inspiration.

But above all I must thank my supervisor Professor Richard Britnell, to whom I owe an immense debt of gratitude. His guidance, advice, and encouragement have been unflagging. He encouraged me to write articles and give papers, and so gave me the opportunity to test out many of the ideas in this book and receive much useful comment and criticism. His interest in and enthusiasm for my research has kept me going through all the ups and downs. He and Jenny have become lifelong friends to Phil and me, and our son Noah. Thank you.

M.T.-H.

Contents

List of Figures   ix

List of Tables   x

1   Introduction and Context   1
    Introduction   1
    The Regional Context   6
    Durham Cathedral Priory   14
    Administrative Strategies: The Accounting System
       at Durham Cathedral Priory   17
    A Snapshot of the Priory's Accounting System: 1480/1   22
    Conclusion   32

2   The Monastic Diet   34
    Introduction   34
    The Provisioning Infrastructure of the Priory   35
    Purchasing and Consumption   36
    Conclusion   71

3   Price, Preference, and Purpose: Factors Influencing
    the Priory's Purchasing Decisions   75
    Introduction   75
    Price as a Determining Factor: Grain   76
    Preference as a Determining Factor: Wine and Spices   89
    Purpose as a Determining Factor: The Priory's
       Cloth Purchases   102
    Conclusion   133

4   Tenurial Purchasing   136
    Introduction   136
    Grain   138
    Meat, Fish, and Other Commodities   145

Sources of Supply   148
Conclusion   160

5 Market Purchasing   162
   Introduction   162
   Market Purchases of Grain and the Regionality of
      Grain Prices   163
   Markets   171
   The Use of Agents   175
   Payment for Goods   177
   Credit   179
   Transport   181
   Conclusion   190

6 The Suppliers of the Priory   192
   Introduction   192
   Numbers of Suppliers and Repeat Suppliers   193
   Wider Relationships between the Priory and its
      Suppliers   195
   Commodity Specialists and Generalists   197
   Families and Locations   203
   Male and Female Suppliers   207
   Case Study: The Suppliers of Cloth   209
   Conclusion   218

7 Conclusion   220
   Standards of Living   220
   The Priory as a Consumer   222
   The State of Trade in Newcastle and the North-East   226
   Concluding Remarks   229

Appendix   The surviving obedientiary accounts,
           1460–1520   231

Bibliography   233

Index   245

List of Figures

2.1 Amount of each type of grain bought by the bursar, 1460–1520 42

2.2 Weekly consumption of wheat by the priory, 1460–1520 46

3.1 Mode price of each grain variety, 1460–1520 79

3.2 Differentials between the price of wheat and of other grains, 1464–1520 80

3.3 Impact of price changes on the amount of wheat bought by the bursar, 1460–1520 82

3.4 Total amount of grain bought by the bursar each year, 1460–1520 84

3.5 Stockpiling and the use of the granary, 1460–1520 86

3.6 Average price paid for wine by the bursar and the amount bought each year, 1464–1520 91

3.7 Prices paid by the priory for dried fruit, 1464–1520 94

3.8 Prices paid by the priory for sugar, 1464–1520 96

3.9 Price paid for hardyn and the amount bought by the bursar, 1464–1520 106

3.10 Price paid for sackcloth and the amount bought by the bursar, 1464–1520 108

3.11 Price paid by the priory for linen, 1464–1520 111

3.12 Price paid for linen and the amount bought by the bursar, 1464–1520 115

3.13 Prices paid by the bursar for livery cloth, 1464–1520 125

4.1 Locations of suppliers to the priory, according to expenditure, 1460–1520 150

4.2 Map showing the distribution of the priory's grain purchases in 1495/6 153

4.3 Map showing the distribution of the priory's poultry purchases, 1465–1515 155

6.1 Distribution of cloth suppliers by average transaction value, 1464–1520 211

List of Tables

1.1 Breakdown of the Durham obedientiaries' expenditure, 1480/1   24

2.1 The quantity of various foods consumed by Durham Cathedral Priory in 1474/5   37

2.2 The amounts of the principal varieties of meat and fish recorded in the sampled bursar/cellarer indentures, 1465–1515   48

2.3 Estimated weight per annum of meat and fish served at Durham and Westminster in the late 15th century   50

3.1 Average mode price of grain and granary movements in adjacent years, 1471–1513   88

4.1 Rental payments made in grain by tenants of Cowpen Bewley, 1495–1510   143

5.1 Grain price indices at Durham compared with those for England overall, 1461–1520   169

5.2 Comparison of harvest qualities for Durham and England overall, 1460–1520   170

5.3 Transport costs for livery cloth consignments, 1465–1505   185

6.1 Place names mentioned in association with wine and iron, 1464–1520   206

6.2 Number of cloth transactions per supplier, 1464–1520   210

6.3 Average number of transactions per supplier for various types of cloth, 1464–1520   212

6.4 Distribution of hardyn transactions between identifiable suppliers, 1464–1520   216

6.5 Distribution of linen transactions between identifiable suppliers, 1464–1520   217

6.6 Cloth-type specialism amongst suppliers of cloth to Durham Cathedral Priory, 1464–1520   218

A1 The surviving obedientiary accounts, 1460–1520   232

Introduction and Context

INTRODUCTION

There is a general view that the middle ages were tradition-bound. Only with the advent of the early modern period, runs the conventional wisdom, did individuals and institutions begin to exercise choice, experiment with new ways of doing things, look around them at their social, economic, and political contexts and invent relevant and intelligent responses. The institutions of the middle ages are generally seen as unreflective, unresponsive, and uninnovative. This is of course a caricature of an attitude, but it is a recognizable caricature of a very common attitude. And when it comes to the church, and especially to monasteries, this point of view is even more firmly and widely held. Monks are seen as being, metaphorically as well as literally, creatures of habit. So if we were to find that a large and ancient monastery was in fact very conscious of both the strengths and weaknesses of its traditions, was prepared to undertake drastic experiments to address the weaknesses, and was exercising rational choice in response to a wide range of changing circumstances, this would be of decisive relevance to our understanding of the medieval mindset and in particular for our understanding of how medieval institutions operated and the range of strategies and options available to them.

This was the case at Durham Cathedral Priory in the later fifteenth century. The findings presented in this study therefore force us to reconsider any remaining prejudice against medieval institutions, and monasteries in particular, as hidebound by tradition and unable to adapt to rapidly changing circumstances. Interestingly, the few recent studies that have explicitly considered questions surrounding marketing and purchasing strategies have concluded that rational choice and considered strategic thinking lay behind much of what they have found. For example, Stone has come to this conclusion in his recent study of medieval farm management and technological mentalities, whilst Dyer found that clergy in the West Midlands were 'discriminating and sophisticated purchasers'.[1] Durham's outstanding archive has allowed an unprecedented level of detail about the purchasing strategies of one of England's foremost monasteries to be uncovered, and it can be seen that the monks were indeed reflective, responsive, and innovative when such qualities were called for. If this is true of a large Benedictine monastery, it is likely to be true to at least the same extent for the vast majority of other households and institutions in medieval England for which comparable evidence does not exist.

Furthermore, this material allows us a unique insight into the nature of medieval consumer behaviour, which throughout history, and particularly from before the early modern period, remains a relatively neglected subject. This neglect seems to have resulted from a combination of deficiencies in the available evidence, together with a lingering sense that the medieval buyer was somehow an inhabitant of a pre-commercial 'golden age', free from the essentially modern taint of consumerism. The economic history of the middle ages has tended to concentrate on international trade, on the big merchant companies, and on estates and farming. That is to say, the main focus of medieval economic history has been on the suppliers of goods. Yet discussions of the development of markets, cash crops, transport, protectionist policies, and so on all presuppose the existence of a large cohort of consumers, ready and apparently eager to buy the goods discussed once they reach the port, market, or fair. Undoubtedly, the consumer was an important consideration in the supply chain, then as now. Whilst medieval and modern consumerism are of course very different phenomena, nevertheless the importance placed on the consumer in modern economic theory should alert us to the relative neglect of the procuring of goods and services in medieval studies. As Dyer has argued, 'Consumption deserves more research, and a long-term aim must be to identify the buyers, to see what they bought, and from whom, and how purchases were organised.'[2]

---

[1] D. Stone, 'Medieval Farm Management and Technological Mentalities: Hinderclay before the Black Death', *Economic History Review*, 54 (2001), 629–30, 634; C. Dyer, 'Trade, Towns and the Church: Ecclesiastical Consumers and the Urban Economy of the West Midlands, 1290–1540', in T. Slater and G. Rosser (eds.), *The Church in the Medieval Town* (Aldershot, 1998), 71.

[2] C. Dyer, *Everyday Life in Medieval England* (London, 1996), 257.

The Durham archives provide a rare and valuable glimpse into the mind of a major medieval consumer. The survival of substantial series of detailed purchasing accounts, together with a supporting cast of letters, rent-books, and other material, has allowed an analysis of patterns of consumer behaviour over a period of some sixty years. This reveals how the monks reacted to changing circumstances such as price movements, harvest failures, and structural changes in the nature and locations of industries in both the short and the long term. Dramatic differences are also revealed between the strategies used in the selection and purchasing of different commodities, so that in some cases we can see diametrically opposed reactions to the same changed variable, such as a price increase, in two different categories of goods. It becomes clear that issues of choice, the availability of competition, taste, fashion, and personal preference must all be factored in with the more commonly discussed concepts of need and tradition in seeking to understand the habits and whims, strategies and choices of the medieval consumer. Moreover, such considerations applied not only to what goods were purchased, but also to a whole range of supplementary questions such as how those goods were bought, and from whom, when, where, in what quantities, and how and when they were paid for.

These insights bring a fuller coloration to the picture of the economic history of medieval England that we have at present. The shape of England's international trade has been discussed by many historians, using records of imports and exports and of the big merchant companies.[3] Several of the latter have attracted analysis in their own right, and certain particularly well-documented industries have also been discussed in some detail.[4] Attempts to dig beneath the surface of the records that we have of economic activity of late medieval England and examine in detail the economic structures, trading networks, and consumption patterns of a variety of levels in society, however, are plagued by the vagaries of the surviving evidence. Whilst a great deal of relevant material has indeed survived, much of

---

[3] e.g. W. R. Childs, *Anglo-Castilian Trade in the Later Middle Ages* (Manchester, 1978), and E. Ashtor, *Levant Trade in the Later Middle Ages* (Princeton, 1983).
[4] Notable studies of merchant companies include E. M. Carus-Wilson, *Medieval Merchant Venturers* (London, 1954); P. Nightingale, *A Medieval Mercantile Community* (London, 1995); and S. L. Thrupp, *The Merchant Class of Medieval London (1300–1500)* (Chicago, 1948). Studies of particular industries include M. K. James, *Studies in the Medieval Wine Trade*, ed. E. M. Veale (Oxford, 1971), and A. R. Bridbury, *Medieval English Clothmaking: An Economic Survey* (London, 1982).

it is inevitably fragmentary or consists of single examples.[5] Nevertheless, much valuable work has been done. For example, Dyer has been
able to shed a great deal of light on standards of living at all levels of
society, whilst the household accounts of noble households have
been discussed by Woolgar.[6] For monastic households, Harvey's
study of Westminster provides an unusually detailed discussion of
many facets of late medieval life (and indeed death).[7] The provisioning of Cambridge and its colleges has been studied by Cobban and
Lee, whilst the costs associated with medieval transactions have been
analysed by North and by Kowaleski.[8]

  In addition, the ways in which medieval consumers used markets
have been discussed in some depth by both Harvey and Dyer.
Barbara Harvey's work on the purchasing of magnate households in
the long thirteenth century has demonstrated the importance of magnate demand in the economy as a whole, and has exposed the essentially sporadic and ambivalent relationship which existed at that time
between such major consumers and the market.[9] Christopher Dyer

  [5] The most comprehensive list of surviving medieval household records is to be
found as Appendix A to K. Mertes, *The English Noble Household, 1250–1600*
(Oxford, 1988).
  [6] The standard text on medieval standards of living remains C. Dyer, *Standards of
Living in the Later Middle Ages: Social Change in England c.1200–1520* (Cambridge,
1989). Detailed studies on particular aspects of consumption include C. Dyer, 'The
Consumption of Fresh-water Fish in Medieval England', in M. Aston (ed.), *Medieval
Fish, Fisheries and Fishponds in England* (British Archaeological Reports, British
Ser., 182; Oxford, 1988), and C. Dyer, 'English Diet in the Later Middle Ages', in
T. H. Aston *et al.* (eds.), *Social Relations and Ideas* (Cambridge, 1983). Woolgar's
work on great households is available in C. M. Woolgar (ed.), *Household Accounts
from Medieval England*, 2 vols. (Oxford, 1992, 1993), and C. M. Woolgar, *The
Great Household in Late Medieval England* (New Haven, 1999).
  [7] B. Harvey, *Living and Dying in England 1100–1540: The Monastic Experience*
(Oxford, 1993); B. Harvey, *Westminster Abbey and its Estates in the Middle Ages*
(Oxford, 1977); B. Harvey and J. Oeppen, 'Patterns of Morbidity in Late Medieval
England: A Sample from Westminster Abbey', *Economic History Review*, 54 (2001);
B. Harvey, *The Obedientiaries of Westminster Abbey and their Financial Records,
c.1275–1540* (Woodbridge, 2002).
  [8] A. B. Cobban, *The King's Hall within the University of Cambridge in the Later
Middle Ages* (Cambridge, 1969), 112–47; J. S. Lee, 'Feeding the Colleges: Cam-
bridge's Food and Fuel Supplies, 1450–1560', *Economic History Review*, 56 (2003);
D. C. North, 'Transaction Costs in History', *Journal of European Economic History*,
14 (1985); M. Kowaleski, *Local Markets and Regional Trade in Medieval Exeter*
(Cambridge, 1995), 179–221.
  [9] B. Harvey, 'The Aristocratic Consumer in England in the Long Thirteenth
Century', in M. Prestwich *et al.* (eds.), *Thirteenth Century England 6: Proceedings of
the Durham Conference* (Woodbridge, 1997).

has extensively considered the location of purchases, looking at markets and extra-market trading.[10] In particular, he has found that much trade took place outside official markets, and in common with Harvey concludes that small towns did not necessarily benefit a great deal from the presence of a large household nearby. Of particular relevance to this study and to its wider implications is Dyer's conclusion that there was little distinction in geographical purchasing patterns between lay and clerical households, despite what one might expect given the greater stability and the collective nature of religious houses.[11]

In this context, the Durham records provide a uniquely rich resource, allowing an analysis of a large consumer's market participation over a long period, and so enabling a slice or snapshot of their economic activities at local, regional, and national levels to be seen. By using a substantial series of accounts from a major consumer, rather than the records of a single town, village, estate, or farm, it is possible to see how a range of such places fit into the provisioning and marketing strategies used by a substantial local institution and so to establish a sense of their relative importance and individual roles. Whilst this is at heart a detailed study of a single consumer, it seems probable that what we find here will have much wider implications for our understanding of medieval consumers and the medieval market.

Above all, the findings presented here enable us to gain some insight into the thought processes behind a major medieval consumer's purchasing and consumption. The strength of the Durham evidence is that its scale and breadth enables us to see beyond the bare facts of what was purchased, where, for what price, and from whom, and to begin to understand the purchasing strategies employed by the monks. We can begin to comprehend not just what they bought and from whom they bought it, but why they made those decisions. In doing so, it will become clear that the caricature of a tradition-bound, unreflective medieval monk with which we began is very far from the truth.

---

[10] C. Dyer, 'The Consumer and the Market in the Later Middle Ages', *Economic History Review*, 2nd ser., 42 (1989); C. Dyer, 'Trade, Towns and the Church'.
[11] Ibid. 67–8.

THE REGIONAL CONTEXT

The pattern of trade in England in the fifteenth century has been characterized as one of depression for the first quarter of the century, followed by recovery in the second quarter, depression again in the third quarter and finally prosperity for the last twenty-five years of the century.[12] The classic picture portrayed has been one of a general atmosphere of decline or at best of stagnation, and particularly of an urban crisis affecting the majority of England's towns.[13] But other historians have seen growth and entrepreneurial development, and have pointed to the flourishing of certain towns as an exception to, or even a refutation of, the received wisdom.[14] Overall, the emerging consensus is that the fifteenth century saw both growth and decline side by side in different areas, with neighbouring towns often experiencing very different turns of fortune.

The north-east region does not appear to have provided an exception to the general pattern of the economy in this period. Pollard has argued that 'like the rest of Europe, north-east England passed through an extended economic crisis in the later middle ages. The major factors were climatic deterioration, war damage and above all, population decline.' He concluded that 'the fifteenth century after 1440 was a bleak era in the economic history of the north-east'.[15] However, the variety of fortunes found across the country seems to have been mirrored in the region. Dobson was unpersuaded by arguments that the north-east suffered badly in this period, concluding that 'the prevailing impression left by the sources we have is of severe adversity successfully faced and eventually surmounted' by all classes.[16] Newcastle, along with other towns such as Chester, Exeter, and Colchester, was notably exempted by Pythian-Adams from the

---

[12] H. L. Gray, 'English Foreign Trade from 1446 to 1482', in E. Power and M. M. Postan (eds.), *Studies in English Trade in the Fifteenth Century* (London, 1966), 1.

[13] See e.g. R. B. Dobson, 'Urban Decline in Medieval England', *Transactions of the Royal Historical Society*, 5th ser., 27 (1977), and C. Pythian-Adams, *Desolation of a City: Coventry and the Urban Crisis of the Late Middle Ages* (Cambridge, 1979).

[14] A. Dyer, 'Urban Decline in England, 1377–1525', in T. R. Slater (ed.), *Towns in Decline, A.D. 100–1600* (Aldershot, 2000). Pythian-Adams, *Desolation*, 19, notes that towns such as Exeter, Newcastle, and Reading may be considered 'the "success" stories', exceptions from the general picture of decay.

[15] A. J. Pollard, *North-Eastern England during the Wars of the Roses* (Oxford, 1990), 43, 78.

[16] R. B. Dobson, *Durham Cathedral Priory, 1400–1450* (Cambridge, 1973), 253.

general picture of decline which he saw as prevalent from the early sixteenth century; he argued that towns like these, 'ports or centres on navigable rivers . . . acted as outlets for their neighbouring industrial hinterlands' and as such 'survived reasonably unscathed'.[17] However, the lack of satisfactory evidence which is endemic to medieval studies is particularly acute for the north-east. The evidence available for the history of medieval Newcastle in particular is notoriously limited, with only a handful of municipal records having survived from before the sixteenth century, forcing Dobson to conclude that it was almost pointless to ask how Newcastle fared in this period, since virtually no evidence could be brought to bear on the issue.[18]

However, the expenditure recorded in the Durham Cathedral Priory obedientiary accounts can shine a ray of light on patterns of trade in the north-east and on the economy of Newcastle in the late medieval period. Using the accounts of a substantial local consumer to investigate the extent and structure of trade in the Durham and Newcastle area provides a fresh perspective on these issues. The wide range of purchasing information from substantial series of years which is detailed in the Durham obedientiary accounts can provide valuable insights into the range and extent of trading activity both in Newcastle itself and throughout the north-east region. As will be seen in the following study, the evidence from Durham Cathedral Priory indicates Newcastle's considerable importance as a centre for trade and distribution in the late medieval period, and moreover that this importance increased over the course of the fifteenth and early sixteenth centuries.

[17] C. Pythian-Adams and P. Slack, *The Traditional Community under Stress* (Milton Keynes, 1977), 16.

[18] Dobson, 'Urban Decline', 19. Despite this limitation, a substantial body of work has been built up by the resourceful use of the documentary evidence that does remain, such as customs accounts. See e.g. J. F. Wade, 'The Overseas Trade of Newcastle upon Tyne in the Late Middle Ages', *Northern History*, 30 (1994); J. F. Wade (ed.), *The Customs Accounts of Newcastle-upon-Tyne 1454–1500* (Surtees Society, 202, 1995); C. M. Fraser (ed.), *Accounts of the Chamberlains of Newcastle-upon-Tyne, 1508–1511* (The Society of Antiquaries of Newcastle-upon-Tyne, Record Ser., 3, 1987). Rents from Newcastle properties belonging to University College, Oxford have also been analysed, in A. F. Butcher, 'Rent, Population and Economic Change in Late-Medieval Newcastle', *Northern History*, 14 (1978). Work on the earlier middle ages has included J. Conway Davies, 'Shipping and Trade in Newcastle upon Tyne, 1294–1296', *Archaeologia Aeliana*, 4th ser., 31 (1953); J. Conway Davies, 'The Wool Customs Accounts of Newcastle upon Tyne for the reign of Edward I', *Archaeologia Aeliana*, 4th ser., 32 (1954); and C. M. Fraser, 'The Pattern of Trade in the North-East of England, 1265–1350', *Northern History*, 4 (1969).

The agricultural and industrial profile of the region around Durham was a mixed one. On a macro level, the agricultural geography of Britain has been characterized as being divided into two broad areas, with pastoral country predominating to the north and west and arable country to the south and east of a line running from Teesmouth or Tynemouth in the north-east to Weymouth or Exmouth in the south-west.[19] In other words, this conventional dividing line bisected the north-east region. In keeping with this, a great variety of husbandry and cultivation can be seen to have been in operation across the region.[20] In the area centred on Durham itself, pasture tended to be concentrated on the moor land to the west, and arable farming on the eastern lowlands, although there were also extensive moor lands to the east.[21] The priory purchased large quantities of cattle, sheep, pigs, many types of poultry, wheat, barley, oats, corn, and freshwater and seawater fish from the region, as well as smaller amounts of other foodstuffs such as honey.[22]

In addition to this wide range of farming activity, the region also possessed notable mineral resources, including iron, lead, and coal, all of which were commercially exploited to some degree throughout the medieval period.[23] Lead mining was only sporadic for much of the fifteenth century, prices having collapsed around 1406, but there is evidence of a significant revival in the industry in 1471/2, and by the 1490s the export market in Yorkshire lead was so profitable that the York merchants attempted to secure a monopoly on its export through Hull.[24] Iron manufacture was concentrated in the area between the river Wear and the river Derwent. This region was exceptionally well endowed with the natural resources for iron-making, being provided with iron ore of lower than average phosphorus content, plentiful fuel in the form of both wood and coal, and

[19] J. Thirsk, *England's Agricultural Regions and Agrarian History, 1500–1750* (London, 1987), 12.

[20] Pollard, *North-Eastern England*, 30–8.

[21] The survival well into the later medieval period of a great deal of wasteland in the north-east is one of the key discoveries of H. M. Dunsford and S. J. Harris, 'Colonization of the Wasteland in County Durham, 1100–1400', *Economic History Review*, 56 (2003).

[22] See Ch. 2 (for details of foodstuffs purchased by the priory) and 5 (for details on the locations from which such goods were purchased).

[23] Pollard, *North-Eastern England*, 38; M. Threlfall-Holmes, 'Late Medieval Iron Production and Trade in the North East', *Archaeologia Aeliana*, 5th ser., 27 (1999).

[24] Pollard, *North-Eastern England*, 74–5.

water power.[25] The total output of this iron industry has been estimated at around 100 tons a year in 1508, increasing to 500 tons a year
from the 1530s, though it seems probable that the industry under-
went significant expansion from as early as the 1480s.[26]

Coal was a much larger concern. The total output of the coal mines
on the lower Tyne was around 40,000 tons in 1550, and whilst this is
overshadowed by the huge growth seen by the seventeenth century,
when production rose to around 800,000 tons per annum, it remains
a major element of the late medieval economy of the region.[27]
Newcastle exported thousands of tons of coal a year across a wide
area including most of northern Europe and into the Baltic.[28] In the
thirteenth century, Newcastle had been one of the four chief wool-
shipping ports of England, alongside London, Boston, and Hull,
although its role in exporting wool had dropped significantly by the
fifteenth century and, unlike developments at some other ports, cloth
had not taken wool's place.[29] Nevertheless, the coal trade meant that
Newcastle maintained its status as an internationally important port.

The international nature of Newcastle's port is clearly demonstrated by the fourteen surviving particular customs accounts, which
cover 133 months between 1454 and 1509. Of the sailings recorded
in these documents, 19 per cent of ships were from Newcastle
itself and 6 per cent from other English ports, whilst 46 per cent
were French, 21 per cent from the Low Countries, 4 per cent were
Hanseatic, and 3 per cent Scottish. The remaining 1 per cent were
Scandinavian or unidentified.[30] In addition to Newcastle's main
exports of coal and wool, sandstone and lead were also frequently
included in cargoes as profitable ballast. Wine was pre-eminent
among the imports into Newcastle, but these also included fish (especially salted herring), luxury foodstuffs (such as filberts, almonds,
figs, raisins, and peppercorns), hops, iron, and a wide range of miscellaneous goods such as flax, alum, soap, oil, pitch, bricks, glass,
kettles, and felt hats.[31]

---

[25] Threlfall-Holmes, 'Late Medieval Iron Production', 116.
[26] I. S. W. Blanchard, 'Seigneurial Entrepreneurship: The Bishops of Durham and
the Weardale Lead Industry 1406–1529', *Business History*, 15 (1973), 79; Threlfall-
Holmes, 'Late Medieval Iron Production', 113–15.
[27] R. A. Butlin, 'The Late Middle Ages, *c.*1350–1500', in R. A. Dodgshon and R. A.
Butlin (eds.), *An Historical Geography of England and Wales* (London, 1978), 178.
[28] R. A. Pelham, 'Medieval Foreign Trade: Eastern Ports', in H. C. Darby (ed.), *An
Historical Geography of England before A.D. 1800* (Cambridge, 1951), 321.
[29] Ibid. 308–11.   [30] Wade, 'Overseas Trade', 32–4.   [31] Ibid. 38–43.

Furthermore, the merchants of Newcastle upon Tyne were a self-conscious and well-organized group by this period. The important traders in wool and coal overseas had incorporated themselves as the Merchant Adventurers of Newcastle upon Tyne, and they achieved some notable successes.[32] In 1463 they were given statutory exemption from the requirement to export all wool via the Calais staple, and in 1489 they gained a royal licence to pay only a quarter of the standard rate of custom and subsidy for five years.[33] Newcastle was second only to York in the region in terms of economic importance and organization.

The urban hierarchy in late medieval England comprised small market centres with populations of between 500 and 1,500; regional centres, including ports and places with specialized industries, with populations of between 1,500 and 5,000; and major towns and cities. London was in a class of its own with a population of over 60,000 in 1500, but other major cities included Bristol, Norwich, York, Exeter, and Newcastle, with populations of over 7,000.[34] The north-east region as a whole was served by around fifty markets, from villages to the cities of Newcastle and York.[35] Amongst these, late medieval Durham might be considered 'a comparatively small market town, with a limited range of trades'.[36] Durham certainly provided a marketplace serving the needs of its immediate area, being well placed in this respect at around fifteen to twenty miles from the nearest other market towns of Newcastle, Darlington, Hartlepool, and Barnard Castle. Indeed, it was no doubt of major importance to the economy of this immediate region, since the presence of the cathedral and castle meant a continual demand for foodstuffs which could not be satisfied from the town itself. The presence of these large consumers meant that Durham could be counted amongst the main market towns and ports which served the region—Richmond, Ripon, Northallerton, Yarm, Darlington, Malton, Whitby, and Scarborough, with Newcastle and York dominant and York predominant as the 'regional capital'.[37]

[32] Few records survive from the merchants' company for this period, but those that do have been published in F. W. Dendy (ed.), *Extracts from the Records of the Merchant Adventurers of Newcastle-upon-Tyne*, i (Surtees Society, 93, 1895).
[33] Wade, 'Overseas Trade', 42–3. [34] Butlin, 'The Late Middle Ages', 143.
[35] Pollard, *North-Eastern England*, 40.
[36] M. Bonney, *Lordship and the Urban Community: Durham and its Overlords, 1250–1540* (Cambridge, 1990), 145.
[37] Pollard, *North-Eastern England*, 40–2.

Durham's physical appearance mirrored its experience of lordship and its claim to national importance, with the cathedral and the
bishop's castle both dominating the small peninsula on which the
town was (and indeed remains) centred. The priory and the bishopric
were the two major landlords of the town and the surrounding farm-
land. Durham itself was administratively complex, comprising four
separate, though adjacent, jurisdictions, each designated a borough.
The bishop was particularly associated with the 'Bishop's Borough'
(the area around the marketplace at the entrance to the peninsula),
and the priory with Elvet and Crossgate boroughs.[38] Both ecclesiastical landlords held a great deal of property throughout the town,
however, and not just in these particular boroughs. For example, the
almoner of the priory received rents from across the city, from a range
of properties including South Street, Crossgate, the marketplace, the
Bailey, Elvet, and St Mary Magdalene.[39] In a very real sense the town
was a creation of the church, and continued to be maintained by its
demand for service industries and particularly the victualling trades.
It was also undoubtedly the case that the cathedral and its bishop
and priory gave Durham a social status and an importance beyond
its size, so that Durham was certainly York's closest challenger in the
ecclesiastical hierarchy of the region and was an important pilgrimage destination. Henry VI himself made a pilgrimage to the shrine of
St Cuthbert in 1448.[40] Bonney concluded, in her study of the town
of Durham, that its significance 'lay not so much in its economic
development, or lack of it, but rather in its political role as the centre
of government for the bishop, with the castle as the visible sign of his
power in the region'.[41]

Despite its island-like appearance, Durham and indeed its region
were by no means cut off from the rest of England. Links beyond the
region were many and various. To begin with, it is clear that there
was no physical bar to travel and the transport of goods to, from, and
within the north-east in this period. The infrastructure of roads and
waterways of England was adequately developed from early in the

[38] Bonney, *Lordship and the Urban Community*, 41–6. An analogous, though less
complex, division was in place in Coventry, which was divided into an earl's half and
a prior's half (J. C. Lancaster, 'Coventry', in M. D. Lobel (ed.), *The Atlas of Historic
Towns*, ii (London, 1975), 3–4).
[39] Bonney, *Lordship and the Urban Community*, 266.
[40] Dobson, *Durham Cathedral Priory*, 174.
[41] Bonney, *Lordship and the Urban Community*, 230.

middle ages, and the main routes were well travelled by the fifteenth century. The first known medieval map of England, that of Matthew Paris from *c.*1250, shows the route from Dover to Newcastle via London, Doncaster, Northallerton, and Durham, and known royal itineraries show a similar route from London to York and Newcastle via Durham in frequent use throughout the medieval period.[42] The coast and rivers provided an additional network of alternative routes, the importance of which is shown by the high proportion of prominent medieval towns built with ready access to navigable water.[43] Durham was unable to take direct advantage of water transport, since the river Wear was not navigable from the sea. However, Newcastle and Hull provided major ports for the region into which goods could be shipped both from abroad and from other English ports, notably London. Other smaller ports included South Shields, Jarrow, Hartlepool, and Sunderland, from all of which the priory purchased fish in this period, alongside a host of other coastal villages which no doubt supported minor fishing industries.

Overall, the evidence available about medieval travel and road systems indicates that the existing infrastructure was adequate well into the sixteenth century.[44] Martin's study of the fourteenth- and fifteenth-century journeys of the warden and fellows of Merton College, Oxford, whilst restricted by a lack of information about specific transport costs, concluded that travel in this period was 'systematic and regular, and . . . undertaken as a matter of course'.[45] Even winter weather does not appear to have posed a regular bar to the travel necessary for trade or business to be carried out; haulage could be carried on in the winter months without attracting undue comment or problems, and the royal household continued to travel around the country at all seasons.[46] This ability to travel and to forge and maintain links across the country was certainly used by the priory. For some centuries the monks of Durham had had notable

[42] B. P. Hindle, 'The Road Network of Medieval England and Wales', *Journal of Historical Geography*, 2 (1976), 209, 215.

[43] J. F. Edwards and B. P. Hindle, 'The Transportation System of Medieval England and Wales', *Journal of Historical Geography*, 17 (1991), 129.

[44] B. P. Hindle, 'Roads and Tracks', in L. Cantor (ed.), *The English Medieval Landscape* (Croom Helm Historical Geography Ser., 1982), 214.

[45] G. H. Martin, 'Road Travel in the Middle Ages: Some Journeys by the Warden and Fellows of Merton College, Oxford, 1315–1470', *Journal of Transport History*, NS 3 (1975/6), 172.

[46] B. P. Hindle, 'Seasonal Variations in Travel in Medieval England', *Journal of Transport History*, NS 4 (1978), 170, 176–7.

connections northwards. The monastic cell at Lindisfarne was of great symbolic importance, whilst that at Coldingham in Scotland was by far the most prominent of Durham's cells in terms of wealth and prestige in the twelfth and thirteenth centuries.[47] After the 1290s, however, the Anglo-Scottish wars continually threatened the stability and prosperity of the monastery at Coldingham, and in 1462 the Scottish link was finally lost to Durham when the English monks were unceremoniously expelled from Scotland.[48]

The priory retained strong connections, however, across England and into Europe. The surviving letters between the prior of Durham and his representatives at the papal Curia, in connection with the situation at Coldingham, show that links with Rome were in place but were hampered by logistical difficulties with transferring money and documents back and forth between the two. The priory maintained at least one agent in Rome, and a Durham monk, Richard Billingham, went out to Rome personally to oversee the handling of the Coldingham case in 1465.[49] Durham Priory had a long history of sending monks to study at Oxford University: from as early as 1278 monks had lived there whilst studying, and in 1381 the monastic cell which had become established in Oxford was formally endowed as a college.[50] Apart from the erstwhile cell at Coldingham, the other cells maintained by the priory comprised five within the region (Jarrow, Monk Wearmouth, Finchale, Farne, and Holy Island), together with one in the north-west, at Lytham in Lancashire, and another at Stamford.

Much of the land in the counties of Durham and Northumberland was owned by the immensely powerful Percy and Neville families, who gave the region a national importance in the political intrigues and power struggles which characterized this period in England's history. Both Edward IV and Richard III were sons of Cecily Neville, and Richard inherited the large Neville estates in Durham on his marriage to Anne, the daughter of Richard Neville, Earl of Warwick. Richard spent significant periods of time in the region, notably as ruler of the 'Council of the North', based in York, and both Richard and Anne were members of the Fraternity of St Cuthbert.[51] But the

---

[47] R. B. Dobson, *Church and Society in the Medieval North of England* (London, 1996), 110.
[48] Ibid. 111, 116.   [49] Ibid. 119–21.
[50] Dobson, *Durham Cathedral Priory*, 343–4.
[51] M. Dufferwell, *Durham: A Thousand Years of History and Legend* (Edinburgh, 1996), 67.

priory was not simply of national importance via such figures as these; the prior of Durham was an important public figure in his own right, particularly in the context of the Anglo-Scottish wars. Prior Wessington, for example, was asked to be a member of the commission negotiating an extension of the truce with the Scots in 1444, although he refused so as not to antagonize the Scots into taking action against the Coldingham cell.[52] Durham Priory appears to have been frequently used by the king as a safe repository for money, jewels, and documents, and the prior was authorized to admit various royal functionaries (such as the sheriff of Newcastle upon Tyne) to their offices, thus sparing them the journey to London.[53]

DURHAM CATHEDRAL PRIORY

It is evident that Durham Cathedral Priory was one of the major monasteries of the country, not merely of the region. It was certainly one of the wealthiest houses in the land. Although income levels were gradually eroded over the end of the fourteenth and beginning of the fifteenth centuries, by the mid fifteenth century a partial recovery had been made, and income levels remained stable for the remainder of the life of the priory.[54] For example, the bursar's income was consistently in the region of £1,400 for the whole of this period, varying by no more than 5 or 6 per cent from this median. Even in the first half of the century, when money was tighter and crises could and did make a considerable impact on the priory's finances, the records do not suggest that any particular degree of hardship was felt by the monks.[55]

Whilst the number of monks belonging to the priory varied over time, it would appear that somewhere between sixty and seventy full members of the monastery was normal throughout the fifteenth century.[56] Accurate figures are surprisingly elusive as the priory kept no standard register of deaths from which such figures can be simply abstracted. However, the monastic population of the priory over this period has been estimated by Mr Alan Piper, by compounding the

[52] Dobson, *Durham Cathedral Priory*, 173. [53] Ibid. 175–6.
[54] R. A. Lomas, 'Durham Cathedral Priory as a Landowner and a Landlord, 1290–1540', Ph.D. thesis (University of Durham, 1973), 284–6.
[55] Dobson, *Durham Cathedral Priory*, 255.
[56] Ibid. 300 gives this figure for the period 1400–50.

lists of monks received into the priory—which are to be found in the
Liber Vitae up to 1482—with any other biographical details to be
found in the archives, and imputing any missing data.[57] Overall, the
average number of monks registered as members of the priory in any
one year over the whole period 1464–1520 was sixty-six. Around
thirty of these men were resident in the priory's various cells or at
its Oxford college at any one time, leaving an average of thirty-six
resident in the mother house over this period.[58]

In addition to the monastic population, the priory would have also
been home to a large number of servants. Whilst the obedientiary
accounts contain numerous references to pensions, salaries, and
stipends for such servants and other dependants of the priory, it is
impossible to know from these accounts how many of the recipients
of such payments were in fact residents of the priory. Other references in the accounts to the purchase of liveries or other garments for
servants who were more clearly defined as members of the household
unfortunately give no indication of the numbers involved. However,
two of the few surviving bursar's rough notebooks include listings
of the servants who received cloth liveries (usually at the rate of three
ells apiece) in the two years 1509/10 and 1510/11.[59] These list
the names of individuals under headings according to their degree
(gentlemen, clerical valets, valets, and grooms) and also include
supplementary lists of the number of servants under each of the
main obedientiaries who were also entitled to receive an allocation
of cloth. It is possible from these lists to gain an idea, if not of the
number of resident servants of the priory, at least of the number who
qualified as the household. A total of 112 servants are listed for
1509/10 and 111 in 1510/11.

The scale of the administrative task faced by the monks of Durham
is therefore clear. A household comprising at least 140 members had
to be fed, clothed, and (for many of them at least) housed. In addition,
the estates which paid for these things had to be farmed or otherwise

---

[57] A. Piper, 'The Size and Shape of Durham's Monastic Community, 1274–1539'
(forthcoming). The *Liber Vitae* has been published in facsimile: A. H. Thompson (ed.),
*Liber Vitae Ecclesiae Dunelmensis. A Collotype Facsimile of the Original Manuscript,
with Introductory Essays and Notes*, i: *Facsimile and General Introduction* (Surtees
Society, 136, 1923).
[58] The figure of 30 monks resident at the cells, varying from year to year but within
only narrow limits, is given by Dobson, *Durham Cathedral Priory*, 300; Piper's analysis
suggests that this figure for the first half of the century held true for this later period.
[59] Durham Cathedral Muniments (hereafter DCM) Bursar's Book H, fos. 204ᵛ,
274ᵛ, 275ʳ.

managed. Finally, the duties of prayer and hospitality which were the ultimate point of these other tasks had to be carried out. Whilst the large servant population was clearly there to help with the daily round, many duties inevitably fell upon the monks themselves. An average resident monastic population of thirty-six (many of whom were junior) had to oversee the carrying out of all these tasks as well as fitting in their religious duties.

In managing so demanding a household, the monks produced copious amounts of documentation, from accounts to charters, letter books to estate records. The survival to the present day of so much of this has meant that the Durham archives have long been recognized as one of the most important collections of medieval monastic records in Europe. The volume and range of the surviving material provides the evidence for an unusually rounded picture of the life and times of the priory to be constructed. In particular, the obedientiary accounts have survived in unique numbers and in exceptionally good condition. The most important, the bursar's accounts, have survived from as early as 1278, and exist in a substantial series from the four-teenth, fifteenth, and early sixteenth centuries.

Much use has been made of this material since extracts from the various account rolls were published by the Surtees Society at the end of the nineteenth century.[60] In particular, the Durham archive provided much of the source material for Barrie Dobson's book on Durham Priory in the first half of the fifteenth century, which pro-vides a comprehensive survey of the social, political, economic, and intellectual life of the priory in those years.[61] In addition, a great deal of work has been done on the estates and estate management pol-icies of the priory by Richard Lomas, drawing on the obedientiary accounts and estate material, while Margaret Bonney made substan-tial use of the priory records in her survey of the geography and eco-nomic activity of medieval Durham.[62]

However, some aspects of the material contained in the Durham Cathedral Priory obedientiary accounts have been seriously neglected,

[60] J. T. Fowler (ed.), *Extracts from the Account Rolls of the Abbey of Durham, from the original MSS*, 3 vols. (Surtees Society, 99 (1898), 100 (1898), 103 (1900)).
[61] Dobson, *Durham Cathedral Priory*.
[62] Lomas, 'Durham Cathedral Priory'; R. A. Lomas, 'The Priory of Durham and its Demesnes in the Fourteenth and Fifteenth Centuries', *Economic History Review*, 2nd ser., 31 (1978); R. A. Lomas, 'A Northern Farm at the End of the Middle Ages: Elvethall Manor, Durham, 1443/4–1513/4', *Northern History*, 18 (1982); Bonney, *Lordship and the Urban Community*.

and this is especially the case for the material from the later fifteenth century. In particular, the vast amount of information relating to the priory's expenditure has only recently begun to receive detailed attention, in the form of Christine Newman's work on employment on the priory estates and the present study.[63]

This study uses the obedientiary accounts to analyse the consumption and purchasing of the priory between 1460 and 1520. The high level of detail contained in many of the accounts, together with the preservation of many of them as a virtually complete series for the period looked at here, has allowed a detailed analysis of both the actual purchases and the purchasing practices of the priory. Whilst purchases in the accounts themselves are organized by commodity types (wine, grain, spices, and so on), a thematic approach has been adopted in the analysis and presentation of this material. This approach is supplemented by the use of case studies where a more in-depth treatment of a particular commodity is desirable, or where the priory's approach to the purchasing of different commodities differed considerably.

ADMINISTRATIVE STRATEGIES: THE ACCOUNTING SYSTEM AT DURHAM CATHEDRAL PRIORY

A medieval Benedictine monastery such as Durham Cathedral Priory typically administered its estates and household by dividing the lands between several of the monks, who were each then responsible for running those estates and for part of the day-to-day running of the monastery using the revenues. These monks were known as the obedientiaries. However, Benedictine monasteries were each governed independently, and the precise nature of the administrative system in each differed to a considerable extent. By the fifteenth century a great many modifications had been made to the original system outlined in the Rule, which had mentioned only a handful of offices (the abbot, prior, cellarer, and weekly kitcheners).

Three broad categories of administrative style have been identified as in use in English religious houses by the late fourteenth or early fifteenth century, the key difference between them lying in the

---

[63] C. M. Newman, 'Employment on the Priory of Durham Estates, 1494–1519: The Priory as an Employer', *Northern History*, 26 (2000).

existence and role of the bursar or treasurer.[64] The first system did not have this officer, but was organized on the principle outlined above, with the priory's lands being distributed between the obedientiaries, who then managed them independently and received the revenues from them to be used in the expenses of their offices. At Battle Abbey, for example, the role of bursar never developed and the cellarer remained the most important obedientiary of the household well into the fifteenth century.[65]

The office of bursar developed in most Benedictine houses from around the end of the thirteenth century, although in some places such an office can be detected much earlier. At Canterbury Cathedral Priory, for example, a central treasury was in operation at the date of the first surviving account, 1198.[66] At this date, the purpose of this office was to enable the rent collecting system to be centralized; revenues could then be divided between the other obedientiaries in fixed proportions, so that variations in income affected all the offices equally. However, the bursar rapidly became a key official in his own right in most houses, and the second of the three systems shows this process at its most developed, being based around a central bursary which received all the revenues from the monastery's lands and distributed them to the various obedientiaries.

The third and probably the more common system was a combination of these two extremes. The main obedientiaries had lands allocated to them individually, which were managed on the old pattern, but these did not comprise the whole of the house's property. A bursar also existed, and received the revenues of all the lands not otherwise allocated. In practice this often meant all or most of the lands acquired by the priory after its original foundation, and the bursar could thus be by far the richest of the priory's officials. In Durham this third system was in place by the late thirteenth century.[67] The main obedientiaries had the income from certain properties assigned to their specific offices, whilst the bursar received the otherwise unallocated estates and revenues, giving him nearly three-quarters of the priory's total income. Typical of the old established obediences were the hostillar, who had an estate worth about £170 a

[64] R. A. L. Smith, *Collected Papers* (London, 1947), 35.
[65] E. Searle and B. Ross (eds.), *Accounts of the Cellarers of Battle Abbey, 1275–1513* (Sydney, 1967), 6–13.
[66] Smith, *Collected Papers*, 23–41.
[67] Dobson, *Durham Cathedral Priory*, 258.

year, and the sacrist, whose annual income was around £80. In contrast, the bursar's income varied between £1,308. 5s. 10³/₄d. and £1,472. 12s. 3d. in this period.[68]

The length of the bursar's account rolls, together with the large sums that he accounted for and the wide range of goods that he was responsible for buying, misled early historians into mistaking his role. The sixteenth-century writer of *The Rites of Durham* stated first that the bursar's job was to receive all the rents pertaining to the house, and then went on to declare that all other officers of the house made their accounts to him, and he discharged all the servants' wages, and paid all the expenses of the monastery.[69] James Raine, writing in 1844, assumed that the different obedientiaries' account rolls were compiled together to create the bursar's roll, which could be taken as 'embodying the whole proceedings of the monastery in a summary way'.[70] In fact, as already noted, the bursar's job was essentially miscellaneous—he was responsible for all income and expenditure not otherwise assigned. This was an extremely demanding job, as the size and complexity of his annual accounts indicate.

Indeed, the priory's administration faced a major crisis in 1438, when no monk would accept the office of bursar, the candidates approached stating that they would prefer imprisonment or transfer to a stricter order. This impasse was temporarily resolved by a bold experiment in which the prior (John Wessington) divided the responsibilities of the office into three roughly equal parts, giving a third of the bursar's income to both the cellarer and granator to manage independently and appointing a bursar with the much reduced job of managing the remaining third.[71]

This new division did not greatly change the basic division of responsibilities between these obedientiaries, but it did mean that the huge burden of the bursar's task of managing the estates, collecting rents, repairing property, and so on was now shared equally between them. Unfortunately, as Dobson shows in his analysis of this unusual period in the priory's history, the years of this experiment were ones

---

[68] Lomas, 'Durham Cathedral Priory', enclosure in end pocket. The lands allocated to each obedientiary are detailed ibid. 298–364.

[69] J. T. Fowler (ed.), *The Rites of Durham* (Surtees Society, 107, 1903), 99.

[70] J. Raine (ed.), *The Durham Household Book: or, The Accounts of the Bursar of the Monastery of Durham, from Pentecost 1530 to Pentecost 1534* (Surtees Society, 18, 1844), p. viii.

[71] Dobson, *Durham Cathedral Priory*, 287.

of unusual economic problems for the priory, and the stringent eco-
nomies that these years entailed reflected badly on the new arrangement. In addition, complaints were voiced that the experiment
simply tripled administrative overheads for no gain. In 1445 the old
system was reinstated by popular demand, and from then on until the
dissolution the bursar remained supreme amongst the obedientiaries.[72]

There were at least twelve obedientiaries at Durham in this period,
but not all compiled accounts. Those who did not could nevertheless
be extremely important members of the community: they included,
for example, the prior, the sub-prior, the master of the novices,
and the prior's chaplain, and their functions are described at length
in the 1593 *Rites of Durham*.[73] On the other hand, a further two
obedientiaries, not mentioned in the *Rites*, are known to have existed
from the accounts they have left. These were the almoner and the
infirmarer, responsible for the monastery's charity hospital and the
monks' own infirmary respectively.

In addition, the surviving account series refer to a number of other
officials or servants who were involved in the provisioning process,
and to documents such as indentures relating to transactions with
such officials which have not been found amongst the surviving
records of the priory. For example, the indenture made between the
bursar and the cellarer in 1480/1 refers to butter being bought 'from
the caterer', and itself includes a 'tallies and indentures' section which
lists a total sum of £92.10s.10d. paid by indenture to three 'purveyors'. However, the fact that so many examples remain of accounts
from each obedientiary whose records have survived in the archive
suggests that those that are not represented were in some sense
subordinate to the main business of the priory, or were intended at
the time they were compiled to be only transitory documents. That
is to say, it seems likely that the account series that have survived
represent the priory's opinion of which records were important. It
should be remembered, however, that the obedientiaries discussed
here are by definition those who compiled accounts which have survived, and that the actual daily business of the priory involved many
more individuals.

After the bursar, the most important obedientiaries were the
granator, responsible for the priory's grain, and the cellarer, theoretically responsible for all the other food and drink required.[74] The

---

[72] Dobson, *Durham Cathedral Priory*, 287–90.
[73] Fowler (ed.), *Rites*, 93–4, 96–7, 101.   [74] Ibid. 99–100.

running of the church was the responsibility of the sacrist, in conjunction with the feretrar who had special responsibility for St Cuthbert's shrine.[75] The chamberlain provided the monks' clothing and bedding, and the communar provided pittances. The *Rites of Durham* described the latter's job with great enthusiasm, as being to provide a fire in the warming-room, to provide spices in Lent, and always to have a hogshead of wine available for the monks' use.[76] Finally, there were also the terrar, who was the priory's rent collector, and the hostillar or guest-master. The *Rites of Durham* declared that the terrar's job was to look after the guest chambers, keep the linen in good order, and make sure that there was also wine available for the entertainment of guests.[77] This was in fact clearly the job description of the hostillar, but the expansion of the bursar's role had resulted in the terrar's job becoming increasingly redundant over the years, and the posts of hostillar and terrar had by the time of the dissolution long been held by the same person and so were confused. Such a combination of offices in the hands of a single monk was not unusual in monasteries by this period, as the old job titles remained even where the jobs themselves became redundant or were combined. In Selby Abbey, for example, one monk was both bursar and cellarer in 1436 and another combined the offices of granger and keeper of the spiritualities.[78]

The accounts that these obedientiaries produced each year all follow the same format, with income listed first followed by expenditure. The categories into which the entries are divided within these broad headings are consistent within each account from year to year, although they vary somewhat between the different obedientiaries. This variation primarily takes the form of the bursar having many more divisions in his accounts—splitting out purchases of wine, corn, oats, barley, cloth, and so on—whereas the lesser obedientiaries, with only one or two entries in each category, tend to lump all commodity purchases and miscellaneous expenses together into a single 'expenses' section. In all cases, however, the section or sections detailing such expenditure are followed by several other sections listing expenditure on pensions, salaries, repairs, and so on. The archives also contain a few examples of the bursar's household books, notebooks in which the bursar jotted down purchases and payments made, and from which he later compiled his yearly enrolled

[75] Ibid. 94, 97–8.   [76] Ibid. 100–1.   [77] Ibid. 99–100.
[78] J. H. Tillotson, *Monastery and Society in the Late Middle Ages: Selected Account Rolls from Selby Abbey, Yorkshire, 1398–1537* (Woodbridge, 1988), 28.

accounts. Unfortunately, these have not survived systematically, and are generally incomplete and in worn condition;[79] but they do exist in reasonably complete condition for 1530/1 to 1533/4, and these have been published by the Surtees Society.[80]

This study focuses on the expenditure of the priory, as recorded in the second half of the obedientiary accounts.[81] However, some income elements are also relevant to the issues looked at here, and have thus been included in this analysis. For example, tithes were occasionally paid to the priory in kind and in particular some of the grain acquired by the priory in most years came via this route, and so the tithe income sections of the accounts have been examined for such payments. Other income elements could also be paid in kind, as will be seen; such payments do not show up in the accounts themselves but in the few surviving rentals, which have also been used here as appropriate.[82] Finally, some of the obedientiary accounts include income elements which represent the profits of selling various by-products of an office. For example, the bursar's accounts include income from selling second-hand garments, leather, wool (apparently only a by-product rather than a major industry at Durham in this period), tallow, and dripping. The cellarer also sold similar kitchen by-products, including tallow, dripping, hides, and sheepfells. But for the most part, the priory's dealings with the market were as a consumer, and the main focus of this study is on the extent and nature of those dealings and of the markets and other environments in which they took place.

A SNAPSHOT OF THE PRIORY'S
ACCOUNTING SYSTEM: 1480/1

The fact that so many of the obedientiary accounts have survived makes possible a detailed analysis of the priory's administrative

[79] Only three such notebooks survive for this period: DCM B. Bk. G contains miscellaneous information relating to 1495/6; DCM B. Bk. H records payments made in 1507/8, 1509/10, and 1510/11, and includes reckonings with the prior and other obedientiaries for those years; and DCM B. Bk. J includes payments made in 1517/18, and some miscellaneous information relating to 1518/19.

[80] Raine, *Durham Household Book*.

[81] The income sections of the obedientiary accounts were the focus of Lomas, 'Durham Cathedral Priory'.

[82] See Ch. 5.

strategies and accounting system in the late fifteenth century.[83] The administrative system which produced these documents was a complex one, and the accounts themselves illustrate the interlocking network of responsibilities and obligations which grew up around St Benedict's original conception. The main problem in trying to recreate this system for most monasteries is the lack of full sets of evidence. Generally, only one or two accounts from any given house have survived for any one year, and only rarely have accounts survived for consecutive years. It thus becomes impossible to tell whether payments recorded as having passed between two offices of the same house were standard practice or unusual; whether payments described as gifts were in fact gifts or had hardened by long practice into obligations, and whether a particular year's accounts record the full spectrum of an officer's responsibilities. It is also difficult to tell quite how the various responsibilities attendant on running a monastery were divided between the monks.

Because Durham Cathedral Priory's accounts have survived in such substantial numbers, however, it is possible to get uniquely close to the ideal of being able to study a full set of accounts. For a single year in this period, 1480/1, eight out of a total of eleven obedientiary accounts and similar documents exist (that is, including the bursar/cellarer indenture which was in fact an expenditure account). The three accounts not represented in the archive for this year are the terrar's, infirmarer's, and sacrist's.[84] To make this study as comprehensive as possible, the following analysis includes accounts from other years for these obedientiaries. The nearest terrar's account dates from 1463/4, but both the infirmarer and the sacrist have accounts from 1485/6 which are used here. The following analysis thus presents a snapshot of the priory's financial system in this period (Table 1.1), and provides an unparalleled insight into the details and structure of late medieval monastic administration.

To assist analysis, expenditure has been categorized under twelve headings: food and drink (which accounted for just under half of all

    [83] The Appendix shows exactly which accounts have survived for each obedientiary over this period.
    [84] The bursar's account roll for 1480/1 is rather damaged in places, and as a result the necessary expenses for this year are indecipherable. In this analysis, the bursar's expenditure is made up of the 1480/1 details for all sections except the necessary expenses section, for which the figures from 1478/9, the nearest available year, have been substituted.

TABLE 1.1. Breakdown of the Durham obedientiaries' expenditure, 1480/1

	Bursar	Bursar/cellarer	Hostillar	Sacrist	Chamberlain	Communar
	£. s. d.	£. s. d.	£. s. d.	£. s. d.	£. s. d.	£. s. d.
Food and Drink	480.9.2.	360.10.4.	6.18.8.	24.14.3.	1.5.8.	2.1.8.
Grains	362.11.7.	—	—	6.0.	—	—
Meat	44.4.10.	150.0.9.	—	20.16.7.	—	—
Fish	2.6.5.	126.5.0.	—	—	—	—
Spices	—	20.15.11½.	2.0.	—	—	1.11.10.
Dairy	—	2.12.9.	—	—	—	—
Other food	22.19.8.	60.6.8½.	—	5.8.	—	—
Wine	48.6.8.	—	6.16.8.	3.6.0.	1.5.8.	9.10.
Cloth/ing	50.15.2.	—	4.17.2.	3.15.4.	21.0.4½.	5.0.
Monks' clothing	6.3.9.	—	10.0.0.	3.4.	16.5.4½.	—
Servants' clothing	29.13.7.	—	2.17.6.	2.11.0.	1.5.11.	3.3.
Hoods, boots, gloves, etc.	13.4.	—	10.0.0.	10.0.0.	2.17.6.	1.9.
Misc. clothing costs	1.2.0.	—	—	1.0.	1.1.	—
Linen	7.15.7½.	—	16.8.	5.8.	7.6.	—
Other textiles	5.6.10½.	—	3.0.	4.4.	3.0.	—

Fuel	9.8.4½.	—	3.o.	—	—	4.o.
Pensions/Stipends, etc.	121.o.11½.	—	54.2.11.	29.19.11.	10.2.10.	9.3.6.
Buildings	88.15.8½.	—	20.8.4.	68.18.1.	1.17.8½.	17.17.2½.
Administration	13.11.0½.	—	5.11.11.	14.8.	2.6.4.	12.9.
Agriculture	15.1.0.	—	15.19.11½.	2.10.2.	—	—
Stables	9.9.2.	—	35.17.9½.	3.o.10.	1.10.9.	2.9.5¾.
Rents	7.8.4.	—	—	5.10.5.	—	34.19.6½.
Transfers	18.2.5.	—	11.o.o.	4.4.11.	38.o.8.	6.3.
Other	20.17.3½.	—	9.12.11.	19.17.9½.	13.1.	7.o.8.
Allowances	22.5.11½.	—	17.15.8.	—	6.10.1.	75.o.o¾.
TOTAL	857.4.7.	360.1.2.	182.8.4.	163.6.4½.	83.7.6.	75.5.1o½.
Total given in roll (without surplus)	814.3.8.*	400.11.2.	not given	164.18.0½.	82.14.o.	

Note:
The sacrist's figures are from 1485/6.
The bursar's figures are from 1480/1, but the 1478/9 necessary expenses details have been used in the breakdown. The bursar's 'necessary expenses' section in 1480/1 totalled £87. 6s. 9d.; because of the bad condition of this section, that for the nearest available year, 1478/9 (totalling £88. 6s. 7d.) was used in this analysis.

Table 1.1. *(cont'd)*

	Almoner £.s.d.	Cellarer £.s.d.	Terrar £.s.d.	Feretrar £.s.d.	Infirmarer £.s.d.	TOTAL £.s.d.
Food and Drink	1.10.4.	6.2.	1.2.0.	—	4.9½.	878.13.10½.
Grains	—	4.8.	1.0.0.	—	—	364.2.3.
Meat	—	—	—	—	—	215.2.2.
Fish	—	—	—	—	—	128.11.5.
Spices	—	—	2.0.	—	—	44.7.1½.
Dairy	—	—	—	—	—	2.12.9.
Other food	—	—	—	—	—	62.3.0.
Wine	1.10.4.	1.6.	—	—	4.9½.	61.15.2.
Cloth/ing	—	2.4.	1.2.8.	4.9½.	7.	85.0.5.
Monks' clothing	2.17.0.	—	—	4.9½.	—	24.2.5½.
Servants' clothing	1.0.0.	—	6.8.	—	—	38.9.8½.
Hoods, boots, gloves, etc.	1.7.0.	—	16.0.	—	—	5.18.7.
Misc. clothing costs	10.0.0.	—	—	—	—	1.4.1.
Linen	—	10.	—	—	—	9.6.3½.
Other textiles	—	1.6.	—	—	7.	5.19.3½.

Fuel	12.0.	—	—	—	18.8.	11.6.0½.
Pensions/Stipends, etc.	26.15.4½.	18.14.6.	5.1.4.	1.11.2.	10.10.	277.3.4.
Buildings	13.16.5.	12.1.6.	13.4.	3.	—	224.8.6½.
Administration	12.9.	2.8.	2.13.5.	1.0.	1.0.	26.7.6½.
Agriculture	3.10.8.	2.9.2.	—	—	—	39.10.11½.
Stables	1.6.7.	—	5.16.4.	—	—	57.1.5½.
Rents	2.11.4.	—	—	—	—	17.19.6¾.
Transfers	2.15.6.	2.0.0.	3.4.	21.2.2.	1.18.8.	134.7.2½.
Other	3.5.5.	2.13.5.	2.11.8.	6.7.	1.11.11.	61.16.4.
Allowances	10.0.	9.4.5½.	—	1.8.	—	63.8.6.
TOTAL	60.3.4½.	47.14.2½.	19.4.1.	23.7.7½.	5.6.5½.	1877.3.9¾.
Total given in roll	62.14.7½.	47.4.6.	19.4.1.	23.7.7½.	5.6.10½.	1695.10.5½.
(without surplus)						1877.18.9½.
						(incl. hostillar total estimate)

Note:
The terrar's figures are from 1463/4.
The infirmarer's figures are from 1485/6.

the priory's expenditure in 1480/1, and has been subdivided as grains, meat, fish, spices, dairy products, other foodstuffs, and wine), clothing and textiles, fuel, payments to individuals (such as pensions and stipends), building and repair works, administration, agriculture, stables, rents, transfers to other obedientiaries, miscellaneous, and allowances. The division of responsibilities between the different obedientiaries was by no means clear-cut. Apart from the unendowed cellarer and granator, each was responsible for the administration of his own estates and revenues; each paid pensions, salaries, or stipends, each to some degree provided clothing for his own servants, and most were responsible for the upkeep of certain buildings. Most of the obedientiaries, therefore, divided their expenditure between all or most of the categories defined above, since they were responsible for all the miscellaneous expenses relating to their particular sphere of influence.

Purchases of food and drink, for example, were handled to some extent by every obedientiary except the feretrar. They were nevertheless particularly the province of the bursar and the cellarer, who between them paid for 96 per cent of all the foodstuffs bought by the priory. The cellarer used the money provided by the bursar to purchase virtually all the meat, poultry, and fish consumed by the priory, whilst the main items of consumption bought directly by the bursar were grains and wine. The bursar was almost solely responsible for these latter items, buying virtually all the grain purchased by the priory in this year (over 99.5 per cent), and 78 per cent of the wine. The only other obedientiaries who bought grain-based products in this year were the sacrist, cellarer, and terrar, and they spent small amounts on bread doles. Providing bread for the priory's meals was clearly the sole financial responsibility of the bursar, although the day-to-day practical responsibility lay with the granator to whom the bursar passed all the grain which he purchased.

The picture is slightly different for wine purchases. Although the bursar was responsible for the bulk of the priory's wine purchasing, a sizeable minority, 22 per cent, of the wine bought by the priory was supplied by other obedientiaries. In particular, the hostillar bought 10 per cent of the total, presumably for use in entertaining the priory's more exalted guests, while a further 5 per cent was bought by the sacrist for use in the church. Moreover, these core supplies were supplemented on a regular basis by 'gifts' from other obedientiaries to the monastery. In 1480/1, the chamberlain spent £1. 2s. 4d. on

wine for the prior and brothers, and a further 3s. 4d. on wine for the
novices; the communar donated 9s. 10d. worth of wine to the prior's
four annual *ludi* (recreation periods); while the almoner gave £1. 2s.
2d. worth of wine to the same feasts, and like the chamberlain also
gave wine costing 3s. 4d. to the novices. All of these are recorded in
the 'Gifts and Presents' sections of the respective accounts, but do
appear to have been regularly given each year and so were probably
considered to have been obligations of the offices concerned rather
than freely given—and withdrawable—gifts.

The only strikingly unusual feature of the distribution of food
and drink purchases between the obedientiaries is the purchase of a
notable amount of meat, 10 per cent of the total bought by the priory,
by the sacrist. This anomaly occurred because the sacrist's traditional
estates included an area given over to pastoral husbandry, and rents
from these farms were paid partially or wholly in kind. It should
be borne in mind that many of the food purchases of the priory,
especially of grains, meat, and fish, were in fact transactions of this
nature.[85] The monastery accounts conceal this fact by a form of
double-entry accounting, in which rents are recorded as having been
paid, and goods as having been bought, at their cash values, even
when in fact no money changed hands. The two recorded transactions are simply two ways of looking at the same actual transaction.
We can tell that this is the case because for a few odd years the
bursar's rentals have survived. These notebooks list the priory's
tenants and the rents due from each, and in the spaces between these
entries their payments are recorded. The typical pattern was for a
rent owed to be paid in several stages and by a variety of means. An
additional complexity could be introduced into the system when
the payments in kind did not add up exactly to the amount owed,
and there are several examples in the rentals of both under- and over-
payments being carried forward to the next year.[86]

The 'transfers' section in this analysis includes all payments
recorded in one obedientiary account as having been paid to another
obedientiary. As well as rents, this category also includes customary
or extraordinary payments ordered by the prior for the subsidy of a
struggling office by a flourishing one, or as contributions to major

[85] See Ch. 5.
[86] R. A. Lomas and A. J. Piper (eds.), *Durham Cathedral Priory Rentals*, i: *Bursars Rentals* (Surtees Society, 198, 1989), e.g. 147, 150.

building projects such as the bell tower. Eric Cambridge has studied these payments as part of his thesis on the priory's architectural history and building works and has found that many had become standard amounts paid to the prior each year as a kind of slush fund, to allow for the priory's non-standard expenses. In the 1480s, these were all paid to the sacrist to subsidize the construction of the new cathedral tower.[87] One interesting point to note about this transfer category is that the feretrar was spending virtually all his income in this way, which illustrates both the extent to which an office once important enough to attract an endowment had dwindled in influence, and also the flexibility within the system which enabled the outward forms of tradition to be upheld whilst the substance was put to new uses.

These accounts, which were presented by each obedientiary to the priory's Chapter around Pentecost each year, were designed as a means of checking that the obedientiaries had honestly and efficiently administered their estates and carried out their tasks. In theory, each obedientiary was personally liable for any shortfall, although the allowances system meant that he could write off certain sums, notably rents uncollected due to the tenure being vacant or waste. The system was therefore based around the assumption that the accounts would be thoroughly audited.[88] However, only a small amount of evidence of auditing procedures having taken place can be found in these accounts, and they contain frequent arithmetical errors which are only occasionally corrected.[89]

The clearest indication of auditing having taken place is the appearance in an account of marginal patterns of dots, which represent the final position of the counters used on the *scaccarium*, the chequered cloth used as an abacus board by the auditors. The presence of such dot patterns, usually alongside some of the subtotals

[87] E. Cambridge, 'The Masons and Building Works of Durham Priory 1339–1539', Ph.D. thesis (University of Durham, 1992), 17–19, 118.

[88] Dobson, *Durham Cathedral Priory*, 254–5. Hatcher notes that the accounts of the Duchy of Cornwall estates do appear to have been audited every year (J. Hatcher, *Rural Economy and Society in the Duchy of Cornwall, 1300–1500* (Cambridge, 1970), 50); and examples of auditors disallowing certain expenses can be found in I. S. W. Blanchard, 'Seigneurial Entrepreneurship', 106.

[89] Snape has suggested that auditing was intended to be carried out at least every year; however, he also notes that, at Worcester at least, this was frequently neglected (R. H. Snape, *English Monastic Finances in the Later Middle Ages* (Cambridge, 1926), 67).

or the grand totals in an account, indicates that these totals have been checked for their accuracy and passed as correct.[90] These confirmatory dot patterns may be seen in only three of the accounts, and in a fourth from just outside this period. They appear against most of the expenditure subtotals and the expenditure grand total on the 1517/18 communar's account; against every subtotal in both the receipt and expenditure sections on one of the three copies of the communar's 1524/5 account;[91] against the surplus of expenditure over receipts at the end of the 1499/1500 cellarer's account; and against several of the subsections in both of the two surviving copies of the 1499/1500 bursar/cellarer indenture.

These dots are not the only possible indication that the accounts have been audited, however. In the 1506/7 terrar's account similar marginal confirmations of the expenditure subtotals and grand total are made, but in the usual pounds, shillings, and pence notation. Other suggestions of auditing procedures having taken place are much less clear-cut, consisting of the presence in the accounts of corrections, especially those made in a different ink to that used in the preparation of the account. Examples occur in the sacrist's account for 1473/4, where a repeated entry in the church expenses section has been erased; in the sacrist's 1485/6 account, where 6d. has been added to the grand total in another ink; and in the chamberlain's 1475/6 account and the cellarer's 1490/1 account, where several amplifications have been made although the sums involved remain unchanged. These corrections are not distinctively auditors' marks, and may well have been made by the scribe himself when he came to read through his work. Even if these corrections are taken as signifying auditing having taken place, the accounts for which we have evidence of auditing are greatly outnumbered by those containing no such evidence. In all, only nine out of a total of seventy accounts that were checked showed any of these various signs of auditing activity.[92]

[90] L. C. Hector, *The Handwriting of English Documents* (2nd edn., London, 1966), 42–3.
[91] DCM Communar's account 1524/5 B. Neither of the other copies of this account (A or C) bears any evidence of auditing having taken place. It should be noted that in another case where three copies of an account survive, the hostillar's account for 1473/4, none of the copies show any signs of auditing.
[92] A total of 70 accounts (not counting duplicates surviving for some years) were checked for signs of auditing procedures having taken place: i.e. all of the surviving sacrist's, terrar's, and chamberlain's accounts, and a sample from the accounts of the other obedientiaries consisting of one account per decade. Of these, only nine (as detailed above) contained such indications.

In addition to this lack of positive evidence of systematic auditing, there are many examples of uncorrected arithmetical errors in these accounts. These are particularly prevalent where large numbers are involved, such as in the bursar's cloth and iron purchases; this, combined with the fact that the errors are of no uniform size or direction, implies that they are indeed simple mistakes in arithmetic rather than bearing any significant meaning. The frequent occurrence of such errors supports the conclusion that little systematic or effective auditing of the obedientiary accounts took place in this period.

The largest degree of error occurs in the almoner's account roll, where the total given at the end of the roll is 4.1 per cent higher than that arrived by summing the individual entries. Much smaller errors occur in the other accounts: the given total is 0.9 per cent higher than the calculated total in both the sacrist's and the infirmarer's accounts, and is 0.9 per cent, 1.1 per cent, and 0.8 per cent smaller in the communar's, cellarer's, and chamberlain's accounts respectively. The fact that the largest inconsistency is a positive one could conceivably indicate a degree of fraud; nevertheless, the final total is lower than the sum of all the entries in three other accounts, and it should be stressed that the overall level of error is very small, a negligible 0.04 per cent.[93]

CONCLUSION

It is clear that the priory's accountancy system was a complex one.[94] In addition to his basic role within the supply pattern of the priory, each obedientiary faced a huge administrative burden throughout the year. Each had servants to clothe, pay, and direct, and each had an estate to administer with all that that entailed—rents to collect, courts to hold, hay to be mown, tithe-corn to be threshed, buildings

---

[93] Much larger errors were sometimes detected by medieval auditors. An example of this comes from the household accounts of Queen Elizabeth Woodville from 1466/7, in which the sum of the miscellaneous expenses section was changed by the auditors from £26.19s.7d. to £22.12s.11d., a difference of 19% (A. R. Myers, *Crown, Household and Parliament in Fifteenth Century England* (London, 1985), 308).

[94] Errors abound in the accounts of Norwich Cathedral Priory, and Saunders has suggested that 'we are driven to the conclusion that the obedientiars lived from hand to mouth. They administered efficiently, but finance may have been a thing apart' (H. W. Saunders, *An Introduction to the Obedientiary and Manor Rolls of Norwich Cathedral Priory* (Norwich, 1930), 154–5).

to be repaired, and much more besides. It is not hard to imagine the apprehension with which the obedientiaries must have contemplated the preparation of their annual account rolls, and their reluctance to accept the larger offices is easily understood.

Nevertheless, it is equally notable that such a system seems to have worked sufficiently well to have been continued and to have permitted the monastery to flourish as it did. The monks appear to have applied a simple but effective strategy to managing their administrative burdens, maintaining the structure laid down in the Rule but adapting the substance and responsibilities of each job as and when occasion demanded. It is fascinating to see the complex web of interlocking responsibilities and cross payments which made up the priory's administrative and accounting system laid bare, like an anatomical diagram. The analogy is an appropriate one, for like a body the priory's structures and systems had grown and evolved: they were certainly not logical, but they equally certainly worked.

2

The Monastic Diet

INTRODUCTION

The first step in analysing the priory's purchasing strategies is necessarily to ascertain what exactly the monks were buying. Once that
is known, we can begin to ask and answer supplementary, deeper
questions about the motivation and reasoning behind such purchasing decisions. In the case of food, for example, which as we have seen
was the largest single item of expenditure for the priory, such questions include whether supply or demand was the driving force behind
the priory's purchasing, and whether a relatively fixed idea of an
appropriate monastic diet was purchased every year or whether
changing factors such as price, availability, or taste were allowed to
influence the priory's purchasing from year to year.

Medieval and modern critics of monasticism have often focused on
the perceived debauchery and extravagance of the monastic diet. One
has only to think of Friar Tuck, or of the religious in Chaucer's tales,
to see how monks were commonly portrayed as more concerned with
the contents of their plates than of their prayers. It is certainly the case
that food and drink loom large in the archival evidence available for
Durham Cathedral Priory. Purchases of food and drink accounted
for nearly half the priory's spending each year, and two important
obedientiaries, the cellarer and the granator, were almost exclusively
concerned with supplying the tables of the monastery. The detailed
lists of purchases available in the obedientiary accounts allow a fairly
accurate picture of the monks' diet to be drawn.

It is generally considered that the monastic diet was equivalent to
that of the aristocracy, being relatively over-supplied with meat,
wine, and spices. Barbara Harvey's analysis of the diet of the monks
at Westminster Abbey in the 1490s largely confirmed this view, and
for the first time provided a detailed breakdown of the elements and

nutritional value of that diet.[1] One major benefit of this study of the purchasing of Durham Cathedral Priory is that it provides in passing a complementary analysis of the monastic diet at Durham. The evidence used here is different, since the kitchener's daily accounts have not survived in Durham—if, indeed, they ever existed—and so a detailed calorific analysis such as Harvey's has not been possible. However, this is compensated for by the longer period that the Durham accounts have made it possible to study.[2]

In this chapter the priory's provisioning infrastructure is briefly considered and the margin of error involved in using purchases as an indicator of consumption is estimated. Each of the major constituents of the priory's diet is then looked at in turn. First the grains consumed, mainly as either bread or ale, are considered. The priory's consumption of meat and fish is then analysed, followed by wine, spices, and other flavourings, fats, dairy produce, and vegetables. In each of these sections the types or varieties of each commodity purchased by the priory are looked at, the priory's consumption is estimated, and comparisons are drawn with other great households for which information is available from this period. Finally, the overall make-up of the diet at Durham Cathedral Priory is summarized.

THE PROVISIONING INFRASTRUCTURE OF THE PRIORY

Provisioning a large institution like Durham Cathedral Priory was a complex business. The accounts of the priory reveal a sophisticated network of departments that shared the responsibility for purchasing the wide variety of foodstuffs required. This complex accounting network was mirrored in the strategies by which foods were handled once they had entered the priory, and also in the uses made of the various geographical and architectural spaces within and around the

[1] B. Harvey, *Living and Dying*, 34–71.
[2] For the purposes of this analysis, the bursar/cellarer indentures have been sampled at as near to decade intervals as the surviving documents would permit. The sample years are 1465/6, 1474/5, 1485/6, 1495/6, 1504/5, and 1515/16. References in this chapter to average yearly purchases are based on these sample years. Accounts other than the bursar's, cellarer's, and granator's records have been used for this analysis only if they contain major and regular contributions to the priory's purchasing of a particular commodity. The sacrist's and hostillar's wine purchases, and the communar's spice purchases are therefore included here, but small ad hoc purchases of foodstuffs are not.

priory. An example of this is the way in which grain was purchased by the bursar, but then handed over to the granator by indenture and discharged on a monthly basis from the granary by the granator, as discussed in the previous chapter.

Particular light is shed on the processes by which foodstuffs other than grain were handled by the remainder sections which occur at the beginning and end of each of the surviving bursar/cellarer indentures. These list the amounts of various commodities which had been purchased but not yet consumed at the time that the account was made. The cellarer organized this list by grouping items held in the same physical space or room, and this reveals how and where various items were dealt with. The movement of food from one stage to another is particularly clear with regard to beef. First, numbers of live cattle are recorded. These were kept on the priory's farms; mainly at Relley, although Bearpark is also mentioned in 1515/16. Secondly, slaughtered cows in the slaughterhouse are recorded, followed by preserved carcasses held in the larder, both salted and 'powdered' (that is, covered in a dry layer of spices). Sheep are also mentioned in each of these states in most accounts. It can thus be seen not only that the priory reared, slaughtered, and preserved its own meat, but also that it had a number of distinctive areas devoted to these activities.

The other food location mentioned is the fish-house, presumably an approximation to a refrigerator. Other miscellaneous goods—oil, honey, spices, rice, dried fruit—are mentioned after fish. Although these are mentioned in a new sentence no other room or cupboard is quoted at this stage, so it is unclear whether these items were kept in the fish-house, or in an unnamed location. The fish-house would seem an unlikely place for dry goods, however, and it may well be that these were kept simply in the kitchen, rather than in a special room, and so it was not considered necessary to specify a location in the accounts.

PURCHASING AND CONSUMPTION

It is clear from the presence of the 'remainder' sections in the accounts that there was not an exact correspondence between the goods purchased and the goods consumed by the priory within any one accounting year. This does not cause a problem in the case of the priory's grain purchases, since for those the granator's monthly

TABLE 2.1. The quantity of various foods consumed by Durham Cathedral Priory in 1474/5, from the bursar/cellarer indentures

Item	Remainder from 1473/4	Purchases in 1474/5	Remainder to 1475/6	Calculated consumption in 1474/5	Purchases v. consumption (%)
Dogdraves	80	2,327	480	1,927	−17.2
Red herring	1,000	57,000	2,000	56,000	−1.8
White herring		23.5 barrels	5 barrels	18.5 barrels	−21.3
Salmon		34		34	0
Salt salmon	0.5 barrels	14.5 barrels	2 barrels	13 barrels	10.3
Seals		4		4	0
Sparling		2,600		2,600	0
Sprats		2 casks		2 casks	0
Pike		3		3	0
Kelyng		420		420	0
Eels		5 barrels		5 barrels	0
Lampreys		180		180	0
Stockfish	40	120	100	60	−50
Cattle	95	175	78	192	9.7
Calves	28	28	20	36	28.6
Sheep	130	584	81	633	8.4
Lambs		175		175	0
Pigs		37		37	0
Piglets		359		359	0
Oil	1 barrel	2 barrels	1 barrel	2 barrels	0
Honey	30 gallons	39 1/2 gallons	40 gallons	29 1/2 gallons	−25.3

records of the grain taken from the granary provide consumption figures. However, the discrepancy is of relevance for all the other foodstuffs purchased by the priory. Clearly, a comparison of the goods purchased in each year with the goods left over from the previous year and those carried forward to the following year would overcome this, giving the amount actually used in any one year. However, it is only rarely the case that all three consecutive accounts have survived intact; indeed, a full comparison can be done only for one year of those looked at here, 1474/5.

Table 2.1 shows for 1474/5 the amount that the priory consumed of each major commodity for which the bursar/cellarer indenture is the chief or only source of information. The purchases recorded for 1474/5 are shown alongside the amount carried into this year from 1473/4 and the amount carried from 1474/5 into 1475/6. The total amount of each commodity that was therefore actually consumed within the accounting year 1474/5 is then calculated. Finally, the percentage difference between the amount of each commodity that was purchased and the amount that was consumed in 1474/5 is shown. The inclusion of this calculation enables an assessment of the margin of error involved in using the purchases each year as if they were consumption figures to be made.

Although for stockfish the percentage difference between the amount recorded in the bursar/cellarer indenture as having been purchased in 1474/5 and the calculated actual consumption for that year was as much as 50 per cent, this figure stands out as unusual. It is probably no accident that such a large difference exists only for a commodity that was by definition particularly suitable for storage, being dried for this very purpose. Overall, taking the direction of the differences into account, the average difference between consumption and purchases for 1474/5, where such differences exist, is – 6.5 per cent. If only the magnitude and not the direction of the differences are taken into account, together with the fact that in many cases there is no difference, the average discrepancy between purchases and consumption is 11.3 per cent. This suggests that it will be appropriate to bear in mind an overall margin of error of around plus or minus 10 per cent when using the purchase figures from the bursar/cellarer indentures as representative of the priory's consumption in any one year.

Grain

The single most important item in the priory's diet was grain. The bursar bought wheat, barley, and oats for the monastery, and also purchased oats, peas, and beans for animal feed. These were all handled by the granator, who kept a monthly record of the grain used over the course of the accounting year. As noted above, these monthly figures mean that the issue raised above, that annual purchases and annual consumption may not be equivalent, does not apply in the case of grain, since consumption figures are specifically included in the granator's accounts. The granator also notes a total amount for 'liveries' and 'allowances' in each year. It is not clear what these represented, but it seems probable that the liveries grain was for dependants or beneficiaries of the priory who were entitled to a grain or bread dole. The allowances amount fluctuated considerably, but was normally very low at around 2 quarters per year. This may well have represented waste from the granary. These two quantities are excluded from the following analysis.

Although it is a shame that daily, weekly, or monthly kitchen accounts such as those used by Barbara Harvey for her study of Westminster Abbey do not exist for Durham for this period, which means that no information survives as to the actual dishes in which the foods bought by the various obedientiaries were used, the granator's accounts do give some information about the uses to which the various grains bought by the priory were put. This information is often implicit rather than explicitly stated, but a general idea of the destinations of each grain may be satisfactorily inferred. It is clear, for example, that the wheat purchased by the priory was used entirely or almost entirely for bread. Although no explicit statement to this effect is given in the accounts, probably because it was considered obvious, in some years the granator's statement of the amount of wheat that remained in the granary is amplified to specify that this quantity included wheat 'milled, not milled and in bread'.[3] It is interesting to note that this also implies that bread and flour made but not yet consumed remained the responsibility of the granator rather than the cellarer. The fact that bread that had not actually been consumed was counted as remaining to the next year rather than being counted as consumed in the month in which it was made also adds credence to the monthly consumption figures given by the bursar for oats and barley. It is worth noting that separate remainder or consumption figures are never given for the small amounts of rye which the priory acquired in most years. These purchases were included with the figures for wheat, the implication being that it was treated in the same way as wheat, and perhaps even mixed with it.

Generally speaking all the barley received by the granator in a year was malted, to become the principal ingredient of ale, but occasionally there was a remainder of unmalted barley. This occurred in only six of the thirty-four years for which granator's accounts remain, in which years the average amount malted was 969 quarters, and the average amount unmalted was 133 quarters (12 per cent of the total).[4] The average amount malted per year for all years in which this figure is given was 984 quarters, so it would seem likely that in the

[3] DCM Granator's accounts, e.g. that for 1494/5.
[4] These years were 1461–4 and 1479–80 inclusive.

years when some grain was not malted this was simply because the excess was surplus to requirements. No suggestion of alternative uses for the excess are given in the accounts, so it is probable that it simply remained in the granary and was malted in the following year.

The situation for oats was more complex; some were malted, some were used for animal fodder, and a small amount was given to the kitchen, presumably for human consumption. The oats mentioned first in the granator's accounts were for either the first or the last of these, oats for animal fodder being mentioned in a separate fodder section along with peas and beans. Some oats were passed to the kitchen in every year for which accounts remain.[5] In twenty-two of the thirty-two years for which these figures are given this was a standard quantity of 16 quarters, and comprised the whole of the oats received by the granator that year. In the remaining ten years, varying amounts between 12 and 20 quarters were passed to the kitchen, giving an average yearly amount of 15.5 quarters. These were probably used in pottage and similar dishes. This seems a very small quantity of grain for pottage and other recipe dishes for a household of this size. It is possible that some of the wheat discussed above, or some of the oats mentioned below as having been malted or bought as fodder, were in fact also used for this purpose.

The granator received a significant, though greatly varying, amount of oats which were malted. This amount varied from 30 quarters in 1464/5 to 256 quarters and 3 bushels in 1461/2, but averaged 99 quarters per year.[6] It is worth noting that there is a close correspondence between the years in which oats for malting were received, and the years in which the granator recorded a surplus of barley which was not sent for malting. As well as these amounts, the barley section of the bursar's and granator's accounts also regularly included an average of 36 quarters of 'havermaltum', malted oats, from Billingham.[7] The inclusion of these with the barley purchases throughout

[5] The amount passed to the kitchen is left blank in the 1489/90 account, and the oats section is missing from the 1508/9 account due to damage to the end of the parchment roll (the last surviving line of the document consists of the oats section heading).

[6] Oats to be malted that are included in this average were received in 1460–4, 1479–81, and 1485/6. They were also received in 1489/90, but this year has been excluded from the analysis since many figures have not been given, and in 1492/3 which has been excluded from the average since the amount malted is not specified.

[7] Thirty quarters were received in 1460/1, 35 in every year for which accounts remain from 1461/2 to 1477/8, 37 in 1480/1, just under 31 in 1485/6, and 37.5 in every other year for which accounts remain from 1479/80 onwards.

the priory's records, together with the correspondence between the presence of additional malt oats and spare barley, suggests that these malt oats may have been used with malt barley in the priory's brewing. Overall, oats made up 6 per cent of the malt used by the priory in this period.

Finally, some oats (an average of 375 quarters per year), and all the peas and beans, were bought for fodder. It can therefore be calculated that of all the grain which was used by the priory in an average year, 24 per cent was for human consumption as bread or as an ingredient in food, 52 per cent was malted and used to make ale, and 24 per cent was for fodder.[8] There does not appear to have been any difference between the oats bought for the monastic kitchens and those bought for feeding horses. They cost the same, and in 1489/90 and 1492/3 the two are not even separated into two sections, as was the normal practice, but are listed together; whilst in 1515/16, 1517/18, and 1520/1 some of the oats listed under the fodder section are noted to have been malted. This raises the possibility that some of the oats listed in the accounts as fodder may in fact have been consumed by the monastic household, although this possibility has been disregarded here.

Although there were variations in the exact proportions of the different grains bought from year to year, the basic pattern remained fairly consistent over this period. Barley formed the bulk of the grain bought by the bursar, with wheat coming second, then oats, and finally a small amount of peas and beans. (Rye purchases were insignificant). On average, a total of 2,118.5 quarters of grains were accounted for by the bursar each year, a sum made up of 1,074 quarters of barley (50.7 per cent), 539.6 quarters of wheat (25.5 per cent), 440.3 quarters of oats (20.8 per cent), and 64.6 quarters of peas and beans (3.0 per cent). The extent to which this quantity and its constituent parts varied from year to year may be seen on the graph (Fig. 2.1).

The granator's accounts include a record of the monthly usage of each of the principal grains. These accounts exist for thirty-three years in the period from 1460 to 1520, but those for 1509/10 and

---

[8] This calculation uses the amount discharged from the granary per year, as found in the granator's accounts, which differs from the amount bought as given in the bursar's accounts. In an average year, the priory used 481.4 quarters of wheat and 15.8 quarters of oats for food, 1,020.8 quarters of barley (including the malt oats from Billingham which cannot be separated out) and 53.8 quarters of oats for malt, and 440.1 quarters of oats and 63.5 quarters of peas and beans for fodder.

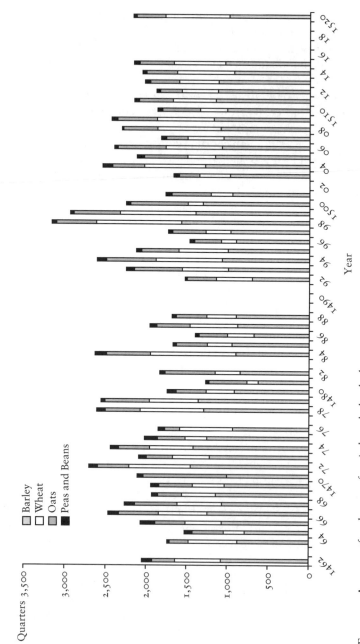

FIG. 2.1. Amount of each type of grain bought by the bursar, 1460–1520

1513/14 are in bad condition with major omissions in the wheat and barley sections, whilst the oats section is missing from the 1508/9 account. In addition, certain accounts have been excluded from this analysis because of irreconcilable inconsistencies in the monthly data.[9] The data used here comes from twenty-nine accounts for wheat, twenty-three accounts for barley, and thirty-two accounts for oats, although it should be noted that in half of these valid oats accounts it is recorded that no oats were used in that year.

An overall view of the priory's grain consumption from these monthly figures shows that in an average year 1,049.4 quarters of barley, 458.5 quarters of wheat, and 91.9 quarters of oats were consumed. Consumption of each of these grains fluctuated from year to year, strongly suggesting these figures represent actual usage and are not merely conventional. No strong trends can be seen in the data for either barley or oats, but for wheat the pattern is different. Here there was a marked upward trend over the latter half of this period, following a dip in the 1470s. Since wheat was a staple item of diet, such an increase seems at first to be surprising. However, whilst the servant population appears to have remained stable, the monastic population changed over this period, and there is a marked degree of correspondence between the changing size of the population and the priory's wheat consumption.[10] It seems probable, therefore, that the wheat consumption figures were closely related to the number of people eating in the priory, rather than reflecting an increased per capita consumption of wheat.

Having considered all the information available in the accounts, an estimate of the amount of grain which was consumed per person in the monastic household can be made, mainly as either bread or ale.

---

[9] For each account, the total amount stated to have been used that year was compared with the total of all the monthly amounts given. Small errors were only to be expected, but major differences (>2% out), which may have arisen from a misreading of damaged sections, meant that that year's account was omitted from this analysis. For wheat, of 31 data sets there was an exact correspondence in all but seven cases. In five cases the error was less than 2%, so these were kept in, and two cases were discarded (1481/2 and 1492/3, with errors of 80% and 7% respectively). For barley, of 31 data sets eight had errors of between 4% and 40% and were omitted (1462/3, 1474/5, 1476–7, 1479/80, 1481/2, 1501/2, and 1512/13). Of the remaining 23, 10 matched exactly and 13 had errors of <2%. For oats, of 32 data sets there was no monthly usage for 16 (these were included), and all of the remaining 16 were included, 14 with an exact correspondence between the given and calculated totals and two with an error of <1%.

[10] For population figures, see Ch. 1.

Harvey has calculated that between 45 and 50 gallons of best ale were made from one quarter of malt barley at Westminster Abbey in this period, and it would seem reasonable to assume that a similar figure would apply in Durham.[11] In total, 1,095.4 quarters of grain were malted at Durham in an average year.[12] If it is assumed that the whole of this quantity was successfully converted into ale, this would have yielded somewhere in the region of 50,000 gallons of ale per year, or 137 gallons per day. Given that the average population of the priory throughout this period comprised around 40 monks and around 110 liveried servants, this seems roughly what one would expect, fitting well with the general concept of a gallon of ale a day being a standard individual allowance.[13]

For bread, the priory used an average of 458.5 quarters of wheat per year, although as has been seen this did not remain constant over the period. Taking this average amount, however, and assuming that the Durham kitchens produced the same number of loaves per quarter of wheat as those of Westminster, it can be calculated that the priory consumed 48,601 loaves or 97,202 lb of bread in an average year.[14] Again, this seems commensurate with standard allowances made in other medieval households, working out at 133 loaves per day. It seems likely that a monk received a loaf a day, and servants slightly less than this. However, this average conceals some notable fluctuations.

The fact that the granator recorded the monthly discharges from the granary means that the data can be checked to see if any

[11] Harvey, *Living and Dying*, 58. Malt oats do not seem to have been used at Westminster in this period, but for the purposes of this calculation it is assumed that oats and barley were equivalent. The amount of malt oats used by Durham was in any case small enough for differences in the relative productivity of the two grains to make very little difference. Oats were malted only in 16 of the 32 years for which records remain, and the average amount of oats used in those years was only 91.9 quarters, or 46 quarters per year over the whole of this period, a negligible quantity compared to the 1,049.4 quarters of barley used in an average year.

[12] i.e. 1,049.4 quarters of barley and 46 quarters of oats.

[13] Servants may well have received a weaker brew than that assumed in these calculations, which would make up the shortfall here of c.13 gallons per day. Wood-Legh notes that the ale bought for a 15th-cent. chantry priest was described as 'best' and that bought for his household as 'second' (K. L. Wood-Legh (ed.), *A Small Household of the XVth Century: Being the Account Book of Munden's Chantry, Bridport* (Manchester, 1956), p. xxiv).

[14] B. Harvey, *Living and Dying*, 59, calculated that at Westminster a quarter of wheat produced 106 loaves, each weighing roughly 2.5 lb before baking and 2 lb when cooked.

fluctuations in bread consumption occurred over the course of the average year, rather than over a progression of years. However, patterns cannot easily be seen in the data as given in the accounts, as the months given are four-weekly blocks dating from the start of the account, in other words from Pentecost each year. Since the date of this feast depended on the date of the previous Easter, the months as given in the accounts are not comparable from year to year, so monthly or seasonal fluctuations are obscured. Even patterns which might be expected to have occurred as a result of the church calendar are not visible, since Lent (for example) is calculated from the date of the subsequent, not the preceding Easter.[15] It was therefore necessary to adjust the data given in the granator's accounts to match the calendar, rather than the church year.

The resultant graph (Fig. 2.2) shows a series of mild peaks and troughs, averaging 8 quarters 6 bushels 2 pecks per week over the whole year. Furthermore, there is a clear peak in the Lenten period, at the height of which the priory's average weekly wheat usage over this period rose to 9 quarters 4 bushels 2 pecks, an 8.5 per cent increase on the overall average. The obvious conclusion is that that the monks' consumption of bread rose in Lent, presumably to compensate for lower levels of other foods. Another peak can be clearly seen around the Christmas period, which may well reflect the entertainment of visitors at this season. It is notable that fluctuations occurred at all, as it has generally been thought that the provision of bread in medieval households was based on conventional portions and would have varied little over the course of the year. This graph suggests that the monastic dietary provision was much more flexible and responsive than has previously been thought.

Meat and fish

An impressive range of different types of animals and fish were bought for the priory table over this period. These included cattle (variously described as oxen, steers, cows or calves, or on one

---

[15] It was this that led to the inclusion of odd weeks in the monthly data, rather than simply 13 four-week months. For example, the granator's account of 1480/1 contains 13 months and 3 weeks, since Easter in 1480 was three weeks earlier than in 1481, falling on 2 and 22 Apr. respectively. Conversely, in 1471/2 only 12 months and 1 week are accounted for, since Easter fell on 14 Apr. in 1471 and 29 Mar. in 1472 (C. R. Cheney, *Handbook of Dates for Students of English History* (London, 1961)).

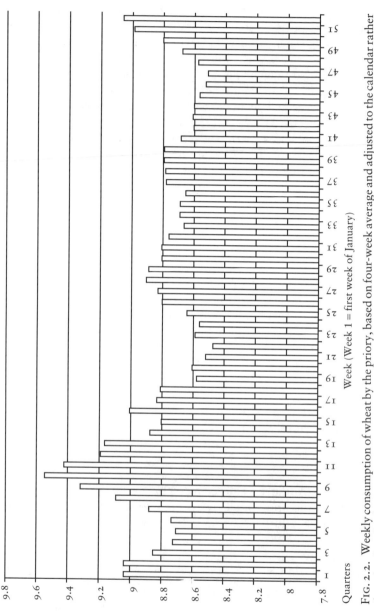

FIG. 2.2. Weekly consumption of wheat by the priory, based on four-week average and adjusted to the calendar rather than the church year, 1460–1520

occasion a bullock), sheep (which were described either simply as sheep or as ewes or lambs), pigs, boars, and piglets, and poultry (pullets, hens, penny-hens, geese, half-penny geese, and capons). On occasion much rarer and more expensive varieties of poultry were also eaten. Cygnets occur sporadically throughout these accounts, with as many as twenty pairs being purchased for the Christmas feast of 1504, whilst four cranes were bought in 1515, at the astounding price of 3s. 4d. each.[16]

The fish bought by the priory were even more varied. The staples were members of the herring and cod families. Herring were described as white (either dried or pickled in brine) or red (smoked), and were joined by herring-sprats, sprats, and sparling. The cod family was represented by dogdraves, ling, stockfish (dried cod), and powdered kelyng (preserved in dry salt). The priory also bought large quantities of salmon and eels, both of which could be either fresh or salted, whilst plaice and sturgeon were occasionally bought. Shellfish were represented by cockles and mussels, and in most years at least one dolphin, porpoise, or seal entered the priory. The priory's fish purchases also regularly included unspecified quantities of assorted fresh fish, including mudfish, pike, pickerel, roach, tench, bream, dace, and fluke.

With such variety in the types of meat and fish purchased by the priory it can be very hard to gain an overall picture. Table 2.2 summarizes the quantities of each of the principal types of meat and fish bought by the cellarer at decade intervals over this period. The overall amount of meat purchased by the priory increased dramatically over this period. To an extent this may be explained by the upsurge in population in the monastery towards the end of the fifteenth and beginning of the sixteenth century. However, such an increase cannot explain the virtual doubling of the number of poultry bought, from 796 in 1465/6 to 1,571 in 1515/16, nor the similar increase in sheep (see Table 2.2). It seems likely that these increases represent a major change in the scale and extent of meat-eating in the monks' diet over this relatively short period—equivalent perhaps to a single monk's career.

Interestingly, a glance at the main fish types bought (see Table 2.2) shows that this change was in no way made at the expense of

---

[16] DCM Bursar/cellarer indentures, 1504/5 and 1515/16.

TABLE 2.2. The amounts of the principal varieties of meat and fish recorded in the sampled bursar/cellarer indentures, 1465–1515

Commodity	1465/6	1474/5	1485/6	1495/6	1504/5	1515/16
Poultry						
Pullets	37				61	409
Capons	147	127	309	297	262	182
Geese	156	270	219	352	307	299
Hens	456	455	503	542	587	681
TOTAL	796	852	1,031	1,191	1,217	1,571
Pigs						
Boars		2	3	3	4	3
Pigs	47	37	37	31	32	48
Piglets	213	359	344	589	653	553
TOTAL	260	396	381	620	685	601
Cattle						
Mixed cattle types	57	60	36	224	98	159
Cows	78	39	158	39	92	49
Oxen	39	56	29	26	69	32
Steers	54	20	20	2		
Calves	26	28	33	43	29	16
TOTAL	254	203	276	334	288	256
Sheep	520	584	520	693	783	928
Lambs	72	175	140	149	315	271
TOTAL	592	759	660	842	1,098	1,199
Fish						
Dogdraves	1,637	2,327	2,163	2,136	2,755	2,751
Dolphin/seal/porpoise	2	4	8.5	10.5	10	5
Barrels of white herring	11	23.5	23	23	30.98	33
Red herring (1,000s)	23	51.5	48.5	51	30.5	18
Stockfish	36	200	120	214	230	720

fish-eating. On the contrary, this too seems to have increased in much the same way, although the pattern is complicated by the rise and fall in popularity of different types of fish within the total.[17] Dogdrave purchases rose, though not smoothly, over this period. More

[17] Woolgar, *Great Household*, 132, notes a similar increase in the amount of meat eaten in several large households in this period, but matched by a decline in the amount of fish consumed.

dramatically, purchases of stockfish went from only 36 in 1465/6 to 720 in 1515/16. The number of barrels of white herring purchased by the cellarer also increased steadily, from 11 in 1465/6 to 33 in 1515/16, although overall the number of herring purchased remained relatively stable, the slight drop seen in the table for 1515/16 being anomalous and not symptomatic of a general decline; in 1520/1, a total of c.79,000 herring were bought (comprising 34,000 red herring and 45 barrels of white herring).

These figures for the meat and fish consumed by Durham Cathedral Priory can be used to draw a rough comparison with the consumption of the same foodstuffs found at Westminster. It should, however, be noted that the relevant figures for the two households are not directly comparable, although the same estimates of edible meat weights per carcass have been used for both. In the first place, the evidence used is of a different nature: the Durham figures are taken from the purchases accounted for by the cellarer on an annual basis, whilst those for Westminster are calculated from the kitchener's daily records of the meals actually served. It is unlikely, however, that the two records are widely disparate, especially since the Durham purchases are averaged over the whole of the period, and since the figures given in Table 2.3 are for the estimated edible weight of meat and fish, taking waste (bones, skin, etc.) into account.

Secondly, the populations of the two monasteries were not identical. For the purposes of this comparison it has been assumed that Barbara Harvey's assumption that the number of extra consumers of the priory's meals (corrodians, servants, and the poor) would have been cancelled out by the monks who absented themselves from the common meals on any one day holds as well for Durham as for Westminster. But the average number of resident monks at Westminster in this period was around fifty, compared to around forty at Durham, and this should be borne in mind when comparisons are made. Moreover, the Westminster figures exclude meat and fish eaten within the abbot's household, for which separate accounts were compiled. Finally, the figures for meat and fish consumption at Westminster are located to different rooms; meat was primarily eaten in the misericord and fish in the refectory, and it is the figures for consumption in these rooms that are given. However, a substantial amount of meat would also have been eaten in the refectory, not as joints but as an ingredient (minced, ground, or otherwise rendered virtually unrecognizable) in made-up dishes. The actual meat figures

TABLE 2.3. Estimated weight per annum of meat and fish served at Durham and Westminster in the late fifteenth century

	Durham kg	%	Westminster kg	%
Meat				
Beef	26,103.8	65.1	1,634.4	24.0
Veal	497.9	1.2	793.6	11.5
Mutton	7,369.9	18.4	3,180.3	46.0
Lamb	761.5	1.9	78.1	1.0
Pork	3,640.9	9.1	961.1	14.0
Poultry	1,746.8	4.4	113.5	1.5
Other	—	—	149.4	2.0
TOTAL	40,120.8	100.1	6,910.3	100.0
Fish				
Cod family[a]	4,995.7	34.1	5,255.1	49.0
Eel	86.3	0.6	491.2	4.5
Herring	7,328.3	50.1	847.6	8.0
Other fatty fish[b]	2,074.3	14.2	321.9	3.0
Total fatty fish	9,489.9	64.9	1,660.7	15.5
Other fish[c]	160.9	1.1	9,115.9	35.5
TOTAL	14,646.4	100.1	10,776.6	100.0

[a] Including cod, dogdraves, stockfish, ling, etc.
[b] Including herring, eels, salmon, sprats, etc.
[c] Including plaice, whiting, and freshwater fish such as pike and roach. Seals are also included here for the Durham figures. Crustaceans and molluscs are excluded from the table.

for Westminster might perhaps be as much as 50 per cent higher than those given here, therefore.[18] Fortunately, it is unlikely that the fish data is as affected by this anomaly; some expensive and luxurious freshwater fish varieties were no doubt served in the misericord, but the volume involved is unlikely to have been great. Fish-days, by definition fasts, were days on which the rules governing attendance at the common meal in the refectory were stricter, so it is likely that the

[18] B. Harvey, *Living and Dying*, 51. Meaty dishes (i.e. those in which meat was one ingredient amongst many) were served in the refectory on about 150 days of the year, whilst on the same number of days flesh-meat was served in the misericord.

fish figures given here are much more nearly equivalent to those for Durham.

With all these caveats borne in mind, however, it can be seen that the amount of fish, and especially the amount of meat, eaten at Durham was far higher than was the case at Westminster (Table 2.3).[19] An estimate of comparable figures might be made by adding 50 per cent to the Westminster meat figures and perhaps 10 per cent to the Westminster fish figures to allow for the quantities of these commodities served in other rooms, and then dividing the resultant totals by 40 for Durham and 50 for Westminster. If this is done, a total annual meat allowance for a Westminster monk of perhaps 207.3 kg can be compared with an equivalent figure for Durham of 1,003 kg, with equivalent fish figures of 237.1 kg and 365.4 kg respectively. Overall, then, it would appear that the inhabitants of Durham Cathedral Priory consumed nearly four times as much meat as those of Westminster, and over 50 per cent more fish.

It is possible, perhaps likely, that a certain amount of this difference could be explained by a higher proportion of the food entering Durham being consumed by servants, dependants, and certainly guests than at Westminster. To some extent, too, the inclusion of the meat eaten at the abbot's table at Westminster would no doubt serve to close the gap. However, the difference between the figures for the two monasteries is so large as to leave little doubt that meat, at least, was a far greater feature of the diet at Durham than at Westminster.

Moreover, the proportions of the various types of meat and fish eaten at the two monasteries were noticeably different. Cattle formed the great majority of the meat eaten at Durham (65 per cent), with mutton taking second place (18 per cent). By contrast, at Westminster mutton was the most common meat, accounting for 46 per cent of the meat eaten in the misericord, with only just over half as much beef being consumed (24 per cent). Taking veal into account the gap closes somewhat, since this was much more common at Westminster than Durham, but the difference is still striking, the two together forming 66 per cent of the meat eaten at Durham and only 36 per cent at Westminster. Whilst these proportions probably reflected farming patterns in the two regions, it is interesting to note that the Durham figures are very similar to those found by Woolgar

---

[19] Data for Westminster Abbey in this comparison is taken from B. Harvey, *Living and Dying*, 48, 53.

at the household of Edward Stafford, Duke of Buckingham, in 1503/4.[20]

The differences in scale between the diets of the two monasteries is less pronounced in the case of fish than meat, but here too the varieties eaten are very different. At Durham, herring accounted for fully 50 per cent by weight of the fish consumed by the priory, compared to a mere 8 per cent at Westminster. Other fatty fish (with the exception of eel) also featured much more strongly in the diet at Durham, due primarily to the much higher consumption of salmon, both salted and fresh, than at Westminster. In compensation, members of the cod family were less common at Durham (34 per cent) than Westminster (49 per cent), and 23 per cent by weight of the fish prepared by the Westminster kitchens were whiting, which were only very occasionally bought by Durham Priory, and in negligible quantities.

'White meats': Eggs, cheese, and milk

According to Harvey, these were immensely popular and important items in the monastic diet of this period.[21] They certainly appear with great frequency in contemporary recipe collections and menus.[22] However, they only rarely appear in the Durham obedientiary accounts, appearing neither in the bursar/cellarer indentures, nor in either the bursar's or the cellarer's purchases. Some eggs do appear in the income section of the bursar's account for 1536/7, when 250 are recorded to have been received from each of Cowpen Bewley and Billingham, but this is an isolated example.[23] The latest surviving cellarer's weekly accounts, from 1449/50, show that despite not

---

[20] There are several similarities between these households. That of Buckingham in 1503/4 had a population of 130 and a total annual expenditure of £2,061, of which £801 was spent on food and drink, figures which are comparable with those seen for Durham. Cattle accounted for 65.7% of the meat eaten by this household in 1503/4, and sheep for 32.5%. (Woolgar, *Great Household*, 12, 113, 134).

[21] B. Harvey, *Living and Dying*, 61–2.

[22] e.g. these items appear in many of the dishes listed in the medieval recipes collected in C. B. Hieatt and S. Butler (eds.), *Curye on Inglysch: English Culinary Manuscripts of the Fourteenth Century (including the Forme of Cury)* (Early English Text Society, supplementary ser., 8, 1985). Many recipes use combinations of such 'white meats', such as the 'Brewet of ayren' (egg soup) which includes water, butter, cheese, and eggs, or the ravioli which consist of grated cheese, eggs, butter, and dough (both p. 118).

[23] Fowler (ed.), *Account Rolls*, iii. 674, 676.

appearing anywhere else in the priory archive eggs were certainly used by the priory in large numbers. From these figures, the average number of eggs consumed by the monastery in a week was 808, a number which rises to 940 if Advent and Lent are excluded from the reckoning.[24] This equates to around 20 eggs per monk per week, a figure which is comparable to that found at Swithun's Priory in this period.[25] The absence of eggs from the obedientiary accounts is easily explicable, since it seems most probable that the priory kept hens and so supplied itself with eggs rather than purchasing them from external suppliers. The cellarer's accounts for 1512/13 and 1515/16 contain payments to workmen in relation to the priory's henhouse (and goosehouse too in the latter account), implying that these structures were in regular use.[26]

Cheese also appears only occasionally in these accounts. The purchase of cheese is mentioned in passing in the cellarer's account for 1525/6, and cheese fats are referred to in his accounts for 1469/70, 1480/1, 1512/13, and 1525/6.[27] It seems likely that cheese was made largely within the priory kitchens, and this is supported by the cellarer's purchase of a cheese fleke—a hurdle for drying cheeses on—in 1465/6.[28] Milk is also largely missing from the documentary evidence, although small quantities are occasionally mentioned in the cellarer's 1449/50 weekly accounts.[29] Extrapolating from these figures gives an estimated weekly average milk consumption for the priory of 2.2 gallons, or 17.5 pints, a much smaller amount than might be expected. It must surely have been the case that this amount was supplemented by milk from the priory's own cattle.

[24] DCM Cellarer's account, 1449/50. Only a few eggs were consumed in Advent (170 in the week commencing 13 Dec. 1449), and none in Lent.
[25] Surviving diet rolls for 1492 show that the monks of St Swithun's priory consumed an average of 764 eggs per week in Nov. and Dec.; there were around 34 monks in the priory at this period, so 22 eggs were consumed per monk per week (G. W. Kitchen, *Compotus Rolls of the Obedientiaries of St. Swithun's Priory, Winchester* (London, 1892), 16, 309–11).
[26] Fowler (ed.), *Account Rolls*, i. 105–6.
[27] Ibid. 93, 97, 105, 108.   [28] Ibid. 90–1.
[29] DCM Cellarer's account 1449/50, months 8, 10, and 12. J. E. T. Rogers, *A History of Agriculture and Prices in England, From the Year after the Oxford Parliament (1259) to the Commencement of the Continental War (1793), Compiled Entirely from Original and Contemporaneous Records*, 7 vols. (Oxford, 1882), iv. 360, states that milk could cost as little as a penny per gallon but was more usually 2d.; if this were the price at Durham in the two months for which no price is given, the quantities suggested would be halved.

Vegetables, herbs, and fruit

The extent to which fresh fruit and vegetables formed part of the monastic diet has always been a matter for conjecture, largely because items grown in a monastery's own gardens never passed through the accounts, just as has been seen above with milk and eggs. It is clear that there were several gardens at Durham, although they have left only a few traces in the accounts. An underground gutter in 'the abbey garden' (perhaps the centre of the cloisters) required repair in 1459/60 and again in 1478/9, and two fothers of flagstones were also bought for that garden in 1459/60.[30] This may have been the priory's pleasure garden, where the monks were accused, in the bishop's visitation of 1442, of repairing for play and loitering after compline.[31]

Other gardens were clearly used, to some extent at least, for the production of food and herbs. The prior and infirmarer each had a walled herb garden for which wall repairs and the purchase of seeds (and even manure in the case of the infirmarer) are recorded.[32] Moreover, the bursar was paying a pension of 5s. 0d. to the prior's gardener in 1536/7.[33] The sacrist and almoner also had gardens: in 1420/1 the almoner bought onion seed for his, but by 1535/6 it was rented by the sacrist in addition to his own nearby.[34] The hostillar had a garden in 1331, when he planted hemp seed there.[35] No specific references to the terrar's garden are to be found, but in 1463/4 the terrar bought 2 quarters 3 bushels of unspecified seeds, for £1. 11s. 8d., 7 per cent of his total expenditure in that year, implying significant gardening activity.

Finally, the cellarer, as one would expect of the obedientiary with special responsibility for the priory's food supply, appears to have had several garden spaces. The main one was known as the Impgarth, a name which may imply nursery activities such as propagation.[36] This was clearly a kitchen garden, as seeds and plants feature regularly in his accounts. For example, in 1466/7 the cellarer purchased 2 lb of onion seed and other seeds for planting there, together with

---

[30] Fowler (ed.), *Account Rolls*, i. 88; iii. 647.
[31] Dobson, *Durham Cathedral Priory*, 70.
[32] Fowler (ed.), *Account Rolls*, i. 271–2; ii. 558; iii. 611.
[33] Ibid. iii, 704. [34] Ibid. i. 228; ii. 419. [35] Ibid. i. 115.
[36] J. H. Harvey, *Early Nurserymen: With Reprints of Documents and Lists* (London, 1974), 18–21.

herbs and vegetables.[37] Onion seed, herbs, and other unspecified seeds are also listed in the 1471/2 account, and in 1500/1 both onion and leek seed are mentioned.[38] The cellarer's accounts also contain references to fish ponds (clearly in use, since they were cleaned in 1459/60), a pigsty, and at least one orchard.[39]

Parallel evidence from other monastic sources is similarly sparse, but it is clear that several gardens belonging to various obedientiaries were standard, and that these gardens were used to grow at least some table crops. The most detailed evidence on monastic gardening from this period comes from Norwich, where some of the gardener's accounts have survived. From these it is clear that Norwich Cathedral Priory had at least three different gardens: the kitchen garden, which grew garlic, shallots, porrets, leeks, colewart, beans, parsley, and other unspecified herbs; the infirmary garden, which grew saffron, and which produced honey for the infirmarer to sell; and orchards, including apple, pear, cherry, walnut, and hazelnut trees.[40]

Both the cellarer and the kitchener of Battle Abbey had gardens which they cultivated: watering cans were purchased for the two gardens in 1464/5, and the cellarer's salary payments in 1478/9 included 16s. 8d. for the gardener's salary and robe.[41] The only crop mentioned is onions, for which the cellarer purchased seed.[42] At Abingdon Abbey, there was a full-time gardener who produced his own accounts. He appears to have been primarily in charge of orchards, for the only produce for which he accounted was fruit and nuts. Some of these were sold – fruit produced in his garden sold for 10s. 0d. in 1450/1, and filberts netted 1s. 11d. – but he was evidently also supplying some to table, as he bought 2s. 8d. worth of fruit in the same year.[43] There were at least five gardens at Abingdon. The gardener had at least a garden and a croft (and the orchards may have been in

---

[37] Fowler (ed.), *Account Rolls*, i. 91; see also 92–4.

[38] DCM Cellarer's accounts, 1471/2, 1500/1.

[39] Fowler (ed.), *Account Rolls*, i. 88 contains references to fish ponds and an orchard. For the pigsty, see DCM Cellarer's account, 1480/1. In DCM Cellarer's account 1500/1, a payment is made for fencing 'le Westorchard', possibly implying a distinction.

[40] C. Noble, *Farming and Gardening in Late Medieval Norfolk; Norwich Cathedral Priory Gardeners' Accounts, 1329–1530* (Norfolk Record Society, 61, 1997), 5, 8–9.

[41] Searle and Ross (eds.), *Battle Abbey*, 140, 151.

[42] Ibid. 136, 150.

[43] R. E. G. Kirk (ed.), (Camden Society, NS 51, 1892), 129–30.

addition to these), and he received rents from the clerk of works and the precentor for gardens leased to them.[44] In addition, the chamberlain certainly had a garden too, for in 1428/9 he spent 1s. 1d. on seeds for it.[45]

Early gardening manuals make it clear that the cultivation of a wide variety of garden crops was common throughout much of northern Europe at this time. Well over a hundred types of fruit and vegetables are mentioned in just two books, *The Feat of Gardening* (1440) and *Le Menagier de Paris* (1393), and this list excludes such common crops as garlic, shallots, and cress (which were presumably so commonly grown as to need no instruction), and saffron and carrots, which may have been the preserve of specialist growers.[46] Moreover, John Fitzherbert's *Boke of Husbondry* (1523) not only advises the husbandman to grow several varieties of pears, apples, nuts, cherries, and plums, but also explains how the necessary grafting may be carried out.[47]

The fact remains, however, that there is only very patchy information available on the crops actually grown in monastic gardens, and little or no record of the amounts of these crops which entered the monastic diet. The bursar/cellarer indentures for 1465/6 and 1474/5 record the purchase of onions costing 5s. 2d. and 5s. 4d. respectively, but the weight or number of onions bought is not given. The lack of detailed kitchen accounts for Durham in this period is a notable gap in the records here, but even the few accounts that do exist for other monasteries, and for Durham in earlier periods, vary in the extent to which they record fresh produce, and the impression given is that items bought at market were recorded but not items supplied by the monastic gardeners. For example, the account of the kitchener of Selby Abbey for 1416/17 includes 4s. 9d. spent on 2 bushels 3 pecks of mustard seed (almost certainly used as a spice rather than planted, since a payment is included for mending the mustard-grinding stones), 5s. 4½d. spent on an unspecified quantity of cabbages and leeks, 1s. 0d. for garlic, 3s. 0d. for onions, and 7s. 6d. for 1 quarter 1 bushel of green and white peas.[48] With the exception of the garlic,

[44] R. E. G. Kirk (ed.), (Camden Society, NS 51, 1892), 128.
[45] Ibid. 105–6.   [46] J. H. Harvey, *Early Nurserymen*, 18–21.
[47] J. Fitzherbert, *The Boke of Husbondrye*, ed. W. W. Skeat (English Dialect Society, 1882), 87.
[48] Tillotson, *Monastery and Society*, 167–8.

which was simply 'purchased this year', the suppliers of these goods are named in the accounts, making it clear that these were indeed market transactions. However, the Selby kitchener clearly did have the use of a garden as well, for in the same year he paid 6d. to a general labourer (by no means a specialist gardener, for he had previously been employed repairing the kitchen ranges) 'for digging in the garden called *Herynghousgarth* for 3 days in order to plant and sow herbs there'.[49]

At Westminster, the kitchener's daily records sometimes gave values to the produce of the monastic gardens and sometimes did not.[50] Whilst it is possible, therefore, that significant quantities of fresh produce were included in the monastic diet but were excluded from the records, from the lists of ingredients used at each meal that are available from Westminster fresh fruit and vegetables do not appear to have been commonly consumed. Indeed, Harvey has estimated that they accounted for only around 0.5 per cent of the calorific intake of the Westminster monks in this period, and that the monks were almost certainly deficient in vitamin C as a result.[51]

Salt

Large quantities of salt were bought by the bursar, an average of 67 quarters 5 bushels 1.5 pecks, which at an average cost of £13. 3s. 2d. made this a major item of food expenditure. The bursar distinguished two particular varieties of salt from his usual purchases, Bay salt (from the Bay of Biscay) and 'Courtladies salt' (perhaps a finer grind). However, there was little or no price differential between these varieties. It is probable that this salt was primarily bought for salting meat, and that we know that the priory bought live cattle, slaughtered them itself, and 'powdered' some of the carcasses confirms this. Whether or not any of the salt bought was used for cooking or for seasoning food in its own right is unknown, but that it was bought only by the bursar rather than by the cellarer makes it seem unlikely. It is possible, however, that small quantities of salt may have been included in the unspecified 'diverse spices' bought by the bursar, cellarer, or communar, and this may have been table salt.

---

[49] Ibid. 167.   [50] B. Harvey, *Living and Dying*, 60.
[51] Ibid. 57, 60–1, 63.

Fats

Oil, butter, and fat occur together in a miscellaneous category of the bursar/cellarer indenture, along with honey and sometimes onions. Two or three barrels of oil were bought each year, and a barrel probably contained 30 gallons.[52] If so, the average amount bought was 76.5 gallons. This could have been olive or rape oil, since both were frequently used in the medieval period. More importantly, the accounts do not specify whether the oil purchased was for use in lights or for cooking. Rogers considered the former to be more common, and so it is possible that this oil was not in fact an item of diet at all, although its purchase by the cellarer would suggest that it was for culinary use.[53] Butter was also bought in each year, but the amount bought was rarely specified. However, in 1515 two purchases of butter were made, one of unspecified quantity but one of 32 stones at 12d. per stone. If this price is taken as standard then it is possible to estimate the amounts bought in the other years from the amount spent in each year, which is always given.[54] From this calculation it would appear that an average of 36.3 stones of butter were bought by the cellarer in each year. Finally, an average of 18.9 stones of fat (presumably lard) were also accounted for in this section.

In addition to these fats purchased by the cellarer, there must also have been fats produced as a by-product from animals slaughtered in the priory. Indeed, it is clear that the priory generated a surplus of these, as the bursar's annual accounts of income regularly show receipts from the sale of tallow and dripping from the kitchen, making £5. 18s. 3½d. in 1480/1. Presumably this was only an excess, and much more would have been used within the kitchens. Occasionally, however, glimpses of such internal uses do show up in the accounts, as in 1478/9 when the bursar's necessary expenses included £5. 5s. 3½d. for wax and fat-skimmings bought from the cellarer for candles.

---

[52] In 1504/5, the cellarer bought 2.5 barrels at £1. 10s. 0d, and 24 gallons at just over a penny each. If oil bought in bulk was slightly cheaper at 1d. per gallon, a barrel would contain 30 gallons. In 1515/16, three barrels 'of greater size' were bought at a higher than normal price.

[53] Rogers, *History of Agriculture and Prices*, iv. 366–7.

[54] Rogers noted the usual price of butter per stone to be around 1s. 1½d. in this period, so 1s. 0d. is not unreasonable (ibid. 360).

Honey

The amount of honey bought in a year more than doubled between the beginning and end of this period, the change point coming abruptly around 1500. The indentures record the purchase of an average of 40.3 gallons per year in the first four decades, and then an average of 89.5 gallons per year in the last two decades looked at here (overall, honey purchases averaged at 56.7 gallons per year over the whole of this period). It is interesting to note that the increase in sugar consumption at the priory noted below did not take place at the expense of honey purchases, but that honey consumption increased alongside that of sugar. Furthermore, unlike sugar, the price of honey did not decrease over this period. This suggests that the falling price of sugar alone is not sufficient to explain the priory's increased demand, but rather that changing tastes may have driven, or at least accelerated, the trend.

Spices[55]

The term 'spices' denoted a wide variety of substances in medieval Europe, and can be usefully subdivided into several categories. The monks themselves accounted under this heading for sugar, but not, as has been seen, for honey or salt; onions, but not garlic or herbs (many of which, in any case, would have been home-grown rather than purchased); certain nuts, dried fruits, and the 'exotic' spices for which we nowadays tend to reserve the word—principally liquorice, aniseed, ginger, cinnamon, nutmeg, cloves, mace, pepper, and saffron. The range of spices that the monks purchased over this period appears to have been fairly constant, although it is unfortunately impossible to penetrate any changes that might be hidden behind the general headings of 'diverse spices' or '. . . and other spices' which occur so often in these accounts. The hostillar's account in fact only gives such an aggregate, but the communar's and bursar's accounts contain more detail. These specify that sugar (in the form of comfits and 'plate', but not any of the other forms common in this period such as loaves or

---

[55] The information on spices and wine given here draws and expands upon M. Threlfall-Holmes, 'Durham Cathedral Priory's Consumption of Imported Goods: Wines and Spices, 1464–1520', in Michael Hicks (ed.), *Revolution and Consumption in Late Medieval England* (Woodbridge, 2001).

powder), aniseed, liquorice, ginger, nutmeg, cloves, mace, pepper, figs, raisins, and onions were bought in most years. Nuts, saffron, and 'torts' (some sort of cake or tart) were also bought in several years. The hostillar bought ginger, cinnamon, and other unspecified spices in each year, and added 'zintar' to this list after 1505/6.[56]

Some more miscellaneous items are also included in the communar's accounts. These include a category described as 'electuary for the novices' each year: no further detail is given, and it seems likely that this was some sort of medicinal cordial deemed appropriate for the young. Other items appear much less frequently. 'Torts', or tarts, are occasionally mentioned—three were bought in 1502–3, and five in each of 1510/11, 1511/12, and 1517/18. An item 'made of comfit' was bought for 3s. 8d. in 1511–12, presumably as a centre-piece for a banquet. Such 'subtleties' were highly prized examples of the confectioner's or pastry chef's art, and edible crowns, lambs, and eagles were commonly set upon the table between courses at a feast. These figures were made of meat paste in the earlier middle ages, but were increasingly fashioned of sugar or pastry—or even non-edible materials such as cardboard—by this period.[57]

The spices for which most information can be gleaned from these accounts are sugar, dried fruit, and pepper, and for each of these consumption may be estimated. The priory accounts do not, of course, give any details of how or when these spices were used. In attempting to answer this question, other sources have been necessary, and those used here are primarily Andrew Boorde's 1542 *Dyetary*, together with certain recipe collections.[58]

Dried fruit accounted for by far the largest part of the priory's spice purchases each year, in terms of both the quantities purchased and the amount spent. In all, 14 per cent of the priory's spice expenditure was accounted for by dried fruit, and these purchases were split between the cellarer, who spent an average of £2. 6s. 5½d. (10 per

[56] Zintar cannot be traced in the relevant published reference works. Mr Weiner, Deputy Chief Editor of the *OED*, has suggested that it may possibly be an otherwise unrecorded deviant spelling of 'sanders', or sandalwood, which commonly occurs in lists of spice purchases alongside ginger and cinnamon, as zintar does in these accounts.

[57] T. Scully, *The Art of Cookery in the Middle Ages* (Woodbridge, 1995), 109.

[58] Two particularly useful collections of medieval recipes are Hieatt and Butler (eds.), *Curye on Inglysch*, and T. Austin (ed.), *Two Fifteenth Century Cookery Books* (Early English Text Society, os 91, 1888). The principles behind the medieval use of spices are discussed in detail in Scully, *Art of Cookery*.

cent of his spice expenditure), and the communar, who spent an average of £1. 3s. 8½d. (around half his total outlay on spices). The dried fruits that were bought included figs, raisins, 'big raisins', currants, and prunes, and are measured in a bewildering variety of ways: in pounds, dozens of pounds, frails, toppets, pecks, and sorts.[59]

When these measures are standardized, the average amount of dried fruit bought by the priory can be calculated to have been 538 lbs per year. However, this was not spread evenly across the period. The communar bought an average of 120 lbs in the 1470s and 1480s, which increased to over 300 lbs by the early decades of the sixteenth century. The cellarer bought an average of 255 lbs throughout the later fifteenth century, but by the second decade of the sixteenth century was purchasing much greater amounts—692 lbs in 1515. Considerable volumes of dried fruit were entering the monastery, therefore, especially towards the end of this period. Divided into forty monk-portions, the average represents just over 4 ozs per monk per week over the whole year, but this rose to around 7½ ozs at the end of the period under consideration here.

Dried fruit was an essentially Lenten aspect of the monastic diet. At Westminster Abbey, it accounted for 2.5 per cent of the calorific value of the monk's food in that season, and was absent from their diet for the rest of the year. Averaged only across Lent, the average quantity purchased would have given each monk around 5½ ozs per day. This is significantly higher than the comparable allowance received by the monks of Westminster in this period, who even in Lent received only 4 ozs of raisins each per week.[60]

It is worth noting that the great increase in the amount of dried fruit bought by the priory over this period reflects a general trend throughout medieval Europe to include more dried fruit in cookery as time went on, as can be seen in a comparison of fourteenth- and early fifteenth-century recipes with those of the later fifteenth and sixteenth centuries.[61] Figs in particular are a ubiquitous ingredient

---

[59] These measures have been standardized for the purposes of this study, using a combination of documentary references, secondary literature, and the relative prices paid by the priory as a guide. These standardizations are as follows: a frail = 40 lbs; a toppet = 20 lbs; a peck = 80 lbs; and a sort = 120 lbs. Key secondary sources are *The Oxford English Dictionary* (2nd edn., Oxford, 1989), vi. 138 and xi. 140; Wade (ed.), *Customs Accounts*, 311; and Rogers, *History of Agriculture and Prices*, iv. 668–9.

[60] B. Harvey, *Living and Dying*, 57, 64.

[61] Hieatt and Butler (eds.), *Curye on Inglysch*, 12.

in the fifteenth-century recipes that have survived, being used in both sweet and meat dishes.[62]

The forms in which sugar was purchased were rather different in the medieval period to those to which we are now accustomed. Powdered sugar, such as is most common now, was perhaps the rarest and certainly the most expensive form in which sugar could then be found. Most sugar was bought in loaves, solid blocks from which sugar was scraped or broken off as required for use. Alternatively, as was the case in Durham, it could be bought in plate form, comprising plates of brittle sugar, rather like the hard toffee that covers toffee apples. The other main form in which sugar was bought at Durham in this period was as comfits, or confectionery, a term which covered a wide range of flavoured sugars and sweetmeats, from sugared almonds and similar sugar-coated seeds and spices, to sugar that had been delicately flavoured with rose water.[63]

The bursar, the cellarer, and the communar all list sugar purchases in their accounts. The bursar purchased between 3 lbs and 8 lbs each year (averaging just over 5 lbs), and the communar between 3 lbs and 7½ lbs (averaging just over 6 lbs). The cellarer did not buy sugar on a regular basis until 1478/9, and the amount that he purchased was much more varied, fluctuating between none and 64 lbs thereafter but averaging around 20 lbs per year. The average sugar consumption of the monastery as a whole over this period can thus be calculated to have been slightly more than 21 lbs each year, or 8.5 ozs per monk per year.

After sugar, the most common spice in the medieval world was pepper. This was the staple commodity of the spice dealers in the middle ages, accounting for over four-fifths of the cargoes brought to Europe from Alexandria by the Venetian galleys at the beginning

---

[62] Dried fruit appears in the vast majority of recipes listed in Austin, *Two Cookery Books*. Typical sweet recipes based on figs, raisins, and dates include 'Fygeye' (p. 24), and fruit-filled pies (pp. 15, 112). Fruit was also included in meat and fish tarts (p. 47), and several other savoury dishes.

[63] A very wide variety of spices, nuts, seeds, and flavourings were used in making comfits: the 1482 'Regimen Sanitatis' of Magninus Mediolanensis listed the best and most delicious comfits then in use as being candied, sugar- or honey-coated ginger; candied pine-nuts, pistachios, and filberts; candied aniseed, coriander, fennel, and juniper seeds; crude dragees; fine table dragees; rose-sugar; marzipan and walnuts candied in sugar or honey. Similarly, Platina described in the 1475 'De honesta voluptate' how 'by melting [sugar] we make almonds . . . pine-nuts, hazelnuts, coriander, anise, cinnamon and many other things into candies'. (Scully, *Art of Cookery*, 129–31, 57).

of the fifteenth century,[64] and sellers of spices and aromatics were generally known simply as pepperers.[65] European imports of pepper increased by between 30 and 55 per cent over the fifteenth century, due at least in part to the progressive impoverishment of the Muslim Levant, which kept prices low on the Eastern markets throughout the second half of the century;[66] however, imports of other spices increased by much greater amounts over the same period.[67] The greater absolute quantities involved may well have reflected a widening of the strata of society that consumed such spices.

Pepper prices and quantities purchased are specified in the cellarer's accounts only after 1502/3, when the communar began to separate pepper out in his accounts. Both clearly bought pepper throughout this period however, as it is frequently mentioned by name in the communar's miscellaneous list of spices purchased but without individual details being given. The cellarer bought between 72 and 108 lbs of pepper per year, averaging 92.5. The cellarer thus provided the vast majority of the priory's pepper, the communar purchasing only between ¹/₂ and 1 lb per year after 1502/3 when his accounts begin to show a quantity. On average, then, the priory purchased around 93 lbs of pepper per year, and this amount remained steady throughout the period. The amount of pepper consumed by an average monk in a year was thus about the same as the maximum amount of sugar reached by the end of this period—around 2¹/₂ lbs per year, confirming the impression gained from the recipes of the period that pepper was very much a staple of the medieval kitchen, and was used in far greater quantities than now.

The total amount spent on spices by the priory in an average year was around £23. This can be compared with what we know of the

---

[64] C. H. H. Wake, 'The Changing Pattern of Europe's Pepper and Spice Imports, c.1400–1700', *Journal of European Economic History*, 8 (1979), 368.

[65] S. L. Thrupp, 'The Grocers of London', in Power and Postan (eds.), *Studies in English Trade in the Fifteenth Century*, 283; Nightingale, *Medieval Mercantile Community*. A case of a pepperer found guilty of selling adulterated saffron, and banned in perpetuity from following the trade of pepperer and selling 'saffron, ginger, pepper, cloves, sugar or any subtle substance pertaining to the pepperer's trade' is discussed in K. L. Reyerson, 'Commercial Fraud in the Middle Ages: The Case of the Dissembling Pepperer', *Journal of Medieval History*, 8 (1982), 67.

[66] Ashtor, *Levant Trade*, 469–70.

[67] Wake, 'Changing Pattern', 372, 393–4; ginger imports increased by 257%, cinnamon by 395%, and other spices by 561% in the 15th cent. Imports of Moluccan spices—cloves, nutmeg, and mace—increased by 292% in the 15th cent. and by a further 500% between 1500 and 1620.

spice purchases of other late medieval households. The monks of Westminster, for example, spent around £14 on spices each year, excluding the cost of spices for the prior's table for which they accounted separately.[68] This is only around 60 per cent of the total spent on spices by the monks and prior of Durham Cathedral Priory, although the addition of the prior's spices to the Westminster total might make 75 per cent more accurate. The population of Westminster was if anything rather larger than that of Durham, averaging fifty as opposed to forty resident monks, and the amounts that the two monasteries spent on wine were roughly commensurate, making this a striking difference.

Some comparisons can also be made with large secular households. Since 'spices were one of the defining characteristics of upper class diet', it would seem likely that aristocratic households would spend at least as much on spices as the priory.[69] However, the household of Sir Humphrey Stafford, Duke of Buckingham, spent £4. 12s. 0d. on spices in 1452/3, less than a fifth of the priory's average. Evidence such as this lends itself less easily to comparison with the Durham figures, but it may be observed that Stafford's wine purchases, at £13. 18s. 0d., were somewhat less than a third of the amount spent by the priory each year.[70] The household thus used disproportionately fewer spices than wine than was the case at Durham. On the other hand, the Earl of Northumberland's household book reveals a similar outlay on wine to Durham Priory—£49 per year— and a rather higher spend on spices, at £25. 19s. 7d. not including the cost of raisins and figs which were also bought.[71] Whilst direct comparisons are not possible, therefore, the priory's expenditure on spices can certainly be seen to have fallen well within the aristocratic range.

Wine

Like spices, wine was a marker of high social status, and again the priory spent heavily on this item of diet. The vast majority of the wine

---

[68] B. Harvey, *Living and Dying*, 37, 57.
[69] Woolgar, *Great Household*, 129.   [70] C. Dyer, *Standards of Living*, 56.
[71] T. Percy (ed.), *The Regulations and Establishment of the Household of Henry Algernon Percy the Fifth Earl of Northumberland at his Castles of Wressle and Leckonfield in Yorkshire, begun A.D.* 1512 (2nd edn., London, 1905), 6, 19–20.

purchased by the priory was ordinary red wine purchased by the tun. Some white wine and claret were also purchased in several years. It should be noted that the 'claret' referred to in these accounts was not the superior red wine that the term denotes today but a spiced wine preparation. Several recipes for the making of this 'claret' have survived from the medieval period. The ingredients used varied considerably, although the main elements were always a sweetener, usually honey, and spices—a simple preparation might use only cinnamon, galingale, grains of paradise, and honey, infused in white or red wine. More complex recipes contain much longer lists of ingredients; perhaps the most impressive includes cinnamon, ginger, pepper, long pepper, grains of paradise, cloves, galingale, caraway, mace, nutmeg, coriander, honey, and brandy (which was itself probably a distillate of a spiced wine).[72]

These red, white, and claret wines were the staple wines of the priory, and tended to share a common price and (presumably) a common quality. There was a tendency for these three varieties to be classed together in the accounts, suggesting that the accountant, at least, saw little to choose between them. In particular, there are frequent entries in the accounts which give a standard price for all three; for example, in 1499/1500 the bursar bought 'Five tuns and one hogshead of red wine, a pipe of claret and a hogshead of white wine at 100s [per tun]'. Sometimes even the respective quantities were unspecified, as in 1504/5 when the bursar's purchases included 'two tuns of red, claret and white wine . . . at 106s.8d [per tun]'. Entries such as these, together with the large quantities purchased, strongly suggest that the monks of Durham viewed most wine as a commodity rather than a luxury, to be purchased in bulk, and to be selected largely by price rather than by considerations of taste.

The exceptions were the particular types of wine purchased less frequently or in smaller amounts; most prominently the sweet wines that were increasingly fashionable in the latter half of the fifteenth century.[73] These were sometimes referred to generically as 'sweet wine' in the accounts, and sometimes described by a variety of names, of which malmsey occurs most frequently. Other varieties are each mentioned only occasionally—bastard in 1464/5; romney and muscatel in 1503/4; and romney again in 1514/15. 'Sweet wine' is

[72] Scully, *Art of Cookery*, 149–51.
[73] C. Dyer, *Standards of Living*, 62, 105.

occasionally mentioned in small quantities in the 1460s to 1480s, but a trend towards buying this type of wine on a regular basis can be seen by the end of the century, with a butt of malmsey becoming a regular annual purchase by the 1490s. For the most part, these varieties were significantly more expensive than the monks' usual wines. 'Sweet wine' or malmsey was consistently around twice the price of normal wine, as was the bastard bought in 1464/5, these purchases costing roughly the same per butt as the monks paid for a tun of their more usual fare. Romney was the exception, being only slightly more expensive than claret at £5. 6s. 8d. per tun compared to £5. 0s. 0d. Unfortunately, the cost of muscatel cannot be calculated since the quantity purchased is unknown.

These sweet wines were almost certainly significantly stronger, that is, more alcoholic, than the staple wines of the priory. They were known in this period as 'high' or 'hot' wines, as contrasted with the 'mean', or lighter, French, Gascon, or Rhine wines.[74] Actual alcohol contents are unknown and virtually impossible to calculate, since variations in viticulture and fermentation techniques are critical in the formation of alcohol and such details are not known for this period. However, it is known that three qualities of wine were produced by most vineyards, using the juice from the first, second, and (diluted with water) third pressings of the grapes respectively. The last, third pressing wine was the common drink of the peasantry in wine-producing regions, and has been estimated to have contained perhaps 5 per cent alcohol by volume.[75] It is certain that the monks of Durham, in common with other wealthy and middling households, would have drunk the first pressing wine, which would have been much stronger. A rough estimate for the alcohol content of the usual wines might be made on the basis of the weakest wines common today, containing around 8 per cent alcohol by volume, but this can only be speculative.

On average, the bursar purchased 7.7 tuns of wine per year in the years between 1464 and 1520. This was made up of about 0.4 tuns of sweet wine and 7.3 tuns of normal wine, with sweet wines becoming more common towards the end of the period, as has been noted. In

[74] A. Boorde, *The Fyrst Boke of the Introduction of the Knowledge made by Andrew Borde, of Physycke Doctor* (1542), ed. F. J. Furnivall (Early English Text Society, extra ser., 10, 1870), 254–5.
[75] Scully, *Art of Cookery*, 141–2.

addition, each year the sacrist purchased a pipe of wine for use in the masses celebrated in the cathedral, and the hostillar bought around a tun, most of which would have been drunk by the frequent guests that the priory was under an obligation to entertain. Although this latter quantity does not seem large, it is likely that only the more exalted guests of the priory were regaled with wine during their stay. In the late thirteenth century, the keeper of the guest house at Beaulieu Abbey was instructed to give wine to dignitaries such as abbots and priors, and to some parsons and knights 'but not all'; the lower levels of the gentry had to be content with ale.[76] Given the Benedictine monasteries' constant worry about the cost of hospitality, it is probable that this distinction was maintained. It seems likely that the wine purchased by the bursar and by the hostillar was consumed by the monks and guests respectively.

If communion wine and guest wines are disregarded in estimating the wine drunk by the monks as a part of their communal diet, then the priory consumed an average of 15,523 pints of wine each year. Calculating the consumption of an individual monk is far from being an exact science, since it is impossible for us to know how many other people may have shared in this amount, or how it was distributed between the monks themselves. It is also possible, perhaps even probable, that this amount was added to by gifts of wine to the monks which do not of course appear in the accounts. However, a rough estimate might be made on the assumption that absenteeism and additional shares might have effectively cancelled each other out, it being highly unlikely that many seculars or corrodians would have had the right to a share of the monks' wine; and that the wine was shared equally between the monks. The average number of monks residing at the priory at any one time was forty,[77] which leads to the tentative conclusion that the average daily allowance of a monk was 1.1 pints (0.6 litres) of wine.

However, it should be noted that this allowance would have been spread very unevenly across the year. In the fast seasons of Advent and Lent wine is extremely unlikely to have been drunk, and the same probably applied to Wednesdays and Fridays throughout the year. In her study of Westminster monks in this period Barbara Harvey

---

[76] S. F. Hockey (ed.), *The Account Book of Beaulieu Abbey* (Camden Society, 4th ser., 16, 1975), 273.

[77] Dobson, *Durham Cathedral Priory*, 54.

concluded that wine would have been drunk on only 100 days of the year, comprising various saints' days, anniversaries, and other celebrations.[78] This would mean an average consumption per monk of 3.9 pints (2.2 litres) on these days—the equivalent of nearly three modern 75 cl bottles. If this is spread over a larger part of the year, the 193 days that are left after the removal of the fast days noted above, then the allowance would have averaged just over 2 pints on those days.

These levels of wine consumption are much higher than those suggested by St Benedict as reasonable provision. St Benedict allowed for this amount to be varied at the discretion of the prior, but almost certainly envisaged such variations as decreasing, not increasing, the allowance; the rule explains that the half-pint or so that is suggested is deemed 'sufficient' having taken the 'infirmities of the sick' into account; and comments, 'We read that monks should not drink wine at all, but since the monks of our day cannot be convinced of this, let us at least agree to drink moderately, and not to the point of excess . . . [and] where local circumstances dictate an amount much less than what is stipulated above, or even none at all, those who live there should bless God and not grumble.'[79] It should also be noted that, in addition to the wine, each monk received a daily allowance of around a gallon of ale. The volume of alcohol they must have consumed is thus startling to modern dieticians, and can hardly be said to have met St Benedict's guideline of moderation.

It is interesting in this context to note that the report compiled by the Bishop of Durham following his 1442 official visitation of the priory contained several criticisms of illicit drinking, although it concluded that the monks were 'men of worthy lives, chaste and sober, suffering neither the shame nor the chains of fleshy faults'—a judgement that cannot be totally dismissed as partial, since it was not unknown for such reports to contain strong condemnations of the visited house. Certain sections of the report make it clear that drinking to excess was recognized as undesirable; but equally, the priory's replies do not suggest that any great seriousness was attached to such

---

[78] B. Harvey, *Living and Dying*, 44, 58.
[79] T. Fry (ed.), *The Rule of St. Benedict* (Minnesota, 1981), 238–41. The quantity of wine recommended as a daily allowance was a 'hemina', which contained 0.273 litres (*c.*¹⁄₂ pint).

criticisms. Article 20 of the report concerns the chamberlain, whom over twenty of the monks had accused of not carrying out his duties satisfactorily; 'and when accusations are laid before the lord prior on this matter, the latter does not take steps to correct it, but says to the monks that this man is a drunkard, and so nothing is done'. Articles 45 and 46 both concern illicit drinking sessions, involving both the monks themselves and also laymen entering the dormitory to join them. The priory's reply is that such sessions are not known of and shall be prohibited, neither statement being entirely convincing.[80]

Whilst the differing size and composition of different households complicates the task of making relevant comparisons, it is clearly desirable to obtain some idea of how the wine consumption of the Durham monks compared with that of the inhabitants of other similarly wealthy households. Barbara Harvey's analysis of the calorific make-up of the diet consumed by the monks of Westminster in this period revealed that, on average, they received an allowance of just over a quarter of a pint of wine each day.[81] The average Durham allowance of just over a pint was thus a great deal higher. At Battle Abbey few accounts remain, but in 1412/13 the daily allowance per monk can be estimated to have been 1.4 pints,[82] higher than the figures seen here for Durham, although this is calculated from a single account and may be abnormally high. Dyer estimated that at both Battle Abbey and the household of the Countess of Warwick (for which the 1420/1 accounts remain), 'the superior members of the household' probably received an allowance of about two-thirds of a pint of wine each per day.[83]

It should be noted here that wine was almost certainly drunk much more commonly, and in greater quantities, in the first than in the second half of the fifteenth century. Decreasing imports after the English loss of Bordeaux indicate that this was the case throughout

[80] Bishop Robert Neville's Visitation Report (9 July 1442), published as the appendix to R. B. Dobson, 'Mynistres of Saynt Cuthbert', Durham Cathedral Lecture 1972 (Durham, 1974); repr. as ch. 3 in Dobson, Church and Society.

[81] B. Harvey, Living and Dying, 64.

[82] Searle and Ross (eds.), Battle Abbey. In 1412/13 seven tuns of wine were bought (p. 105). It is unclear exactly how many monks were then in residence, but in 1394 there were 27, and 25–30 was the standard range. If there were 27, this would give 1.4 pints per monk per day assuming no other sharers in the wine; if 30, this would become 1.1 pints, matching the Durham figures.

[83] C. Dyer, 'English Diet in the Later Middle Ages', 194.

the country,[84] and Dyer has suggested that the practical effect of this decreasing consumption was spread across all wine-drinking ranks, with rich households cutting back daily allowances and lesser households no longer drinking wine on a regular basis.[85] This picture is confirmed by a comparison of the wine purchases of Durham Cathedral Priory in the first and second halves of the century. The average yearly wine purchase of the Durham bursar was 15.1 tuns in the period from 1415/16 to 1439/40,[86] which was twice that recorded for 1464/5 to 1519/20. The average number of monks inhabiting the priory remained stable throughout the fifteenth century, so that, high though the levels of the latter part of the century may seem, they represented a halving of the amount that was being drunk by the Durham monks half a century previously.

The large, though differing, quantities of wine that all these households consumed may be partially explained when it is realized quite how beneficial to health wine was perceived to be. Andrew Boorde's *Dyetary*, a manual on the healthful qualities and dangers of all sorts of food, with diet suggestions for various complaints, which was first published in 1542 and widely read, devotes a long paragraph to a panegyric on the benefits of drinking good wine—albeit in moderation. Wine was alleged to 'quicken a man's wits . . . comfort the heart . . . scour the liver [perhaps more true than they knew] . . . rejoice all the powers of man, and nourish them . . . engender good blood . . . comfort and nourish the brain and all the body, and resolve phlegm . . . it is medicinable, especially white wine, for it . . . cleanses wounds and sores'. 'Furthermore', Boorde adds, 'the better the wine is, the better humours it engenders.'[87]

In addition, it has been asserted that different levels of wine-drinking helped to define the internal hierarchies of the medieval

---

[84] James, *Medieval Wine Trade*, 58–9. The more usual drink in England was ale: in 1497 an Italian visitor to England noted that 'the majority, not to say everyone, drink [ale]'. Another Italian, in c.1500, commented that the English were 'very sparing of wine when they drink it at their own expense . . . not considering it any inconvenience for three or four persons to drink out of the same cup . . . The deficiency of wine, however, is amply supplied by the abundance of ale and beer'. (C. H. Williams (ed.), *English Historical Documents*, v: 1485–1558 (London, 1967), 190, 195.)

[85] C. Dyer, *Standards of Living*, 105.

[86] Calculated from the table in N. Morimoto, 'The Demand and Purchases of Wine of Durham Cathedral Priory in the First Half of the Fifteenth Century', *Nagoya Gakuin Daigaku Ronshu*, 20 (1983), 101.

[87] Boorde, *Fyrst Boke*, 254.

aristocracy.[88] In particular, the laying in of casks of wine was a mark of the richest households.[89] Buying a tun, pipe, or hogshead of wine, rather than purchasing it by the gallon as required, entailed a considerable capital investment. It also meant that the volume of wine had to be drunk in the next few months or be wasted—at best, wine began to deteriorate after six or seven months, due to the hardly sterile processing conditions of the middle ages, although the stronger, sweeter wines kept for longer due to their higher alcohol content.[90] François Villon, criticizing the opulent lifestyles of French monks in the middle of the fifteenth century, noted in particular the detail that 'they have good wines, often drawn from the wood [*embrochez*]'.[91] By buying and drinking wine in these quantities, the monks of Durham were clearly showing that they considered themselves to be near the top of the social ladder.

CONCLUSION

This chapter has of necessity been concerned with the overall averages that show the shape of the diet of Durham Cathedral Priory. The diet of two different individuals within the priory may have been very different: a monk's portion would have been much larger and more varied than that of a servant or corrodian of the priory, and the prior's table would no doubt have included a much wider variety of luxury foodstuffs—sweet wines, spices, game, and freshwater fish— than that served at the general common meals of the priory. Moreover, the monastic calendar meant that the type or quantity of food served was rarely the same two days running, for meals were organized around fast days and feast days, and fast and feast seasons. The more expensive foodstuffs such as cygnets, pike, and other fresh fish and game were often noted in the accounts to have been bought specifically for certain feast days, such as Christmas or St Cuthbert's day.

[88] C. Dyer, *Standards of Living*, 62.

[89] An Italian reporting on England in *c*.1500 specifically noted that 'few people keep wine in their own houses, but buy it, for the most part, at a tavern' (Williams (ed.), *English Historical Documents*, 195).

[90] James, *Medieval Wine Trade*, 165. Boorde commented that 'high wines, such as Malmsey, may be kept long' (*Fyrst Boke*, 254).

[91] François Villon, stanza 32 of 'Le Testament' (*c*.1461); trans. in *Poems*, ed. J. Fox (London, 1984), 39.

Such variations are impossible to glean from the annual enrolled accounts of the priory, and it is unfortunate that the cellarer's weekly accounts do not exist for this period. However, the most recent of these weekly accounts to survive, those for 1449/50, have fortunately survived for the entire year. The cellarer's spending on food for the monastery fluctuated considerably from week to week around the average of £5. 5s. 4d., but the only notable trend was that spending dipped considerably in Advent, to an average of £4. 7s. 0d. per week, whilst in the Lenten weeks of 1449/50 spending was slightly higher than normal, averaging £5. 18s. 0d.

However, it must be noted that spending alone is an unreliable guide to diet due to the widely varying costs of different types of food. The types of food purchased by the cellarer in Advent were not noticeably different from those purchased throughout the year. Fish, though, was a relatively expensive item of diet, and it was certainly the case that during Lent the monks' diet was dominated by fish, to the exclusion of other meat. In the first week of Lent in 1450, the kitchen took delivery of 2,500 herrings, 39 dogdraves, 19 salmon, 19 stockfish, five bushels of mussels and two of cockles, three seams (horse-loads) of unspecified fish, 6½ fresh salmon (the others were probably salted), and 7d. worth of whiting. The only other foodstuffs bought that week were 5d. worth of onions and 2 lb of almonds.[92] The following week, in which over £10 was spent, saw a considerable store of fish being laid in: 3,391 herrings, 64 dogdraves, 31 salted salmon, 32 stockfish, £1. 4s. 4d. worth of whiting and 120 lampreys.[93] By contrast, the diet of a month beforehand had balanced fish with other meats; in a typical week in January, the cellarer's fish purchases comprised 560 herring, 3 salmon, 4 dogdraves, 34 'beadnell fish', 2 bushels 2 pecks of mussels, 2 seams of unspecified fish, and 3s. 2d. worth of whiting. In addition, he had bought 4 cattle, 11 sheep (and an additional 3d. worth of mutton, presumably ready butchered), 2 pigs, 5 calves, 42 hens, 1 capon, 16 piglets, butter, and 420 eggs.[94]

In addition to these variations due to the church's cycle of fast and feast, some purely seasonal variations in the monastic diet can also be seen from these accounts. In spring, lambs and poultry feature more

---

[92] DCM Cellarer's account, 1449/50, month 11 (week commencing 8 Mar. 1450).
[93] Ibid., month 11 (week commencing 15 Mar. 1450).
[94] Ibid., month 9 (week commencing 10 Jan. 1450).

strongly, whilst at the height of summer very few fish were eaten, probably because the heat meant that they spoiled too quickly. For example, in one week towards the end of August the cellarer's total fish purchases comprised only 8 dogdraves, 12 salmon, 3 seams of unspecified fish, and 1s. 5d. worth of whiting.[95] Shellfish were bought only between December and March, whilst game birds occur in these accounts only in the autumn and early winter, between September and December.

To summarize the diet of the priory, however, and to make comparisons with the situation elsewhere, it is necessary to return from this level of detail to the annual averages looked at throughout this chapter. Compared with the findings from Barbara Harvey's study of Westminster, it has been seen that the monks of Durham ate roughly the same amounts of bread and drank roughly the same amounts of ale, but consumed much more meat (and within this, much more beef and less mutton) than the Westminster monks. This higher level of meat consumption was not compensated for by a lower consumption of fish, since the Durham monks also ate at least as much fish (including vastly more herring and other fatty fish and much less cod and whiting) as their brothers in the south. The proportion of fresh produce at both houses is hard to establish, but may well have been very low. Luxury products—spices and wine—were consumed in large quantities at both Durham and Westminster, although in both cases Durham appears to have indulged itself rather more than Westminster. Overall, the diet which these accounts reveal is one of plenty and variety, though with too much meat and too little fresh fruit and vegetables to be considered healthy today. Both dietary staples and luxury goods were apparently bought and consumed freely, although the level of the latter does not appear to have been disproportionately high when compared to levels of consumption at other great households of the same period.

It seems likely that both the difference in the quantity of meat, and the relative proportions of different types of meat and fish eaten at the two houses, were due to their very different locations. The high proportion of meat eaten at Durham may well reflect the pastoral bias of farming in the north of England, for example. To this limited extent, this examination of the monastic diet at Durham in the late middle ages suggests that regional differences in availability may well have

[95] Ibid., month 4 (week commencing 23 Aug. 1449).

been one factor in determining the priory's purchases. However, so far this analysis has not shed any light on the other reasons behind the monks' choices of diet elements; on the vexed question of whether variations in availability from year to year, changing prices, fashion, personal preference, or social considerations were relevant factors in their purchasing decisions. The following chapter addresses these questions, and compares the factors influencing the monks' choices of staple and luxury foodstuffs and their choices of cloth, another socially visible commodity with connotations beyond the satisfaction of basic needs.

3

Price, Preference, and Purpose: Factors Influencing the Priory's Purchasing Decisions

The obedientiaries who were responsible for provisioning the priory had first to decide what commodities to purchase and how much of each was required. This chapter focuses on how these decisions were made, by looking at the various factors that might have influenced or limited the obedientiaries' choices. Certain basic needs such as clothing and sustenance clearly had to be met, but within these categories considerations of tradition, cost, social status, availability, and preference shaped the specific ways in which these needs were satisfied, and the extent to which basic need became irrelevant as a factor in consumer choice.

By looking at what the obedientiaries actually bought for the priory, it is possible to deduce some of the reasoning behind their choices. This chapter takes the form of three case studies which illustrate the varying extent to which different factors influenced choices in staple, non-staple, and socially significant commodities. The first case study looks at the bursar's grain purchasing over this period. Grain provided the priory with the principal raw ingredient for bread and ale, the staple items of late medieval diet for all members of society. It was a necessity with a relatively inelastic demand yet was subject to unreliable supply fluctuations as harvest quality depended on annual weather conditions. Secondly, the wine and spices purchased by the priory are analysed. With luxury imported items such as these, the effects of fashion and availability on the priory's purchasing are particularly clear. Demand for these commodities was technically elastic, but the priory's response to price changes varied between individual varieties. The third case study concerns the cloth and clothing bought by the priory. Whilst some degree of clothing was clearly a necessity, much of that purchased by the priory was imbued with social significance, being designed to illustrate in a tangible way the strict social hierarchy on which the monastery, and indeed the society in which it was situated, was predicated. For some cloths this was the overriding factor in the obedientiaries' purchasing decisions, whilst for other, more utilitarian textiles the situation was more straightforwardly based on need and market conditions.

PRICE AS A DETERMINING FACTOR: GRAIN

Mode price: a note on terminology

Any discussion of the priory's grain purchasing which refers to the prices paid must first note that every year saw a mode price, that is a seemingly standard price for each grain type in each year at which the majority of that grain type was bought by the bursar in that year. This price was not a frozen or customary price since it could change quite dramatically from year to year, indicating that it was in some way a reflection of the prevailing market conditions. Nor was it a price set in stone by the priory for each year, as in many years there are some examples of transactions taking place at other prices, and in some years the mode price is much less prevalent than in others. Nevertheless, the existence of such a price may imply that a fixed price was set for each year—perhaps by reference to some external event such as 'the price in Durham market on Michaelmas Day'—and was then generally accepted as the norm by the priory and its suppliers alike, except when fluctuations in supply and demand were sufficient to cause its abandonment and the re-establishment of the market price in the priory's dealings.

No reference survives in the accounts as to where, when, or how the seemingly normative mode price was set. However, two sets of grain prices are given for 1424/5 in the prior's Marescalia roll for that year. Only five fifteenth-century examples remain of these rolls, which primarily record breaches of weights and measures legislation, and the other four lack equivalent information; however all four are missing either their beginnings or ends or both, so may have originally contained this information. The first example appears at the beginning of the roll recording the proceedings of the prior's Marescalia court held at Staindrop on Monday, 22 January 1424, immediately prior to the list of indictments and judgements, and reads: 'Wheat 8s.8d. per quarter. Barley 5s. Oats 2s.4d.'[1] The second comes at the end of the short roll for the court held at Elvet on the Feast of the Conversion of St Paul (Thursday, 25 January) 1424, and states: 'Wheat price per quarter 9s.6d., Barley 5s.6d., Oats 2s.2d.'[2] These prices were presumably the prices at the respective markets on the respective dates, and are in all cases rather higher than the mode prices paid for these commodities by the bursar in that year, which were 6s. 8d. for wheat, 4s. 5½d. for barley, and 1s. 8d. for oats.[3]

Transactions made at prices other than the annual mode price were exceptional, especially in the first half of this period. For thirty-six of the forty-eight years for which the bursar's expenditure has survived, wheat was bought by the bursar at only a single price. In five years there was a single exception, and in seven years there were several exceptions: such variations were largely confined to the 1460s and to the period from 1505–20.[4] A broadly similar pattern can be seen in the barley prices, with thirty-one years having only a single price, seven years having a single example of a deviant price, and greater variation occurring in eleven years.[5] For barley, however, the temporal divisions are rather less clear-cut than for wheat, although only one example of a non-mode price being used falls within the central period from the mid 1470s to the mid 1490s. The prices of oats and of peas and beans were even less prone to variation: the same price was paid by the bursar for all the oats that he bought in thirty-nine

---

[1] Fowler (ed.), *Account Rolls*, ii. 363.
[2] Ibid. 367.   [3] DCM Bursar's accounts, 1423/4.
[4] For wheat, the mode price was the only price in 1462/3, 1465/6, 1467/8, 1470–5, 1478–82, 1484–8, 1492–1501, 1503/4, 1506/7, and 1508–11. Years in which there was a single exceptional price were 1468/9, 1504/5, 1506/7, and 1512–13, although it should be noted that the accounts for the last two years contained only a few entries, and the deviant entries were for large quantities of grain, 132 quarters 5 bushels 1 peck and 126 quarters 3 bushels 3 pecks respectively. There were several entries at prices other than the mode price in 1464/5, 1469/70, 1476/7, 1504/5, 1514–15, and 1520/1. These figures exclude the small amounts of rye which were included in the wheat section of the bursars' accounts but which usually had a different mode price.
[5] For barley, the mode price was the only price in 1462/3, 1464–5, 1470–2, 1474/5, 1476/7, 1478–80, 1484–8, 1492–6, 1500–1, 1503–4, 1505–6, 1508–10, 1515, and 1520. A single deviance occurred in 1466/7, 1473/4, 1482/3, 1487/8, 1504/5, and 1514/15, and several deviances can be found in the accounts for 1467–9, 1475/6, 1497–9, 1507/8, and 1511–13.

years, one transaction involved a variant price in each of ten years, and there is only a single example of more variation than this, whilst the price of peas and beans displayed any variation at all only in four years.[6] Many of these exceptional prices occurred in what were clearly market transactions rather than payments in kind by tenants (see Chapters 5 and 6 for discussion of these two modes of acquisition), and it seems likely, therefore, that the mode price was a price set by the priory for the calculation of rent payments in kind. In what follows, any reference to annual prices refers to the mode prices unless variant prices are specified.

Price movements

The mode prices of the different types of grain bought by the bursar fluctuated widely from year to year (Fig. 3.1). In addition, they also moved relative to one another, so that whilst in general wheat was the most expensive, followed by barley, peas and beans (which comprised a single category in the accounts), and finally oats, this pattern did not hold in every year. For example, in 1480–2 the prices of barley and of peas and beans were the same, as were the prices of wheat and of peas and beans after 1506/7.

Such movements in the relative prices suggest that the different crops were affected to different extents by adverse weather conditions. In general, however, the prices of the different grains moved more or less together, such that it is possible to see a general pattern of 'good' and 'bad' years in this data.[7] In particular, there is a clear synchronicity of movement of the prices of all four varieties in the periods 1464–6, 1478–88, and 1492–5.

The way in which the prices of the different grains moved relative to one another is revealing. As Fig. 3.2 clearly demonstrates, the price of wheat was the decisive factor in these relative movements. The *differences* between the price of wheat and the prices of barley, oats and peas and beans are graphed alongside the actual price of wheat, and it can be seen that virtually the same curve is described by each

---

[6] The price of oats varied from the mode more than once in 1465/6, and once only in 1472/3, 1482/3, 1498/9, 1505/6, 1512/13, 1515/16, and 1520/1. The price of peas and beans varied once in 1464/5, 1504/5, and 1507/8. In 1520/1 there was more than one entry at the deviant price (6s. 8d.) and only a single entry at the mode price (5s. 4d.), but 12 quarters were bought at the latter and only 6½ at the former price.

[7] See also Ch. 5.

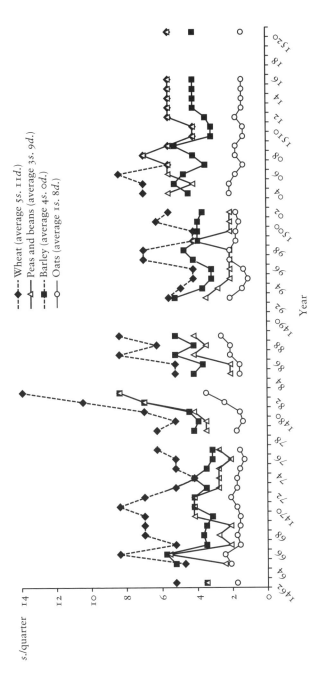

FIG. 3.1. Mode price of each grain variety, 1460–1520

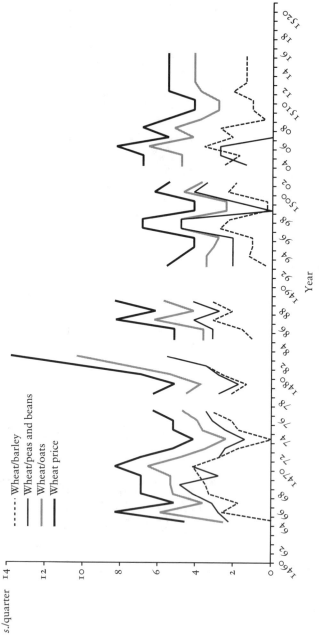

s./quarter

------ Wheat/barley
—— Wheat/peas and beans
—— Wheat/oats
—— Wheat price

FIG. 3.2. Differentials between the price of wheat and of other grains, 1464–1520

line. The implication of this is that wheat prices rose and fell proportionally to but much more violently than the prices of the other commodities looked at here.[8] That is to say, wheat prices fluctuated in the same direction as the prices of the other commodities, but more so. The most likely explanation for this phenomenon is that as wheat was considered by far the most desirable grain demand for it was less elastic than for others, so that similar shortages in supply across all crops affected wheat prices to a greater extent.

The impact of price changes on purchasing

It is an axiom of much discussion of medieval diet that wheat was the grain of choice in good years, and that in years of bad harvest wheat was supplemented with other grains to a greater or lesser extent depending on the status and wealth of the consumer. This pattern was to some extent regional, with wheat predominating in the south and east of the country but other grains which grew well elsewhere always playing a more important part in the diet of those living in other regions.[9] However, although Durham Priory did record the acquisition of some rye to mix with wheat in most years, only very small amounts were involved. Nevertheless, it is interesting to note that the proportions of wheat bought by the priory did change to some extent in inverse proportion to the fluctuating wheat price.

[8] This may be seen through an example of what would happen in the graph if the prices of the different grains moved in various hypothetical relationships. The average price of wheat in this period was 5s. 11d., and the average price of barley 4s. 0d. If the prices of wheat and barley rose and fell with complete synchronicity, i.e. maintaining a 1s. 11d. difference so that when wheat rose to 7s. per quarter barley cost 5s. 1d. per quarter, then the 'wheat/barley' line on the graph would be flat, showing a constant value of 1s. 11d. If wheat and barley prices rose and fell proportionally, so that when wheat prices rose to 9s. 0d. barley would also rise by 52%, i.e. to 6s. 1d., then the graph would look similar but subtly different to that seen in Fig. 3.2. That is, the wheat price and wheat/barley differential lines would rise and fall together, but the fluctuations in the differential line would be less pronounced, reflecting the fact that percentage changes translate into smaller movements when smaller absolute values are in question. If the price of barley remained constant, but the price of wheat fluctuated, then the difference in price would move in accordance with that of wheat, and it is this last pattern which can be seen here. However, since the price of barley did not in fact remain constant this pattern must be interpreted as the price of wheat moving proportionally more than that of barley, and indeed oats and peas and beans.
[9] N. S. B. Gras, *The Evolution of the English Corn Market from the Twelfth to the Eighteenth Century* (New York, 1915; reissued 1967), 37; C. Dyer, *Standards of Living*, 55–7.

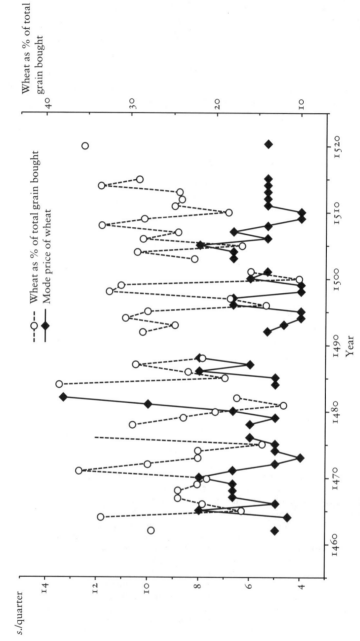

FIG. 3.3. Impact of price changes on the amount of wheat bought by the bursar, 1460–1520 (as % of total grain purchases)

Overall throughout this period 36.6 per cent by volume of the grain bought by the bursar was wheat, a proportion which varied between a lowest point of 8.5 per cent and a high of 39.9 per cent. There was no simple mechanical relationship between the price of wheat and the proportion bought, but they were certainly related. That is to say, whilst the same wheat price in different years by no means meant that identical proportions of wheat would be purchased by the priory, nevertheless when the price of wheat increased the priory tended to decrease the percentage of wheat purchased, and vice versa. This is illustrated by Fig. 3.3.

The relationship between increasing prices and a decreasing proportion of wheat being bought is most clearly illustrated in the crisis years of 1480–2, when grain prices increased dramatically. The average wheat price over the period 1460 to 1520 was 5s. 4d. per quarter, but this rose to 6s. 8d. in 1480/1, 10s. 0d. in 1481/2, and 13s. 4d. in 1482/3. The proportion of wheat bought by the priory in these years fell to 19.5 per cent, 10.6 per cent, and 16.7 per cent respectively. Whilst this shows the effect of increasing prices, that the proportion of wheat actually rose slightly in 1482/3 when the price was at its height also demonstrates that this was a trend rather than a strict correlation. On the same note, the lowest proportion of grain purchased by the priory in this period, 8.5 per cent, occurred in 1500/1 when the wheat price was only moderately above the average, at 6s. 0d. per quarter. It may well have been the case in 1482/3 that the priory's stores of wheat had been depleted over the previous two years of high prices (see the following section on stockpiling for a discussion of the priory's use of the granary), and could no longer be called upon to supplement its wheat purchases.

A similar picture may be seen for the total amount of grain bought by the bursar for the priory from year to year. Fig. 3.4 shows the relationship between the average annual mode price for all types of grain, weighted to take into account the different amounts of each bought, and the total quantity bought by the bursar for each year. The picture is not a straightforward one, but some interesting observations may be drawn. In the first place, it may be seen that there is some relationship between price and the amount of grain acquired by the priory. Where the price increased a great deal, notably in 1481–2 and to a lesser extent also in 1470–1 and 1496–7, the amount bought dropped. Similarly, drops in price, such as in 1494 and 1499, saw an increase in the amount bought. In general it would appear that, whilst there

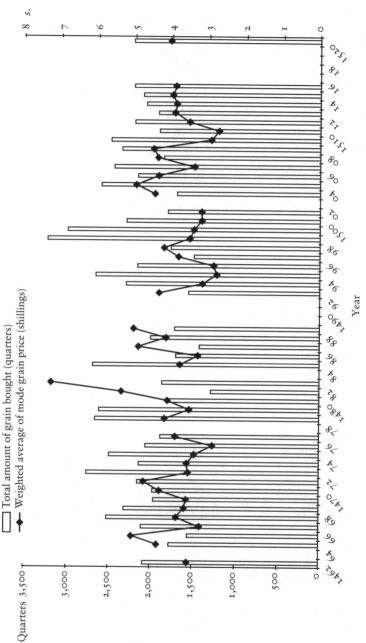

FIG. 3.4. Total amount of grain bought by the bursar each year, with weighted average of mode grain prices, 1460–1520

was not a direct correlation between price and amount bought, nevertheless the amount bought approached its highest level of *c*.3,000 quarters when the price approached its lowest level of *c*.3 shillings per quarter, and dropped as the price increased, approaching its lowest level of *c*.1,500 quarters when the price went above *c*.5 shillings per quarter. This implies a surprising degree of elasticity of demand in a commodity so fundamental to diet. An effective minimum demand for grain for the priory was around 1,500 quarters a year, with purchasing to this level being unaffected by price changes. It is also clear that purchasing above this level was correlated with changing prices to some extent: for example, there are only two instances of large quantities of grain over 2,500 quarters being purchased when the average price was over 4*s*. 0*d*. per quarter, compared to six occasions when the price was below this level. In addition, the years in which the price was lowest, whilst not seeing the very highest quantities purchased, do show a much higher level, 1,896 quarters being the minimum amount purchased when the price was below 3 shillings per quarter.

It appears, then, that there was no consistent policy in place either to buy the same amount of grain in each year regardless of price or conversely to spend roughly the same amount each year. The priory was to some degree reactive to price, but other factors than simply price were involved in the purchasing decisions that were made. The minimum amount that the priory required for its needs was the most important of these; the priory bought at least 1,282 quarters 4 bushels of grain each year regardless of price, whereas purchases over this level were much more responsive to price changes.

Stockpiling

The priory's grain purchasing strategies may well have been affected by the existence of the granary. Its presence gave the monastery the ability, should they so wish, to stockpile grain in cheap years to offset shortages that might occur in expensive years. In addition, the state of the supplies contained within the granary from time to time may have influenced the priory's purchasing decisions on a short-term basis. These issues can be investigated by an examination of the amount of grain added to or removed from the granary store in each year, an analysis which is made possible by the fact that the granator's accounts each include the amount of grain left over from

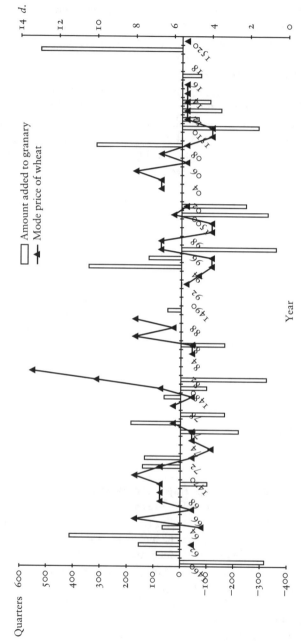

FIG. 3.5. Stockpiling and the use of the granary: the relationship between wheat price and changes to the priory's stock levels, 1460–1520

the previous year and the remainder left at the end of the current year. By a simple process of subtraction, the amount by which the granary was supplemented or depleted over the course of the year is uncovered. This can be compared with the mode price found in the bursar's accounts (Fig. 3.5).

It can be seen, by looking at the years with positive and negative grain store movements separately, that the average amount of wheat by which the granary was supplemented (in years when it was supplemented) was 186 quarters and the average amount of wheat by which it was depleted (in years when it was depleted) was 187 quarters. The similarity between these two figures immediately suggests that the priory practised a policy of maintaining a reasonably constant level of grain in the granary, if not from year to year then at least on average over a few years. The gaps in the series of granator's accounts mean that this cannot be studied in greater depth, but it seems likely that the size of the granary and the risk of spoiling from damp or vermin limited the extent to which large stocks were considered desirable.

The issue of the effect of price movements on stockpiling decisions is rather more complex. A price is lacking for three of the eleven years in which the movement in the granary stocks was greater than average in either direction, and for half of the years in which greater than average amounts of grain were added to the priory. For those years in which both grain movement and price information do remain no clear-cut pattern emerges. For example, in 1501/2 and 1508/9 opposite storage strategies were used despite the price being just over 5d. per quarter in both years. It is possible that this might have been because this was a borderline price, although the average wheat price over the whole of this period was 6d. per quarter. However, the same situation also occurred in 1494/5 and 1510/11, years in which wheat cost only 4d. per quarter, the lowest price recorded throughout the period of this study. It must be concluded that there was no dividing line of a certain price above which grain was taken from store and beneath which grain was added to the granary.

In addition to this lack of a clear price division, there is also no clear relationship between the price paid each year and the size (as opposed to the direction) of the amount of grain added to or removed from the granary. For the one year in which grain prices were startlingly high, at 10d. per quarter, in 1481/2, the amount used from the granary is only the third highest. Similarly, when prices were at their lowest by

TABLE 3.1. Average mode price of grain and granary movements in adjacent years, 1471–1513

Year	Price (d.)	Grain added (quarters)
1471	6.7	142
1472	5	134
1475	5	−218
1476	6	185
1479	5	62
1480	6.7	−98
1481	10	−322
1494	4	344
1495	4	121
1496	6.7	−356
1500	6	−324
1501	5.3	−243
1510	4	−288
1511	5.3	−63
1512	5.3	−148
1513	5.3	−106

no means the smallest amount was taken from the granary. Furthermore, a notable amount was removed from the granary in 1510/11, when prices were at their lowest.

The conclusion that there was no noticeable link between grain price and stockpiling is counter-intuitive. It is possible that the priory's differing reactions in different years in which the same price applied were complicated by external factors which changed over time. In an attempt to eliminate such differences, Table 3.1 shows the grain movements for adjacent years for which both price and granary information has survived.

Whilst some of these figures, such as those for 1479–81, do fit the expected pattern others, such as those for 1475–6, show exactly the opposite tendency. Particularly notable is the data for adjacent years in which the price remained constant. In 1494–5, whilst the price remained at 4d. per quarter, the difference between the amount added to the granary in the two years was 223 quarters, a figure well over the average yearly movement. These results demonstrate that other issues than price must have been important in determining the monastery's grain storage policy, issues which may well have varied from year to year. It would seem probable, given the lack of any consistent pattern in the granary movements, that these were reactive rather than planned; for example, the granary store might have been heavily depleted if it were found to be deteriorating in a particular year due to weather conditions or the quality of that year's harvest. Conversely, a particularly good harvest might have resulted in a great deal of surplus grain being acquired via rent payments or tithes.[10]

PREFERENCE AS A DETERMINING FACTOR:
WINE AND SPICES[11]

Wine

The wine purchasing of Durham Cathedral Priory throughout the late fifteenth century and into the sixteenth century is characterized by the consistently large volume of wine purchased by the monks each year, seemingly regardless of any fluctuations in either supply or price. Throughout the middle ages, individuals and lesser households bought wine as they drank it, from taverns or retailers by the gallon or pint; but large customers like the priory and substantial households bought their wine wholesale, in quantities based on the vast barrel, the tun, which held 252 gallons.[12] It is the three largest of these standard measures, the tun, pipe, and hogshead, that appear most frequently in these accounts, although smaller amounts are occasionally mentioned; as in 1468/9, when the bursar recorded the purchase of 6 gallons of wine 'to refill a pipe'.

---

[10] See Ch. 4.
[11] This section draws upon and corrects M. Threlfall-Holmes, 'Provisioning a Medieval Monastery: Durham Cathedral Priory's Purchases of Imported Goods, 1464–1520', MA thesis (University of Durham, 1997), 16–22, 27–39.
[12] 1 tun = 2 pipes = 4 hogsheads = 252 gallons = 1,008 quarts = 2,016 pints. Non-standard measures used in these accounts included the butt (here taken to have held the same as a pipe), the roundlet (usually containing 18½ gallons), and the barrel (usually containing 31 gallons). These measures are discussed in W. R. Childs (ed.), *The Customs Accounts of Hull 1453–1490* (Yorkshire Archaeological Society Record Ser., 144, 1986), 253–6; and under each term in the full *OED*. Their use at Durham is discussed more fully in Threlfall-Holmes, 'Provisioning', 16–17.

As a cash purchaser of large quantities of wine, the priory was highly exposed to fluctuations in price. However, all the evidence from these accounts demonstrates that the monks absorbed the cost differences rather than adapt their consumption in the affected years. The large quantities of wine purchased by the bursar for the priory were fairly constant over the period in question, and variations do not correlate with price movements (Fig. 3.6). Only one year, 1465/6, stands out for an unusually low amount being purchased, and this was not a year in which wine was particularly expensive. It is not clear why such a low amount of wine should have been purchased that year, but perhaps the wine from the previous year had kept particularly well.

In the years when wine prices rose particularly steeply, notably in 1475/6, 1486/7, and 1487/8, it is possible that the quantities purchased by the bursar may indicate some minor degree of retrenchment. The bursar bought 5 ½ tuns in 1475/6 (compared to 8 tuns in the previous year), 8 in 1486/7, and 7 ½ in 1487/8, having bought 9 tuns in the preceding two years. However, differences of these magnitudes are not confined to years when there was a major price rise, and the volumes purchased by the bursar regularly fluctuated by as much as a tun. In addition, it must be noted that there are some years when the amount spent by the bursar rose dramatically because of an increase in the price of wine, rather than volume being cut back to keep spending level. For example, in 1484/5 the amount spent on wine was £69. 4s. 4d., 144 per cent of the average yearly spend of £48; and in 1486/7, the amount spent went up to £75, the highest spend in these years and 156 per cent of the average. This readiness to pay the highest prices for wine rather than retrench may be seen also in the first half of the century, when the bursar spent as much as £89. 14s. 1½d. on wine in 1443/4.[13] Sweet, stronger wines were more expensive than the usual table wine bought by the priory, but fashion appears to have had a hand here and, as has been seen, these wines were bought with increasing frequency over this period, a butt a year being a regular annual purchase by the sixteenth century.[14]

However, whilst the monks consistently chose to pay high prices over the alternative of having low stocks of wine, there is no reason to

---

[13] Here and elsewhere, figures for the first half of the century are taken from Morimoto, 'Demand and Purchases', 84–115.

[14] See the discussion of the priory's consumption of wine in Ch. 2.

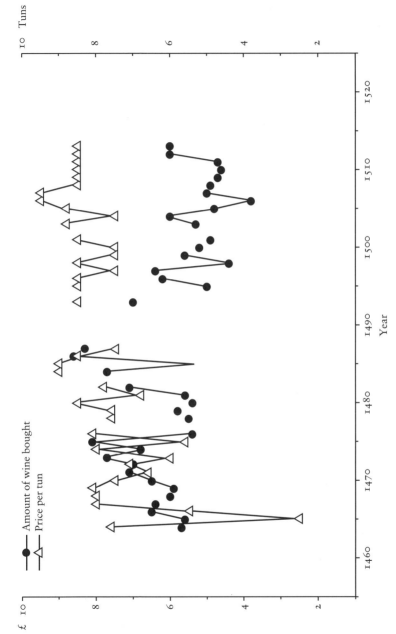

FIG. 3.6. Average price paid for wine by the bursar and the amount bought each year, 1464–1520

believe that they did not keep a careful eye on the prices that they paid for their supplies. There is some evidence to suggest that the bursar shopped around over a wide area for his wine, buying in Hull rather than Newcastle if prices there were more favourable. Overall, 6 per cent of the amount spent by the bursar on wine between 1464 and 1520 is recorded as having been spent in Hull, and this was concentrated across a few years in which wine bought at Hull accounted for a significant proportion of the priory's purchases. In particular, in 1481/2, 93 per cent of the wine bought by the bursar was purchased at Hull; as was 65 per cent in 1487/8. An explanation for this unusual concentration of purchasing away from Newcastle might be found in the fact that in 1486/7 (when the bursar bought 3 tuns of wine in Hull), and in 1487/8, the Hull wine cost £8 per tun compared to £9 per tun paid at Newcastle. Wine prices in Newcastle had nearly doubled since the previous year: in 1485/6, Thomas Swan sold 4 tuns to the priory for £5. 6s. 8d. a tun, whilst in 1486/7 the same merchant's price for a similar quantity (5 tuns) had risen to £9 a tun. It seems unlikely that the same merchant would sell to the same corporate customer in consecutive years two wines of such widely different quality as to account for such a difference in price. In 1486/7, the year this increase occurred, the bursar bought 3 tuns of wine from Robert Chepman of Hull for £8 each; the discovery of such a large difference in price between Hull and Newcastle in this year may well explain his decision to purchase most of his wine in Hull the following year.

Comparable information on prices for 1481/2, the year in which 93 per cent of the bursar's wine purchases were made at Hull, is unfortunately unavailable. The bursar did not purchase wine in Newcastle that year, the remaining 7 per cent being accounted for by wine bought from the terrar of the priory, and the accounts of both the hostillar and the sacrist are missing. However, the price of wine in Hull that year, at £5. 10s. 0d. per tun, was slightly higher than the price in Newcastle the previous year (£5. 6s. 8d. per tun); and the price in Newcastle the subsequent year, 1482/3, is higher still, at around £7. The implication is that price movements in 1481/2 may well have followed a similar pattern as can be seen in 1487/8, with rising prices experienced in Newcastle sending the bursar to Hull to see if wine was cheaper there: and presumably returning to Newcastle in the following year as prices equalized between the two markets.

Short-term local fluctuations such as this were only to be expected, but wider events could also have an impact upon the prices of imported goods such as wine. The prices paid by the priory for wine over this period (see Fig. 3.6) illustrate the effect on wine prices of the loss of Bordeaux and the political manoeuvring caused by the instability of English politics in the third quarter of the fifteenth century. Prices increased to a peak in 1475/6, but then dropped dramatically following the removal of heavy French duties with the Treaty of Picquigney in 1475, and its commercial counterpart signed in January 1476.[15] Apart from the brief but violent rise in the mid 1480s, perhaps a result of Henry VII's order that all wine be carried in English ships, prices generally remained at a consistently lower level between 1490 and 1520—between 4d. and 6d. a gallon—than they had done in the previous quarter-century, when prices had fluctuated between around 5d. and 8d. per gallon.[16] While it would not be true to say that the priory's demand for wine was elastic, since from year to year their purchases did not respond even to the most pronounced price fluctuations, over the whole of this period wine purchases did tend to increase as prices decreased (Fig. 3.6).

Dried fruit

Unlike wine, changes in supply and price did have a direct impact on the priory's purchases of some spices, and as with wine changing fashions in taste also seem to have affected them. The spices for which most information can be gleaned from these accounts are dried fruit, sugar, pepper, ginger, aniseed, and liquorice. In the following section, the priory's purchases of each of these will be briefly considered. By far the largest category of spices bought by the priory, both by volume and expenditure, was dried fruit. The prices paid by the priory for dried fruit varied widely in the first half of this period, but both dropped and became more consistent after 1500.

The average amount of dried fruit bought by the priory was 538 lbs per year, but this was not spread evenly across the period (Fig. 3.7). The communar bought an average of 120 lbs in the 1470s and 1480s, which increased to over 300 lbs by the early decades of the sixteenth century. The cellarer bought an average of 255 lbs throughout the

---

[15] James, *Medieval Wine Trade*, 47–8.   [16] Ibid. 49–50.

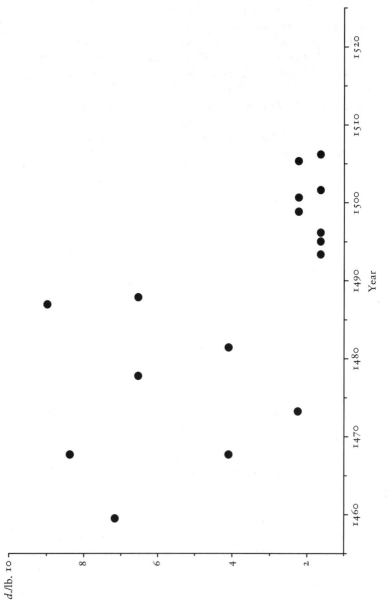

FIG. 3.7. Prices paid by the priory for dried fruit, 1464–1520

later fifteenth century, but by the second decade of the sixteenth century was purchasing much greater amounts—692 lbs in 1515. It would seem likely, therefore, that the priory's demand was elastic, and that the major drop in prices that took place around 1500 stimulated increased demand. It is worth noting that the great increase in the amount of dried fruit bought by the priory over this period reflects a general trend throughout medieval Europe to include more dried fruit in cookery as time went on, as can be seen in a comparison of fourteenth- and early fifteenth-century recipes with those of the later fifteenth and sixteenth centuries.[17]

Sugar

Perhaps the most complete price series in these accounts is that for sugar, the bursar, the cellarer, and the communar all listing sugar purchases in their accounts. This data shows some extremely interesting price movements. As Fig. 3.8 illustrates, sugar prices more than halved over this period, descending in two main steps rather than maintaining a steady downward trend. Between 1478 and 1482, the price of sugar dropped dramatically from a mode price of 20 d. per pound to 12 d.; and then dropped again to around 7d. per pound c.1495. The increased variation in price which occurs towards the end of this period was probably a characteristic of prices in the earlier decades too; a greater variety of evidence is available for these later years, so less uniformity in the data is to be expected.

Sugar prices were dropping throughout Europe in these years as a result of the new Portuguese navigations and subsequent colonial developments, which included a large-scale development of sugar production and trade in and from the new territories.[18] However, it is notable both that the drop in price in Durham came over a decade later than in Flanders, and that prices in Durham (and presumably the north-east in general) were significantly higher than elsewhere, up to double the price in the Low Countries.[19] This may well reflect the

[17] Hieatt and Butler (eds.), *Curye on Inglysch*, 12.
[18] H. Van der Wee, *The Growth of the Antwerp Market*, 3 vols. (The Hague, 1963), ii. 127–9; J. A. Van Houtte, *An Economic History of the Low Countries* (London, 1977), 176.
[19] See Threlfall-Holmes, 'Durham Cathedral Priory's Consumption of Imported Goods', 153.

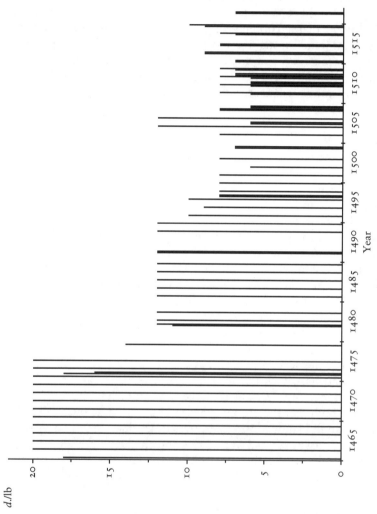

Fig. 3.8. Prices paid by the priory for sugar, 1464–1520

additional transport costs involved in either importing sugar to Newcastle, or transporting it via London. It is also possible that low demand for spices in the Durham and Newcastle area resulted in low levels of competition in the trade; only a handful of merchants appear to have supplied the priory with spices compared to nearly a hundred selling wine.[20]

As with dried fruit, the priory's purchases of sugar show a marked increase over the period under consideration here, rising from around 6 lb per year in the 1460s and 1470s, to 60 or 70 lb by the early decades of the sixteenth century.[21] By the 1520s and 1530s, over 100 lbs of sugar were being bought each year, and the average per monk had thus risen to 2.5 lbs per year, much higher than the average for the period but still relatively low by today's standards. A detailed look at the purchases made by the bursar demonstrates the close relationship between price and amount purchased over this period. The bursar bought 3 lbs per year in the 1470s, when sugar cost 20d. per pound, and was buying around 6 lb per year by the 1490s, when the price had dropped to 10d. per pound or less. In 1505/6 and 1506/7, the price briefly rose from 6d. to 12d. per pound, and the volume purchased by the bursar immediately dropped to 5 lbs, rising to 6 lbs again in 1507/8 when the price dropped to 8d. The quantities bought by the cellarer make the same point more dramatically; he bought no or virtually no sugar in the 1460s and 1470s, and only small amounts (6 to 26 lbs) in the 1480s. By the 1500s much more was being bought: 49 lb in 1503, 50 lb in 1504, and 42 lb in 1506, whilst the four surviving accounts from 1520 to 1536 show the purchase of between 63 and 104 lbs per year. Strong elasticity of demand is shown by these figures, the volume of sugar purchased by the priory in these years more than doubling over the period as the price halved.

Ginger

Ginger was a very popular ingredient throughout the medieval period, being considered an excellent aid to digestion.[22] In particular, ginger

---

[20] See Ch. 6.

[21] As with dried fruit, sugar consumption was rising throughout Europe in this period (Hieatt and Butler (eds.), *Curye on Inglysch*, 9–12).

[22] Boorde, *Fyrst Boke*, 286.

was popular in comfits, and was a common ingredient in a wide variety of meat- and milk-based dishes.[23] The officers of Durham Priory bought ginger regularly—it was one of the few spices mentioned by name each year in the hostillar's accounts, and was listed individually by the communar throughout this period. Ginger also occurs in the bursar/cellarer indentures, but differs from most of the spices acquired by the priory in being bought only sporadically by the cellarer, the purchases of the communar providing the priory with a regular supply of between 1/2 lb and 1 lb per year. The amount bought by the hostillar was not stated in the accounts but was clearly small, whilst the cellarer bought no ginger at all in 1485/6 and 1504/5, 1/2 lb in 1465/6 and 1474/5, 4 lb in 1515/16, and the unusually high amount of 13 lb in 1495/6. Only the communar's purchases provide enough information for an analysis of purchasing trends to be attempted, but the pattern found here is very interesting.

The prices paid for ginger at Durham varied fairly widely over this period, between 1s. 4d. and 3s.4d. a pound, a price range similar to that noted by Thorold Rogers for this period.[24] However, the actual amount spent by the communar on this spice did not vary to the same degree—being between 16d. and 24d. per year—since the amount he purchased varied with these changes in price. A very clear correlation can be seen here between price and demand: the communar bought 1 lb per year when ginger cost less than 2s. per pound, but only 1/2 lb when the price rose above that level. Two shillings per pound was clearly felt to be the turning point, as when ginger cost exactly this much quantities of 1/2 lb, 3/4 lb, and 1 lb were purchased.

Pepper

The lack of more than a single data source for pepper until after 1502/3 means that fewer conclusions can be drawn for pepper. It would seem, however, that no great changes took place in the priory's purchasing of pepper. The price paid varied from year to year, with a low of 13d. per pound paid by the cellarer in 1465/6, and a high of 24d. per pound paid by the communar in 1502/3. However,

---

[23] Austin (ed.), *Two Cookery Books*, e.g. 10–11, 17, 25.
[24] Rogers, *History of Agriculture and Prices*, iii. 528–35.

these fluctuations were not indicative of any trend, and in general pepper prices appear to have remained around the 16–20*d.* mark throughout this period.[25] As has been seen in Chapter 2, the amount bought by the priory appears also to have remained stable.

Aniseed and liquorice

Purchases of aniseed and liquorice are recorded in the bursar's and the communar's accounts, with only one purchase recorded in the bursar/cellarer indentures.[26] The bursar consistently purchased 1 lb of aniseed and 1/2 lb of liquorice in virtually every year until 1507/8, when these quantities suddenly rose to the new levels of 6 lbs and 1 lb respectively, where they remained for the rest of the period. Price changes do not appear to have been behind this increase in the amount of these spices bought by the priory. Although aniseed and liquorice prices are not given separately until after 1507/8, the total paid for the amount of the two that was bought prior to that date makes it clear that prices had not changed over this period. From 1507/8, the prices of the two commodities are given separately, at 3*d.* (occasionally 4*d.*) per pound for aniseed, and 6*d.* per pound for liquorice dropping to 3*d.* or 4*d.* per pound after 1511/12. Before the change point, 6*d.* per year was paid for the two together, which is consistent with the 1507/8 pricing of 3*d.* and 6*d.* per pound respectively. The only price change evidenced here, then, was the late drop in the price of liquorice. This occurred five years after the volume bought doubled, ruling out price change as a factor in that purchasing decision. In any case, this price drop has no parallel in the case of aniseed, yet the volume of this purchased by the bursar did not double but increased sixfold.

Interestingly, the prices and price changes for aniseed and liquorice that are recorded in the bursar's accounts do not find parallels in the

---

[25] Although it might be expected that the Portuguese entry into the pepper business from 1500 onwards would have driven prices steeply downwards, it seems that the Portuguese were careful not to over-supply the market, but to keep imports at a level that would maintain the price on the European market (Wake, 'Changing Pattern', 387–8). Nonetheless prices did drop slightly, and the prices paid by the priory fit the pattern found in Antwerp, with a lowest point around 1515, when the Portuguese had achieved their major victories at sea (Van der Wee, *Antwerp Market*, ii. 129).

[26] In 1495/6 2 lbs of aniseed were bought by the cellarer, but no other purchases are recorded in the sample years looked at here.

communar's records. These show the price of aniseed dropping quite early in this period, from 6*d*. per pound in 1474/5, to 5*d*. in 1489/90, and then to 4*d*. from 1496/7 onwards. The price of liquorice was around 4*d*. per pound in 1474/5 and 1480/1, 6*d*. per pound in 1489/90 and 1496/7, and then 4*d*. from 1499/1500 onwards, this drop thus preceding that shown in the bursar's accounts by ten years. Unfortunately, comparable price series for these commodities are not published, so it is difficult to get a feeling for which of these patterns is the deviant. It is possible that the reason the price drop came earlier for the communar was because he was purchasing larger quantities than the bursar, around 4 lbs of aniseed and 1–1½ lbs of liquorice per year. However, the prices paid by the bursar did not drop when the quantities he purchased rose to these levels; and in any case, one would expect relative price changes to have appeared in both accounts at the same time, even if bulk discounts meant that the absolute prices differed. Nor can these differences be explained entirely by differing sources of supply, although little evidence for this survives and so this may have been the case in some years. The communar states the merchant from whom aniseed was purchased only in three years, and never for liquorice. In 1474/5, aniseed was bought from William Cornforth, in 1480/1 from John Farne, and in 1505/6 from John Farne's widow. These are all familiar names from the bursar's accounts, although direct comparison is not possible in 1480/1 since the bursar's account for this year is badly damaged. In 1505/6, the bursar bought his aniseed from John Eland. However, in 1474/5 both obedientiaries purchased their aniseed from William Cornforth of Newcastle yet they still paid different prices, the bursar paying 6*d*. for 1 lb of aniseed and 1/2 lb of liquorice, the communar paying 1*s*. 0*d*. for 2 lbs of aniseed.

It is interesting that the priory should have bought these spices in comparable quantities to the other spices looked at above, since they were much less common in the recipes of the time. It seems likely that these two items were used primarily for medicinal, rather than strictly culinary, purposes—although the two were by no means sharply differentiated in the medieval mind. The medicinal qualities assigned to them by Boorde do not read any differently from the characteristics he attributes to everything from pepper to strawberries: aniseed 'is good to cleanse the bladder . . . and makes one have sweet breath', whilst liquorice 'is good to cleanse and open the lungs and

breast, and loosens phlegm'.[27] However, it is perhaps significant that
neither liquorice nor aniseed is mentioned at all in the major surviving fifteenth-century recipe collections, and anise, the parent plant
of aniseed, is mentioned only five times in the collections looked at
here.[28] If it were indeed the case that these spices were used primarily
as a medicine, then the sudden increase in volume seen in the middle
of the first decade of the sixteenth century is explicable. Mortality,
both at Durham and elsewhere, appears to have suddenly increased
in this decade, with deaths often attributed to 'sweating sickness'.[29]
The jump in purchasing of these spices in and after 1507/8 may well
be the mark that this high mortality and the monks' attempts to stem
it have left in the accounts.

Wine and spices: concluding remarks

Clearly there were significant variations in the priory's demand and
pattern of changing demand for different commodities within this
overall heading. However, the wines and spices bought by the priory
can be seen as a class of goods with which the priory displayed certain
characteristic purchasing behaviours. First, demand for these commodities was essentially elastic, in the basic sense that they were
not staple foods. The priory's purchases generally show a tendency
to increase purchases of these luxury items when prices dropped,
although the element of display and status which the consumption of
these goods incorporated ensured that short-term fluctuations were
not necessarily mirrored in the priory's purchasing. Secondly, being
imported goods, changes in the political situation and in the economic well-being of areas far distant from the priory impacted upon
prices and upon the supply of these goods. Thirdly, the impact of
fashion and changing tastes must not be forgotten. Europe-wide
trends such as the increasing popularity of strong sweet wines and an
increasing tendency to purchase a wider variety of spices can be seen
mirrored in the priory's purchases over this period. Whilst elasticity

[27] Boorde, *Fyrst Boke*, 281, 287.
[28] Austin (ed.), *Two Cookery Books*; Hieatt and Butler (eds.), *Curye on Inglysch*.
[29] Forthcoming data from the Cambridge Population Study shows this phenomenon (private communication from Mr Alan Piper, Chief Archivist of the Durham
Cathedral Muniments).

of demand can be seen over the longer term for most of these commodities, it seems likely that in the year-to-year purchasing of the priory considerations of taste, preference, and fashion were thought to be the determining factors for these goods.

PURPOSE AS A DETERMINING FACTOR:
THE PRIORY'S CLOTH PURCHASES

The priory purchased a wide variety of cloths, including woollens, linen, serge, hardyn, canvas, sackcloth, haircloth, blanketing, and shirting. These fall into four major categories: livery cloths, other clothing, linens, and cheaper, coarser cloths. Black and white furs were also bought, for trimming the gowns of the major officials of the priory, and some manufactured items such as gowns, gloves, and hoods were also purchased. In total, the average yearly cost of all these goods to the priory was over £71, around 4 per cent of the priory's total annual expenditure, for which an average of 1,474 yards of cloth were purchased each year.

The priory's cloth purchases show a clear distinction between cloths for which social significance was the overriding factor in choosing what to purchase, and utility cloths for which function and price were the only or major considerations. In the first category came outer clothing and certainly the livery garments provided by the priory to its officials, servants, and dependants. Vestments also came under this heading, with all their liturgical significance and potential for defining and reinforcing a divinely ordained hierarchy, as did certain furnishings such as the prior's expensive table linen. Utilitarian cloths, meanwhile, were used for undergarments and everyday clothing and for a variety of household and estate functions. In the following section, these cheap cloths are considered first. Price was the most important factor in the priory's purchases of such cloths as hardyn, sackcloth, and haircloth, and a high degree of elasticity of demand and responsiveness to price changes can be seen. The discussion then turns to linens, an intermediate category which contained some relatively cheap, coarse cloths used for general household purposes and fitting the above pattern, but also some much more expensive textiles used for socially sensitive functions such as table linen and vestments. Cloths bought with display or social differentiation in mind are then considered. The priory's purchases of vestments, garments, and the priory's livery cloths are described, apparent factors in the choices made in these areas are discussed, and finally the social context is examined and comparisons with contemporary practice at other monastic and secular households are made.

Hardyn, haircloth, sackcloth, canvas, and blanketing

The cheap cloths that were bought in the greatest quantities by the priory were hardyn and sackcloth. In addition to these, haircloth occurs twelve times, canvas twice, and blanketing once in these accounts. For most of these purchases no use for the cloth bought is specified, but occasional references both from the Durham material and the records of other similar houses make it clear that these cheap textiles were employed for a variety of domestic purposes, ranging from household uses such as bedding through kitchen functions as rags, rough sieves, and containers, to uses as building materials. For example, Battle Abbey bought canvas in 1442/3, 1465/6, and 1478/9 for binding pipes in the running water system.[30] Again at Battle, in 1399/1400 the purchase of sackcloth and horsehides for sacks and other unspecified uses in the bakehouse is recorded.[31] The granger of Selby Abbey purchased both sackcloth and cloth for making sieves in 1404/5, whilst the kitchener purchased cloth for horses' girths and canvas for making sacks for the poulterer in 1416/17.[32] Sacks were almost certainly the use to which most of the sackcloth bought was put, and these were probably made up within the monastery, as the evidence from Selby suggests. The Durham bursar's necessary expenses frequently included payments for thread, and in 1464/5 this was specified to have been purchased 'for sewing sacks and other necessaries'. Other uses specified for such cloths in the Durham accounts were 4 yards of hardyn purchased by the communar in 1508/9 which were described as being for his exchequer, and the bursar's purchase of 10 yards of bolting cloth (for use in refining flour) in 1464/5. The almoner's inventory from 1515/16 included a number of cloth items which were probably made of the kinds of textiles under consideration here, such as girths, horsecloths, and a number of blankets.[33]

---

[30] Searle and Ross (eds.), *Battle Abbey*, 136, 144, 150.
[31] Ibid. 95.   [32] Tillotson, *Monastery and Society*, 135, 167.
[33] Fowler (ed.), *Account Rolls*, i. 253.

None of these uses for such cloths would have involved them being in any sense on show, or having any impact on public perceptions of the priory. The sole examples of these cheap cloths being used in a public way are occasional purchases of haircloth for use as altar cloths which may be found in some monastic accounts from the earlier half of the fifteenth century, including one example of this happening at Durham. In 1446/7, for example, the sacrist of Selby Abbey bought haircloth for the altar of St Katherine and St Cuthbert, whilst in 1436/7 the master of the infirmary at Durham also bought one haircloth for an altar.[34] It would seem probable that these were intended for dressing the altar in penitential array for Lent, and this practice may well have been continued in the period under consideration here.

Canvas was bought only in 1465/6 and in 1466/7, and it is therefore surprising to see quite large quantities, 113 and 86 ells respectively, appearing in those years. The price in 1465 was 3.2d. per ell and in 1466 3.5d., but clearly no conclusions about the priory's responsiveness to canvas prices can be drawn from such a small amount of data. The fact that only two purchases of canvas occur in these accounts suggest that it was to some extent a speciality cloth, purchased only for specific purposes. In support of this, there is some external evidence to suggest that canvas may have been an imported cloth. Unlike the other cheap cloths discussed here, which are not mentioned in the surviving Newcastle customs accounts, canvas appears several times as an import into Newcastle.[35] In addition, references to canvas in the Cely letters suggest that it was commonly bought in Calais rather than England, and in one case specify the purchase of Normandy canvas.[36] It would seem likely that the priory bought this canvas for a specific unrecorded purpose in 1465–6.

Similarly the accounts record only a single purchase of blanketing, made by the chamberlain in 1504/5. In this year he purchased 160 yards, 100 priced at 6½d. per yard and 60 at 6d. per yard. The large quantity involved suggests that he may have been replacing blankets throughout the monastery; unfortunately, since only ten of the

---

[34] Tillotson, *Monastery and Society*, 223; Fowler (ed.), *Account Rolls*, i. 274.
[35] Wade (ed.), *Customs Accounts*, 19, 22–6, 32, 56–8, 128, 231, 267, 271.
[36] A. Hanham (ed.), *The Cely Letters 1472–1488* (Early English Text Society, 273, 1975), 125.

chamberlain's accounts for these years have survived it is not possible to deduce the lifespan of a medieval monk's blanket. Blanketing may have been used for some warm clothing as well as for blankets themselves. Two entries in the Selby Abbey accounts give the uses for which this fabric was purchased: the keeper of the guest house bought 12 ells in 1413/14 which was indeed used for making blankets, but in addition in 1441/2 the pittancer and chamberlain bought a small amount which was used to make a pair of slippers which were given as a gift.[37]

Slightly more information has survived about haircloth, but again this was not a very common commodity and insufficient data exists for conclusions to be drawn about the priory's purchasing habits. Purchases are recorded in only twelve years out of those looked at here, and occur only in the bursar's accounts. A function is specified only once, when the 40 yards of haircloth bought by the bursar in 1478 were described as being for the malt-kiln, though further details are not given. The quantities purchased remained fairly stable over this period, averaging 47.1 yards per year in the years when purchases were made. Prices too were stable, both the mean and the mode price being 4d. per ell and the price varying from this figure only on four out of the twelve occasions on which haircloth was bought.

Of all these utility cloths, the most significant in terms of the amount bought by the priory was hardyn. This was a coarse fabric made from the hards of flax or hemp; that is, from the woodier parts of the fibres, otherwise discarded after being combed out to leave the finer fibres for making linen. Hardyn was extremely cheap, and became even cheaper over this period, the price per yard falling from 3d. to 2½d. between 1467 and 1492, remaining at 2½d. until 1494, and from 1495 onwards becoming a steady 2d. per ell, although with some sudden fluctuations back to earlier, higher prices recurring after 1507.[38]

Hardyn was almost exclusively bought by the bursar, and was probably used for menial household and estate purposes. The only

---

[37] Tillotson, *Monastery and Society*, 253, 111.

[38] The only exceptions to the 2d. price after 1495/6 came in 1507/8, when the bursar bought 16 out of 177 ells at the higher price of 3d.; in 1508/9, when the communar's 4 ells cost 3d. per ell, and in 1509/10, when the bursar paid 2½d. for just under half his purchases of hardyn.

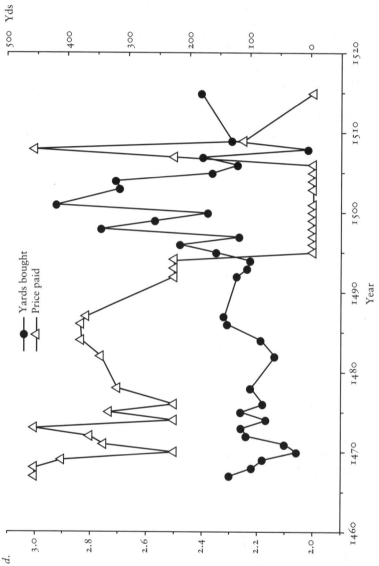

FIG. 3.9. Price paid for hardyn and the amount bought by the bursar, 1464–1520

other purchases to be found in these accounts are in 1486/7, when the sacrist's church expenses included 8 ells of hardyn, and in 1508/9, when the communar bought 4 ells for his exchequer as already noted. The bursar bought relatively large quantities of this cheapest of textiles, an average of 148.6 ells per year. However, this average conceals the fact that the amount bought was much lower towards the beginning, and higher in the later years, of this period. Split by decade, this can clearly be seen; the average bought was 86.4 ells in the 1460s and 1470s, 102.4 in the 1480s, 176.3 in the 1490s, and 220.8 after 1500. The priory's purchases of hardyn show a clear correlation with the changing price, suggesting that the price being charged was the main factor in the choice of hardyn as a material, and in the decision of how much of it to buy in a given year (see Fig. 3.9).

Sackcloth, the other of the miscellaneous cloths of which substantial purchases were made, appears only in the bursar's accounts, where an average purchase of 96.9 ells per year is recorded. There is no marked upwards trend in the volume of sackcloth bought, as occurs for hardyn, though prices again can be seen to have dropped over the period, from between 2.75d. and 3.85d. per ell in the 1460s, to a mode price of 3d. up to 1493, and to a mix of 2.5d. and 3d., weighted towards the lower of the two, thereafter. The drop is less dramatic than for hardyn, and so it is perhaps unsurprising that the correlation between prices and purchases is not so clearly defined here (Fig. 3.10). Indeed, the two seem often to have moved together, suggesting that the priory's demand for sackcloth was relatively inelastic. However, there were some years in which the price changed a great deal and does appear to have impacted upon the priory's purchasing decisions. When the price rose to 4d. from 3d. in 1486/7 the amount bought dropped considerably, although it should be noted that no noticeable reduction in the priory's purchases occurred in 1503/4, when sackcloth was at 4.5d. per yard, its most expensive in this period. Conversely, in 1507/8 the price the bursar paid for sackcloth dipped briefly to 2d., and in that year the quantity bought by him was abnormally high, at 246.5 yards. Although this was not the highest purchase seen in this period, it seems probable that the low price in that year prompted some stockpiling to take place, an interpretation supported by the fact that the volume bought by the bursar in the following year was unusually low, at 32 yards.

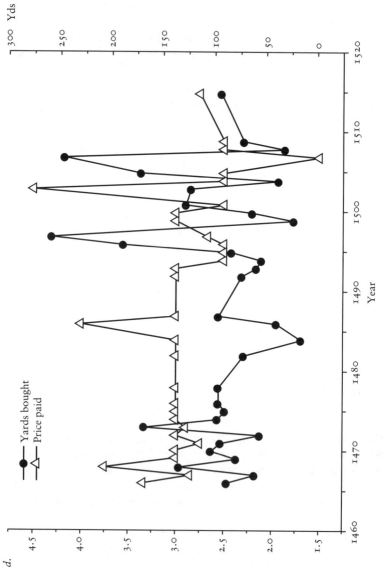

FIG. 3.10. Price paid for sackcloth and the amount bought by the bursar, 1464–1520

Linens

In an average year the priory purchased a total of 495.6 ells of linen, at a wide variety of prices and for a variety of uses. This quantity was shared between three of the obedientiaries, the sacrist buying an average of 28.6 ells of linen per year, the bursar 148.1 ells, and the chamberlain 318.9 ells. Linen textiles was a very broad category in the middle ages which included both relatively cheap domestically produced cloths and the rather more expensive Flemish and Holland linens, and both types were bought by Durham Priory in this period.[39] With the exceptions of Flemish cloth and Holland cloth, the provenance of the linens bought by the various obedientiaries is not recorded in their accounts. As their name implies, Holland and Flemish cloths were imports from the Low Countries, and there are several examples of the import of Holland cloth into Newcastle in the surviving customs accounts.[40] The main supplier of these cloths to the priory was William Cornforth, who also supplied many of the priory's spices and some other imported goods.[41]

Several small quantities of linen for which no further description is given were also imported into Newcastle in this period, and on one occasion for which records have survived were exported too.[42] It cannot therefore be assumed that all linen not otherwise described was in fact of domestic manufacture. However, it seems extremely probable that the cheaper cloths were made locally. Circumstantial evidence to this effect comes in the form of familiar local suppliers' names and the absence in the accounts of transport costs for these fabrics. Certainly there was a domestic linen industry in England throughout the middle ages, especially concentrated in the north and east of the country—in Scotland, Yorkshire, Lancashire, and East Anglia.[43] It is

[39] The Durham accounts do not tend to specify that Holland and Flemish cloths were types of linen, but it is clear that this was the case; in 1471/2 the bursar accounted for the purchase of 54 ells of linen cloth 'called flemysshcloth'. See also Hanham (ed.), *Cely Letters*, 321, and Wade (ed.), *Customs Accounts*, 55, 193.

[40] Ibid. 55, 193, 262, 266, 270–1, 273–4. On some of these occasions the cloth was further described as being 'coarse holland cloth' (pp. 262, 266, 271).

[41] Threlfall-Holmes, 'Provisioning', 95–6.

[42] Wade (ed.), *Customs Accounts*. For linen imports, see pp. 20, 22, 24–6, 55–7, 60, 118, 120, 122, 124, 127, 133, 141, 145, 147–8, 150, 182, 189–90, 194, 196, 260–1. In addition, 'coarse' linen was imported on three occasions: see pp. 28, 238, 259. Linen was exported from Newcastle on 4 May 1457 (pp. 37–8).

[43] N. Evans, *The East Anglian Linen Industry: Rural Industry and Local Economy, 1500–1850* (Pasold Studies in Textile History, 5, 1985), 1.

also known from archaeological evidence that flax was grown in the Durham and Newcastle areas.[44]

The linens bought by the priory varied in price a great deal, both between years and within a single year, so a more meaningful picture of the prices paid by the priory may be gained from a scatter diagram (Fig. 3.11) which shows all the prices paid by the priory for linen in each year, rather than from a consideration of the average price paid each year. Linen could cost the priory between 3d. and 1s. 4d. per ell, but the overwhelming majority of consignments were in the 4d. to 6d. per ell range, which might therefore be called the 'normal' price.

The highest prices paid were unusual. The single purchase at 1s. 4d. per ell in 1508/9 was for table linen for the prior, and the 12d. paid in 1494/5 was also for linen for the prior. Other than these, the highest price paid for linen was 9d. or 10d. per ell, and both prices occur only a few times each in these accounts, and for relatively small amounts of the total linen bought in each year. The 30 ells of linen bought by the bursar at 10d. per ell in 1494/5 are particularly interesting in that they were bought from a named London merchant, a Thomas Ayer. It would seem likely that these much more expensive linens were in some way physically different from the normally priced type—probably of heavier weight, or perhaps with an elaborate weave pattern.

It was certainly the case that the only named linens to appear in these accounts, Holland and Flemish cloths, were amongst the higher priced linens bought by the priory, costing between 7d. and 10d. per ell (the average price being 8d.). The relatively narrow price band in which they appear confirms that these names were used of similar cloths and were used consistently in the first two decades looked at here. Both appear only occasionally and only in the bursar's accounts, and in relatively small quantities—the average amount bought counting both types together was 40.4 ells per year, and it should be noted that this is an average for the years in which they were mentioned (seventeen), rather than an average over the period (of thirty-eight surviving bursar's accounts), which would produce the much lower figure of 18.1 ells per year.

[44] J. P. Huntley and S. Stallibrass, *Plant and Vertebrae Remains from Archaeological Sites in Northern England: Data Reviews and Future Directions* (Architectural and Archaeological Society of Durham and Northumberland Research Report, 4, 1995), 70–1.

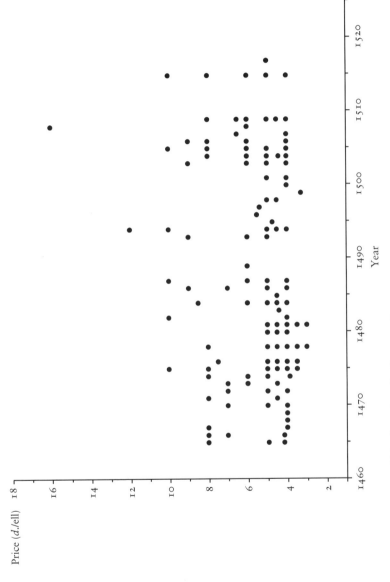

FIG. 3.11. Price paid by the priory for linen, 1464–1520

It should be noted that named Flemish and Holland cloths are mentioned only in the first part of the period, from 1465 to 1487. However, in this period they are virtually the only cloths bought in their price range, whereas after 1487 several unspecified linens costing similar amounts per ell can be seen. It seems likely, therefore, that the change was one of scribal habit or common nomenclature rather than reflecting a real change in the type or origin of the cloth bought by the priory.

Archaeological evidence from medieval sites has found that linen was being used for a wide variety of purposes, including underwear, bedlinen, headcoverings, aprons, burial cloths, toilet paper, and (in the case of raised weaves) towels.[45] Unfortunately, the intended uses for the linen purchased by the priory are only rarely stated in these accounts, but other uses may be surmised. Some was used for ceremonial purposes in church, being made into ecclesiastical garments such as albs and amices, and this is discussed in the section on vestments which follows. Table linen is also sometimes mentioned. On one occasion 4 ells of linen purchased by the bursar at 4d. the ell were described as having been made up into two tablecloths for the table in front of the kitchen window.[46] In the following year, 15.5 ells of linen at the very high price of 1s. 4d. the ell were bought for napkins and hand towels for the prior's table.[47] It is unsurprising that table linen for the prior represented by far the most expensive linen purchased by the priory in this period, as medieval table linen could be extremely elaborate in design and costly in execution. That bought for the prior was by no means the most expensive available, or out of place on the table of a noble of his standing.[48] On the other hand, the extremely wide price range for such items is shown by the purchase by the Durham cell at Monk Wearmouth in 1468/9 of 60 ells of linen

---

[45] E. Crowfoot, F. Pritchard, and K. Staniland, *Textiles and Clothing c.1150–c.1450: Medieval Finds from Excavations in London* (London, 1992), 80–1. This work goes on to point out that linen was made in a wide range of patterns in London, as the 1456 gild regulations demonstrate in a list of different types which includes 'crossewerk', 'cross diamounde', 'smale knottes', and 'damask knottes with chapelettes'. The differing degrees of complexity, and perhaps also different weave densities and fabric weights, involved in these different patterns may be a factor in explaining the wide price range found for linens in the priory accounts.

[46] DCM Bursar's account ('necessary expenses' section), 1507/8.

[47] Ibid. 1508/9.

[48] D. M. Mitchell, ' "By your Leave my Masters": British Taste in Table Linen in the Fifteenth and Sixteenth Centuries', *Textile History*, 20 (1989), 49–77.

for sheets, napkins, and hand towels, at only 3*d*. the ell.[49] Another example of the destination of some of the priory's linen comes in the communar's accounts. On three occasions, in 1489/90, 1508/9, and 1517/18, the communar purchased small amounts of linen for his exchequer. It is not clear what the purpose of this cloth was, but it might perhaps have been for the periodic replacement of the exchequer cloths, marked out for the accounting procedure. The communar was certainly not a regular cloth purchaser, the only other mention of any cloth in his accounts being 3*s*. 4*d*. worth of serge bought in 1499/1500, also for the exchequer.[50]

These stated uses, however, account for only a small amount of the nearly 500 ells of linen bought by the priory in an average year. The uses to which the remainder was put can only be guessed at from the obedientiary responsible for purchasing it, and from occasional entries in similar accounts from other monasteries. The large amounts of linen bought by the chamberlain were probably, given his other responsibilities, for the personal use of the monks both as bedlinen and for undergarments. At Selby Abbey, the chamberlain paid cash sums to the monks for them to provide clothes for themselves by 1441/2, but still purchased some small amounts of linen for towels to be hung in the cloister.[51] It seems likely, from his remit and from the assortment of other cheap textiles which appear in his accounts alongside linen, that the linen bought by the bursar was destined for a hundred and one miscellaneous domestic applications. Examples might be uses in the kitchen, the brewhouse, and the bakehouse such as dishcloths, cheese-cloths, cloths for straining the mash for ale, and bolting-cloths for sieving flour. The more expensive linens that he bought may have been used for towels, everyday tablecloths, and so on: the 1512 household book of Henry Percy, fifth Earl of Northumberland sets out that 70 ells of linen, at 8*d*. the ell, are to be bought for his household each year, to be used for such things as tablecloths for the knight's table in the Great Hall, hand towels for the earl himself, napkins, cupboard cloths, pantry towels, and dresser cloths for the kitchen.[52]

---

[49] J. Raine (ed.), *The Inventories and Account Rolls of the Benedictine Houses or Cells of Jarrow and Monk-Wearmouth in the County of Durham* (Surtees Society, 29, 1854), 211.

[50] DCM Communar's accounts ('necessary expenses' sections), 1489/90, 1499/1500, 1508/9, 1517/18.

[51] Tillotson, *Monastery and Society*, 111.

[52] Percy (ed.), *Regulations and Establishment*, 16.

Neither the bursar nor the chamberlain were noticeably price responsive in their linen purchases. It is hard to be sure about this since the price range at which linens were bought was so wide, and the amounts purchased also varied a great deal from year to year, but as can be seen from the graph of the average price paid for linen with the amounts bought by the bursar in each year (Fig. 3.12), purchasing does not appear to have been correlated with price changes. In some years, notably 1492/3 and 1498/9, upward movements in price do coexist with downward movements in the quantity purchased, or vice versa. However, other years, such as 1492–6, show the reverse pattern, with price movements and the amount purchased by the bursar apparently moving together.

Overall, it does not appear that the absolute price of linen was an important factor in the purchasing decisions of the bursar or chamberlain, though it is of course likely that the relative prices charged would have been taken into consideration when choosing suppliers or even types of linen for a particular task. Linen, therefore, would appear to have occupied a kind of halfway house between utility cloths and the 'display' cloths to which this discussion will now turn.

Vestments

More than any other cloth or clothing bought by the priory vestments were symbolic, and considerations of display and precedent were undoubtedly the main factors in choosing them. Whether the intention was to glorify God or to emphasize the medieval social and ecclesiastical hierarchy, or whether the two were indistinguishable in the minds of the monks, the result was the same; the most spectacular and costly textiles to enter the priory were those destined for use in the church and chapels under the monastery's control. Perhaps partly because of their cost they were only rarely bought, and thus only a few references to such garments occur in the priory archives. Those that do exist, however, suggest that whilst the priory had no intention of skimping on their ecclesiastical splendour they nevertheless saw no reason to be unnecessarily extravagant. They wanted the best, but they also wanted to buy it at the best price possible, and once bought they wanted it to last.

The extravagant nature of the fabrics used for vestments, and also the priory's continued concern for, if not economy, at least budgeting can be seen in a letter from the prior of Durham to his trusted

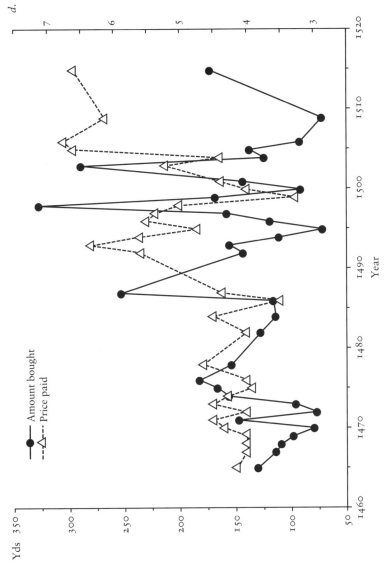

FIG. 3.12. Price paid for linen and the amount bought by the bursar, 1464–1520

steward, Robert Rodes, who was in London on business in May 1456. The prior asks him to purchase six copes of blue velvet, and to have them ornamented with gold flowers as in the sample he had previously sent; also to provide orphreys with embroidery to go with the said copes, at the price of 8 marks each as he had quoted to the prior. Further, he is asked to provide an additional six copes of the same blue velvet and to have these latter embroidered with smaller and fewer gold flowers. This is presumably intended as an economy, as the prior goes on to specify that Robert should expect to pay 6d., or 7d. if necessary, per flower. The total sum available for spending on all these things is £103. 6s. 8d., although the prior is clearly expecting there to be some change, as he requests that 5 marks be paid to a third party out of this, and that anything left be spent on providing additional vestments.[53] Another letter from the same year shows both this concern for price and the importance of precedent in the provision and selection of cloth for vestments as for liveries: the prior discusses the prevailing price of cloth of gold at some length, but goes on to ask that cloth might be supplied at qualities and prices most closely approximating those that the priory had had before.[54]

Apart from these letters very few references to the purchase of vestments survive, and none from this period. Fowler records two instances from the beginning of the fourteenth century: in 1401/2 the bursar's account recorded the purchase of a white vestment for the prior's chapel, at a cost of £2. 0s. 0d., whilst in 1416/17 the almoner spent £2. 0s. 10d. on mending vestments and service books and purchasing a new vestment for the chapel at Helton.[55] The few surviving inventories for the priory do not suggest that a large collection of vestments was kept. The feretrar's inventory for 1441/2 shows that he was in possession of only four whole sets of vestments. He lists a whole set of green vestments, together with curtains, cloth to surround the altar, an altar cloth, and a frontal; a red vestment with matching altar cloth and frontal; an old green vestment with altar cloth and frontal; and a grey and red velvet vestment with two altar cloths and a frontal. The sacrist's inventory for 1404/5 includes a pair of chests for vestments, a white mitre, and a crozier (with a head of ebony inlaid with precious stones), thirteen brocade cloths (possibly

[53] DCM Reg. Parv. III, fos. 79ᵛ–80ʳ.   [54] Ibid., fo. 88ᵛ.
[55] Fowler (ed.), *Account Rolls*, iii. 604; i. 225.

processional canopies), ten blue cloths with arms, two old cloths and a vestment for St Benedict's altar, and a few other individual cloths, including '2 new cloths for Corpus Christi with the remains of a brocade for making orphreys'.[56]

The only references to vestments in the sacrist's and other obedientiaries' accounts for this period are for mending and making up rather than purchasing new vestments, and this fits with the presence in these inventories of old vestments and of cloth for making vestments. The sacrist paid 13s. 8d. in 1472/3 for making five vestments, and a further 12d. for dyeing linen to line them with. No cloth for these is purchased in that year; but since only a few of the sacrist's accounts survive for this period it may have been recorded in an account now lost, or the cloth may have been old and was only now being made up. Other than that, the only references to vestments in the obedientiary accounts for this period are to linen accessories, such as albs and amices, rather than to the elaborate and expensive vestments themselves. These garments were also mended when required; in 1465/6 the purchase of linen is immediately followed by an expenditure of 2s. 11d. 'for making albs and amices and mending an alb', and mending is also recorded in 1473/4.

The sacrist's accounts have survived for only nine years, but in each of these except that for 1487/8 the purchase of linen is recorded, often specified to have been 'for albs and other neccessaries'. The quantities of linen purchased by the sacrist varied a great deal: 8 ells in 1486/7, 14 ells in 1484/5, 15 ells in 1485/6, 20 ells in each of 1472/3, and 1474/5, 44 ells in 1473/4, 45 ells in 1483/4, and 63 ells in 1465/6. The widely varying amounts of linen which were bought by the sacrist in different years make it clear that the provision of such garments and accessories was not a regular, yearly charge but something that was done as required. Clearly, old garments were worn for as long as they remained in good condition, and repaired when necessary. This makes it abundantly plain that whilst the priory would spend whatever was necessary on keeping up appearances, they were not in the business of being unnecessarily extravagant. God and his church demanded the best, but they would drive a hard bargain for the cloth of gold they wanted, and would look after it when they got it.

[56] Ibid. ii. 394–5.

Clothing

The standard clothing requirements of a monk were quite limited, consisting of a habit, a shirt (*staminum*), three or four undershirts (*femoralia*), and perhaps an outer garment (*vestis*) for wear whilst riding.[57] These basic needs were seen to by the chamberlain, who purchased large quantities of white and black serge and a small amount of woollen cloth for the monks' habits. Little information is given about these cloths in the accounts, and since the chamberlain's accounts have survived for only ten years in this period it is not possible to draw any conclusions about the price responsiveness or otherwise of his purchases of these cloths, although one would expect that, like the linens looked at above, purchases would have been largely impervious to any but very dramatic changes in supply or price. The chamberlain's accounts contain reasonably large quantities of black and white serge, which were almost certainly intended to clothe the majority of the monks resident in the priory. The white serge, of which the chamberlain bought an average 93.2 ells per year, at an average price of 7.7d. per ell, was specified in the accounts to have been for shirts. No intended use is mentioned in connection with the average 152.9 ells of black serge that were bought each year at an average price of 10.3d. per ell: however, the colour, quantity, and lack of alternatives elsewhere in the accounts all strongly imply that this material formed the monks' habits.

In addition to the black serge, the chamberlain also bought a certain quantity of woollen cloth each year. The amounts of woollen cloth that the chamberlain purchased in each year fluctuated widely, between 28.5 ells in 1509 and 153 ells in 1504, but the average amount bought each year was the equivalent of 67.4 ells.[58] It seems probable that whilst the black serge provided the monks' habits, the

---

[57] J. Greatrex (ed.), *Account Rolls of the Obedientiaries of Peterborough* (Northamptonshire Record Society, 33, 1984), 28, 33. At Peterborough each monk was issued with all of this clothing except for the habit, for which they apparently received a cash payment. For the regulations on the *vestis* see W. A. Pantin (ed.), *Documents Illustrating the Activities of the General and Provincial Chapters of the English Black Monks, 1215–1540* (Camden Society, 3rd ser., 45, 47, and 54, 1931–7), ii. 66–7, 124.

[58] The woollen cloths purchased by the priory came in both wide and narrow varieties. In calculating the total quantity of cloth purchased, given here in terms of standard (wide) cloth, an ell of narrow cloth has been taken to be equivalent to half an ell of wide cloth.

woollen cloth purchased by the chamberlain provided outer garments to those monks not already provided with these garments by the bursar's livery distribution. Other miscellaneous items of clothing may also have been provided for by the woollen cloth: in 1417/18, the chamberlain of Abingdon Abbey noted the purchase of woollen cloth worth £1. 8s. 6d. 'for the feet'—presumably for socks.[59]

As has been seen, the average number of monks attached to the monastery in this period was around sixty-six, so an average of 152.9 ells of black serge to provide habits would give 2.3 ells to each monk.[60] This figure seems realistic enough, and is comparable with the 27 ells of woollen cloth purchased by the bursar in most years for the outer robes of the priory's nine main obedientiaries, which works out at 3 ells each.

These quantities of cloth per gown can be compared with a contemporary benchmark in the form of the maximum permitted lengths of cloth that were specified for the lower ranks in the 1510 sumptuary law. Men below the rank of knight (with certain exceptions, including 'spiritual men') were not permitted to use more than 4 yards of broadcloth in a long gown or 3 in a short gown, whilst no servant below the degree of gentleman was allowed to use more than 3 yards in a long gown or 2½ yards in a short gown.[61] It would seem from this that an average of around 3 yards of broadcloth may be taken as an effective minimum for a full-length garment, and that therefore the priory was by no means extravagant in the clothing of its monks. The prior stood out alone in having an outer gown made with 6 ells of the highest quality material purchased by the bursar. The main obedientiaries, next in prestige to the prior, had only 3 ells of broadcloth in each of their gowns, the same as was contained in the habits of the remaining monks.

For servants the picture is slightly less clear since the number of servants for whom the bursar's annual livery purchases were intended was not stated in his accounts. For 1509/10 and 1510/11, however, lists of the livery distributed to the priory's dependants survive in the bursar's notebook or household book. That for 1509/10 has bracketed together to one side of the page a note to the effect that the amount of cloth involved in these liveries was 3 ells per gentleman,

[59] Kirk (ed.), *Abingdon Abbey*, 86.
[60] For the population of the priory see Ch. 1.
[61] Williams (ed.), *English Historical Documents*, v. 250–1.

and 5 ells per two valets or grooms, so 2¹/₂ ells each. There was clearly some variation in actual practice, as certain individual entries differ from this standard. For example, the cellarer's valet received 3 ells, whilst the sacrist's six valets received the standard 15 ells between them, and the chamberlain's servant was given 3¹/₂ ells. Most of the servants listed with individual amounts of cloth noted received 3 ells, although quantities of 3¹/₄ ells, 3¹/₂ ells, and 3³/₄ ells were also recorded. In other words, the priory's servants were receiving quantities of livery cloth identical to those received by the monks themselves, albeit of lower quality.

These cloths were bought by the piece, and were presumably made up into garments on the monastic premises, although this activity has left little trace in the accounts.[62] The other purchases of apparel which occur in these accounts are those in which 'garments' are purchased, usually for servants or household members, by various obedientiaries. Whilst it is possible that these transactions may have been simply customary, in other words may in fact represent cash payments rather than the purchase of actual made-up garments, the fluctuations in the prices paid by the same obedientiaries from year to year make this unlikely. For example, the sacrist's accounts survive for the three consecutive years from 1472/3 to 1474/5, and in these years he paid 7s. ¹/₂d., 8s. 2d. and 5s. 6d. respectively for valet's garments. Were these simply customary payments one would expect to see much more standardized sums appearing.

Whole garments were bought on a regular basis by the almoner and the sacrist, and on one occasion in this period by the bursar.[63] The expenditure section of the almoner's accounts begins with a wardrobe subsection, the contents of which varied little over this period, comprising two furred tunics, for the almoner himself 'et socio suo' (20s.); a furred garment for the master of the grammar school (11s., including 11d. worth of fur); and a garment each for the

---

[62] In the 13th cent. the chamberlain purchased cloth which was dyed black, cut, and made up in the monastery, as described in M. R. Foster, 'Durham Cathedral Priory 1229–1333: Aspects of the Ecclesiastical History and Interests of the Monastic Community', Ph.D. thesis (University of Cambridge, 1979), 74. However, no traces of such activity are to be found in the chamberlain's accounts for this period.

[63] The only example of such a purchase in the bursar's accounts comes in 1472/3, when the last entry in the wardrobe section of the bursar's account reads: 'Paid to Jacob Bonelet for 2 garments for him and his servant, 13s. 4d.' No explanation is given in the account of the reason behind this unusual entry.

almoner's valet (6s. 4d.), coachman (6s. 4d.), and groom of the stables (5s. 0d.). The sacrist's list of retainers was somewhat longer: his necessary expense account regularly included the cost of garments for three unspecified servants at an average cost of 6s. 6d. each, and for between five and seven (though usually six) valets, at an average cost of 4s. 9d. each. The accounts do not include any further detail about these garments, so the amount or quality of the cloth that they contained cannot be ascertained.

The use of garments as a social symbol—as payment, badge, creator of bonds of loyalty, and to define social status—can be seen at its most developed in the priory's use of livery, which alone accounted for around £40 of the £71 spent on textiles by the priory in an average year. Each year, the bursar spent this sum on black woollen cloth and black fur for smart new outer garments for the prior and the nine chief obedientiaries, on coloured cloth with white fur for the gentlemen, and on coloured cloth alone for the valets and grooms who were on the priory's payroll. In all, around 350 ells of cloth were bought each year for these liveries. The types of cloth deemed suitable for the wear of each degree of person within the monastery appears to have been very highly stratified, with the five grades of wearer being set out one by one in the accounts and different cloth bought for each.

The livery cloths were accounted for by the bursar, and their importance and value is reflected in that they were the subject of the first subdivision of his expenditure accounts. The list of purchases within this section followed a rigid format. First, the cloth bought for the gowns of the nine major obedientiaries was accounted for, followed by that for the prior's gown. Next came cloth for gentleman servants, valets, and finally grooms. For each of these, a different value of cloth was purchased. The gentleman and valet categories were normally specified to cover both clerical and lay servants, and although no distinction was made between them in terms of cloth value, it was occasionally the case that different colours of cloth were bought for the two. The accounts went on to note the purchase of black furs for the obedientiaries' gowns, then for the prior's gown, and then white furs for the gentlemen's gowns. Hoods for the prior's steward and chaplain are also recorded, but are not discussed here as they remained standard throughout the period, at a cost of 6s. 8d. each with no further details given.

Occasionally there were slight variations to this pattern. In four years, the purchases of cloth and fur for the nine main obedientiaries of the priory (excluding the prior) were replaced by what appears to have been a cash payment to the individuals involved.[64] In these years the entries for cloth and black fur for the use of monk officials do not occur in the bursar's wardrobe accounts, being replaced with a single entry recording the payment to the nine monks involved of 10s. 0d. each. This payment is specified in the 1486/7 and 1487/8 accounts to be for their 'kirtils with fur', whilst in 1498/9 the usual number of black furs were bought in addition to this payment. It should be noted that this payment of 10s. 0d. was very slightly less than the combined value of the cloth and fur that were more commonly bought. Tailoring costs are not mentioned anywhere in the accounts in connection with these livery cloths, but if they accounted for the difference one would expect the cost of a whole garment to be higher than that of its constituent parts, not the other way round. It may be that a cash alternative was considered desirable by the obedientiaries and so slightly less could be given; however, if that were the case it would be expected that this commutation would be common practice rather than occurring in only four of the years looked at here. It does, however, appear to have been the case that the obedientiaries concerned received garments in these years which were equivalent to those allocated to them in years when the accounts record the purchase of cloth directly by the bursar. This is implied by the entries in the income section of the bursar's accounts which note the money received from the sale of the obedientiaries' garments from the previous year; no difference can be seen in the income received or the way in which the garments are described in the years following those in which direct payments are recorded in the accounts.[65]

Only very occasionally do the accounts give any more detail about the cloths purchased than a brief indication of their colour ('black' for the monastics and 'coloured' for the servants) and the social status of their intended wearers. It is not clear what colour the 'coloured' cloths usually were, nor is it possible to tell whether there was in fact a standard shade or if different colours were used in different years. More detail on colour occurs only in a single account in this period, that for 1499/1500, in which the entry for gentlemen's cloth includes the words *coloris tawnys*, and that for grooms' cloth *eiusdem coloris*. Both these phrases are crossed out in the account,

---

[64] DCM Bursar's accounts, 1486/7, 1487/8, 1497/8, 1498/9.
[65] DCM Bursar's accounts, e.g. for 1486/7, 1487/8, 1488/9.

but whether this was because they were inaccurate, or were considered extraneous, it is not possible to tell. The only other references to the colours of the livery cloths come from just outside this period; in 1446/7 the bursar bought green cloth for the servants' liveries and supplemented this with smaller amounts of red cloth, whilst in 1449/50 the colour of the servants' cloth was described as 'red medley'.

The other non-standard term that occurs in connection with these livery cloths is *stragulati*, striped cloths. This description occurs in two years, 1467/8 and 1473/4. In both cases a distinction is made between clerical and lay gentlemen and valets. In every other year the clerical and lay are not distinguished, but in these two years extra entries occur. 'Coloured cloth' is bought as usual for clerical and lay gentlemen at one value and clerical and lay valets at another value, but in addition 'striped cloth' is bought at the same two values for the lay gentlemen and the lay valets only. The clerical/lay distinction is nowhere made in the case of grooms, but in these two years the cloth purchased for their use is a combination of the usual 'coloured' cloth and striped. These striped cloths appear to have been at least partially supplementary to, rather than part of, the usual cloth requirements. Between 3 and 4 broadcloths were usually purchased for the gentlemen each year. In 1467/8, 3 cloths and 2 ells were bought, with the addition of a further 3½ striped cloths, whilst in 1473/4 3½ cloths each of coloured and striped cloths were bought. Similarly, the usual 6 cloths for valets became 5 striped in addition to 3½ (1467) or 4 (1473) normal cloths. To a lesser extent the same applied to the cloth bought for the grooms: the 6 cloths usually purchased became 3 normal and 4 striped in both these years.

It would seem probable that the colour of the livery cloth chosen by the priory varied from year to year, and that in these years a mixed pattern was decided upon. The purchase of both striped and coloured cloths for servants seems to have been a fairly common practice in this period. The Peterborough Abbey receiver's accounts for 1443/4 lists the purchase of several different colours of cloth for servants, including *panni radiati le Chaumpe Murrey* (a grey striped cloth) and blue medley.[66] It would seem, however, that such striped cloths were considered rather too frivolous for men of clerical status.

Apart from these occasional references to stripes, then, the fact that the livery cloths for the obedientiaries of the priory were black

---

[66] Greatrex (ed.), *Account Rolls*, 164.

and those for the servants were coloured is all that is disclosed in these accounts about the actual cloths bought. However, the five grades of wearer are clearly mirrored in the sharply differentiated prices paid for the cloth intended for each. For example, in 1465/6 an ell of cloth bought for the prior cost 4s. 0d., for the main obedientiaries just over 2s. 9d., for the gentlemen 2s. 1d., for the valets just under 1s. 10d., and just over 1s. 6d. for the grooms. In 1509/10, the equivalent prices were 4s. 0d., just under 3s. 0d., just under 2s. 4d., just over 1s. 11d., and 1s. 8d. respectively. Although the cost of cloth for the prior did not change in this period, and the small price rise that occurred in the mid 1480s did not change all the prices in exactly the same proportion, the resulting alteration in the differentials between the five price levels is slight. On only four occasions are the five degrees outlined above not present in the accounts in this stratified manner: in 1475/6, the prior's livery is not mentioned (although his usual furs are still purchased); in 1500/1 and 1515/16, for no apparent reason the 'valet' class is not present (with no concomitant rise in the volume of cloth purchased in other categories); and in 1486/7, the gentlemen and valets are classed together and the same type of cloth (at the lower of the two prices, that current for valets' cloth) is purchased for both. The clear stratification of these prices is shown in Fig. 3.13.

It can be seen from the graph that the cloth bought for the prior's livery cost well over 100 per cent more than that for the grooms. However, the only warning given in the accounts that these cloths were very different items is their widely differing prices. The combination of the two facts should alert us to a major danger in comparing medieval cloth prices from different sources, or even from within the same source in the absence of the clues given here as to the intended destination of the cloth: it is very possible that ostensibly similar cloths may in fact have been of greatly differing qualities without such a difference being noted in the surviving records. In the case of the Durham livery cloths, it is possible to distinguish the black cloth intended for the monk officials and for the prior from the coloured cloths purchased for servants' liveries; but even within these two groupings prices varied a great deal. The cloth bought for the prior was over a third more expensive than that bought for the major obedientiaries, and a similar differential applied between the gentlemen's and grooms' cloth. A significant margin of error must therefore be presumed to exist in any comparison of cloth prices where the

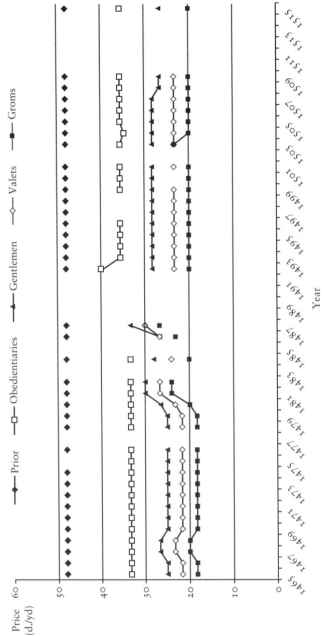

Fig. 3.13. Prices paid by the bursar for livery cloth for the prior, obedientiaries, gentlemen, valets, and grooms of the priory, 1464–1520

sources do not make it tolerably certain that like is being compared with like.[67]

It is clear that the different price levels paid by the priory for cloth for the livery of different grades of dependants must have represented very different qualities of cloth, as was considered appropriate to the status of the respective wearers. It was common practice at the time for liveries to be given which both proclaimed the wearer's association with a household or other grouping, and at the same time made his or her status clear. For example, the liveries of the City of London were graded to differentiate between mayor, sheriffs, gentlemen, yeomen, and so on, 'possibly in the colours and quality [of the cloths] and certainly in the quantity given'.[68] A similar gradation to that seen for Durham is also to be found in other clerical establishments, for example at Peterborough Abbey and in the household of the Bishop of Hereford.[69] At Sion Abbey in 1481, livery cloth for gentlemen cost 3s. 6d. per yard, that for yeomen cost 2s. 6d., and that for grooms 1s. 10½d., whilst in 1489 equivalent cloths cost 3s. 6d., 2s. 8d., and 2s. 0d. respectively.[70] Thorold Rogers also noted such a hierarchy of cloth prices at New College, Oxford.[71]

Furs were also bought as part of the priory's livery purchases by the bursar for the prior, some monks (the nine main obedientiaries for whom he bought livery cloths) and the gentlemen servants of the priory. The price and description of these furs remained constant throughout this period, with the exception of the three years mentioned earlier in which furs for the monks were not listed separately but were included in the cash payment made to them for their livery as a whole. Apart from these three years, in every year for which accounts have survived the bursar purchased 16½ black furs costing 1s. 6d. each—3 for the prior and a total of 13½ for the main

[67] A similar example from a very different context of different prices being the only differentiator between different cloth qualities is quoted by K. Staniland, 'Clothing Provision and the Great Wardrobe in the Mid-Thirteenth Century', *Textile History*, 22 (1991), 248; Bartholomew Tyer of Lyons was requested in 1244 to supply, amongst a long list of other items, '100 cloths of *Arest* without gold, 40 cloths of gold of higher price, 20 cloths of gold of greater price than the aforesaid cloths'.

[68] A. F. Sutton, 'Order and Fashion in Clothes: The King, his Household and the City of London at the End of the Fifteenth Century', *Textile History*, 22 (1991), 263.

[69] Greatrex (ed.), *Account Rolls*, 11, 116–17, 164, 183, 197; C. Dyer, *Standards of Living*, 78.

[70] Rogers, *History of Agriculture and Prices*, iii. 500–1.

[71] Ibid. iv. 496–502, 564–6.

obedientiaries, which represents 1½ each.[72] It is interesting to note that the difference in status between the prior and his main obedientiaries is here marked only in a difference of quantity, rather than of quantity and quality as is the case with the livery cloth. The fur intended for the livery of the gentlemen servants of the priory, on the other hand, was differentiated from that purchased for the monastic liveries in all of the three ways seen for the livery cloths: quantity, price, and colour. Each year the bursar purchased between 8 and 12 white furs, costing 11d. each, for these servants. The lists of servants' liveries which have survived for 1509/10 and 1510/11 record that the priory had 10 gentlemen servants in those years.[73] The bursar's accounts for the latter year have not survived, but in 1509/10 the standard purchase of 8 white furs was made, suggesting that each gentleman received four-fifths of a fur.

The type of fur which the bursar purchased is not stated in these accounts. However, from the colours bought and the prices paid it seems likely that they were lambskins, the most common fur in general use in England throughout the later middle ages, but by no means a fashionable or prestigious one.[74] As far as can be ascertained from surviving account rolls from other monasteries, lamb seems to have been a fairly usual monastic purchase, and the prices paid by the Durham bursar were in the usual range of prices for furs identified in other accounts as being lamb. For example, in 1398/9 the bursar of Selby Abbey purchased 10 lambskins for the esquires' livery at 1s. 3d. each, in 1404/5 the abbot's receiver at Peterborough Abbey purchased 15 lamb furs costing 1s. 3d. each, and in 1433/4 the latter official purchased two lamb furs at 2s. 0d. each and another two furs at 2s. 3d. which were probably lamb.[75] The recipients of the Peterborough furs are not named, so they may have been monks or servants. However, they certainly did not include the abbot, for whom a much more expensive fur was bought in 1433/4, 14s. 8d.

---

[72] In the bursar's account for 1507/8 the prior's fur is described as white. The price remains the same, however, and it seems likely that this was a scribal error.

[73] DCM B. Bk. H, fos. 204ᵛ, 274ᵛ–275ʳ.

[74] E. M. Veale, *The English Fur Trade in the Later Middle Ages* (Oxford, 1966), 133, 176.

[75] Tillotson, *Monastery and Society*, 74; Greatrex (ed.), *Account Rolls*, 117, 164. The 1433/4 entry states that two unidentified furs were bought for 4s. 6d., and then that two 'other lamb furs' were bought for 4s. 0d., the use of the word 'other' suggesting that the first two were also lamb.

being spent on the purchase of a single new fur and the mending of another for him.[76] At an earlier period it would seem that the prior wore budge (a more expensive, imported lambskin) and the chief obedientiaries squirrel; it is unsurprising that this had changed, since all the rarer furs were becoming extinct or greatly increasing in price by the fifteenth century, a process which contributed to the declining fashion for furs already noted.[77]

Livery and the priory's standard of living

Cloth and clothing have always been important, since visible, indicators of social standing and of wealth, and most societies have used textiles in some way to define and advertise status, hierarchy, and tradition.[78] In medieval Europe in particular the use of fabrics in this way, as definers of social stratification, was taken for granted at all levels of society. The disquiet felt by those in power when those below them on the social ladder copied their fashions took statutory form in the various sumptuary laws passed from time to time throughout this period. These frequently had economic motives behind them, such as to encourage home production and exports and limit imports, but their provisions make it clear that a prime intention was also 'the desire to preserve class distinctions, so that any stranger could tell by merely looking at a man's dress to what rank in society he belonged'.[79] Since it seems likely that the reason these laws were so frequently re-enacted was because they were widely ignored, it is interesting to observe that the practice at Durham Priory shows definite parallels with the sumptuary laws passed in England in this period.

Acts of Apparell were passed by Parliament in 1463, 1483, 1510, and 1515, all containing broadly similar prohibitions but with a tendency to increase the provision for exemptions over time. For example, the Act of 1510 excluded all women from its provisions whereas the Act of 1483 had specifically included the wives and

[76] Greatrex (ed.), *Account Rolls*, 164.
[77] Veale, *English Fur Trade*, 8; Fowler (ed.), *Account Rolls*, i. 165, 169, 178, 215; ii. 495, 505, 507, 562.
[78] A. B. Weiner and J. Schneider (eds.), *Cloth and Human Experience* (Washington, 1989).
[79] F. E. Baldwin, *Sumptuary Legislation and Personal Regulation in England* (Baltimore, 1926), 10.

daughters of husbandmen and labourers, whilst the 1515 Act provided for a greater degree of flexibility for servants in the royal households.[80] The 1510 legislation provides a useful (if somewhat limited in scope) benchmark against which to assess the generosity or otherwise of the priory's cloth provision to its servants and inhabitants, since its provisions include several clauses prohibiting certain classes of people from wearing garments containing more than certain amounts of cloth, as has been seen, and also from wearing cloth valued at more than certain sums per yard. This act specified that broadcloth costing above 2s. 0d. per yard was not to be worn by 'servant of husbandry nor shepherd nor common labourer nor servant unto any artificer out of the city or borough nor husbandman having no goods of his own above the value of £10'.[81]

This statutory price mark can be compared with the amount paid by the priory for its servants' livery cloths in 1509/10: just under 2s. 4d. the yard for gentlemen, just over 1s. 11d. for valets, and 1s. 6d. for grooms. It is interesting to note that the cloth values for the Durham liveries in this year circle the figure of 2 shillings, seemingly aware of its symbolic importance—only those servants who are categorized as gentlemen are bought cloth over this value, whilst the cloth for the next level down, the valets, is just marginally under this level. In addition, the 1510 statute specifies that servants beneath the rank of gentlemen were not permitted to wear any kind of fur, a prohibition which evidently matched the practice at Durham where furs were purchased for the prior, monks, and gentlemen only.[82]

A similar lack of ostentation would appear to have prevailed in the quality of the cloth purchased for the monks' clothing. Comparisons of the amount paid by the priory for such cloth with other contemporary sources of cloth price information show that the cloths bought by the priory were by no means extravagant by the standards of the day. This was perhaps just as well, since there was a strong tradition in this period of equating the wearing of exaggerated fashions and costly garments with sinfulness. The vision of Edmund Leversedge, which was written in 1465, described devils and angels wrestling for a

---

[80] W. Hooper, 'The Tudor Sumptuary Laws', *Economic History Review*, 30 (1915), 433–4.

[81] Williams (ed.), *English Historical Documents*, 250–1.

[82] Ibid. 250. The same distinction was in force at Westminster Abbey in this period (B. Harvey, *Living and Dying*, 168).

man's soul, the devils citing their victim's fashionable dress as evidence that he clearly belonged to them. The man is eventually saved, but is sternly warned never to wear such clothes again. The condemned fashions are described in some detail—he is to refrain from wearing padded shoulders, very short tunics, long pointed shoes, long hair, high hats, and tight hose. In prescribing a modest standard of dress, the 'Vision' notes not only that henceforth his gown should be mid-leg in length and black in colour, but also that the black cloth should cost only 2s. 6d. or 2s. 7d. per yard, further evidence that the quality of cloth was generally described only by reference to its price.[83] The cloth bought by the priory in this period compares well with the yardstick of extravagance laid down by Edmund's vision: with the exception of the 4s. 0d. per yard paid for the cloth for the prior's gown, the most expensive cloth purchased by the priory was the black bought by the bursar for the main obedientiaries' gowns, at 2s. 7d. the yard in the 1460s and just under 3s. 0d. the yard by 1510.

By contrast, cloth purchased by the royal household and for the households of the higher nobility could be breathtakingly expensive. The most expensive textiles—velvet, silks, cloth of gold, and so on—were priced more on a par with jewellery than with normal clothing. An example of the extravagant expenditure on textiles which was commonplace in such households may be found in the Duke of Norfolk's draper's bill for 1483, which came to a grand total of £156. 16s. 2d. The two single largest items of expenditure were £40 for 15 yards of cloth of gold, and £38. 8s. 4d. for 9¾ yards of damask; these textiles therefore cost £2. 10s. 0d. and £3. 18s. 9½d. per yard respectively. The most expensive textile bought was ½ yard of crimson (perhaps mixed with gold) which cost an astonishing £4. 0s. 0d. per yard. In addition, large amounts of luxurious velvet and satin were bought, in various different dyes, costing between 7s. 0d. (for black satin) and 16s. 0d. (for purple velvet) per yard.[84] The royal household spent on an even grander scale, as the long lists of golden, velvet, and ermine-trimmed garments in the wardrobes of the kings of this period demonstrate.[85] Although the priory accounts do not include any

[83] W. F. Nijenhuis (ed.), *The Vision of Edmund Leversedge* (Nijmegen, 1991), 10, 60–1, 121.

[84] J. P. Collier (ed.), *The Household Books of John, Duke of Norfolk and Thomas, Earl of Surrey, 1481–1490* (London, 1844), 416–17.

[85] Sutton, 'Order and Fashion in Clothes', 255–8.

expenditure on this scale, such luxury materials as these were certainly present (in somewhat smaller quantities) in the priory in the form of the precious vestments described above.

Even the more everyday cloths bought by the royal and magnate households, such as woollen broadcloths for outer clothing, were often priced at up to twice the amount paid for the highest quality cloth bought by the priory, that for the prior's robe. Although such cloths were the preserve of the very highest households, cloths of higher price than those bought by the priory were purchased by a wide stratum of the nobility. The Stonor family, for example, purchased a range of cloths; a bill from 1478/9 shows that the russet and tawny broadcloths worn by the chief members of the family cost between 6s. 0d. and 7s. 6d. the yard.[86] The cloth prices paid by Durham Cathedral Priory would appear to place the monks' clothing, somewhat surprisingly, alongside that of the lesser nobility and gentry families such as the Pastons. In 1449 Margaret Paston asked her husband to obtain black broadcloth at 3s. 8d. or 4s. 0d. the yard for a hood for herself, and in the mid 1450s she reported to him that she was having difficulty finding suitable broadcloth for liveries at the price she wanted to pay, which was a maximum of 3s. 0d. the yard.[87]

The lack of much evidence of cloth purchases from other monastic establishments in this makes it hard to tell whether the relatively modest standard of dress at Durham was typical or atypical. One directly comparable example comes from Peterborough Abbey in 1504/5, when the livery purchases included 14 ells of black cloth for the abbot and his officials, at a cost of 5s. 0d. the ell. In addition, whole garments were bought for four categories of servant—gentlemen, principal valets, second valets, and grooms—at 8s. 0d., 6s. 8d., 6s. 0d., and 5s. 0d. respectively—but these prices are not, of course, directly comparable with the Durham figures for cloth by the ell.[88] It can be seen, however, that the black cloth was significantly more expensive than that bought by Durham at the same date, 20 per cent more for the prior/abbot and around 65 per cent more for the chief obedientiaries. However, it would be irresponsible to refine too much

[86] C. L. Kingsford (ed.), *The Stonor Letters and Papers, 1290–1483*, 2 vols. (Camden Society, 3rd ser., 29 and 30, 1919), ii. 75.

[87] H. S. Bennett, *The Pastons and their England* (3rd edn., Cambridge, 1990), 54.

[88] Greatrex (ed.), *Account Rolls*, 183.

upon a single example, and such differences could potentially be accounted for by transport costs: Durham was buying from Leeds in 1504/5, but the source of the Peterborough cloth is not stated in the accounts. For cloth for servants, the closest comparison comes from slightly earlier in the century, when the accounts of the cellarers of Battle Abbey record the purchase in both 1435/6 and 1442/3 of woollen cloth for the livery of the cellarer's servants at 1s. 10d. per yard.[89] The degree of the servants is unknown, but this figure is very close to those seen for valets and grooms at Durham in 1465/6, at just under 1s. 10d. and just over 1s. 6d. respectively.

Overall, therefore, the cloths bought by the Durham obedientiaries may be split into two major groupings. All were bought primarily because they were fit for the purpose for which they were intended, but for some that purpose was essentially practical, whilst for others it was to define and maintain social distinctions in a strictly stratified hierarchy. The cheapest cloths bought show a strong degree of price responsiveness, purchases increasing when prices fell and decreasing when they rose. Demand for some other cloths such as linen and serge was relatively inelastic since clothing, bedlinen, and so on were a constant requirement and a certain standard was no doubt assumed to be necessary. The demand for the livery cloths was apparently totally inelastic, although the lack of any great fluctuations in price means that this was not tested in this period. Certainly, however, the priory's purchases of these status-defining cloths show clearly that the firm and rigid delineation of the varying steps of social status was a primary object here. There is some evidence to suggest that the bursar shopped around for the best deal when his reliable supply in York dried up in the mid 1480s, but in general the livery cloths are the one area in the priory's purchasing for which a long-term relationship with a single supplier can be seen, suggesting that here at least consistency, reliability, and perhaps even tradition were considered more important than price.[90] Yet even when buying the most expensive cloths to enter the priory, the vestments, the epitome of cloths for which display, magnificence, and beauty were paramount, the priory never lost sight of price altogether. Relatively, if not absolutely, the obedientiaries still hoped for good value.

---

[89] Searle and Ross (eds.), *Battle Abbey*, 116, 136.   [90] See Ch. 6.

CONCLUSION

Finally, it may be valuable to take an overview of the price movements of all the commodities considered here, and to look at both the overall trends of prices and the overall purchasing strategies pursued by the priory in response to or in defiance of such changes. Most price series in this period were characterized by fluctuation, and there was no general price trend, either inflationary or deflationary, which could be said to have been in operation across all or most commodities at this time. The different commodities looked at here show a range of price movements, differing from each other not only in degree but also in direction.

Wine, dried fruit, and sugar prices fell noticeably over the period, but no equivalent trend can be seen in the prices paid by the priory for other spices such as pepper or ginger. For cloth, the prices of all the livery cloths (except that bought for the prior, which remained static) increased slightly over this period, whilst the prices of the cheaper cloths such as hardyn and sackcloth fell significantly. Within the overall heading of grain most varieties show if anything a slight decrease over time, but for barley the reverse is the case, although for all the grains bought by the priory annual fluctuations in price far outweigh any such changes. This lack of any strong directional tendency in the prices paid by the priory overall fits with the inflationary trends observed more generally for the later medieval period, which saw prices remain static or rise very slightly in the second half of the fifteenth century, begin to rise after 1500, and increase more steeply as the sixteenth century progressed.[91]

Overall, the period examined here was one of price stability; that is to say, the often violent fluctuations in the prices of various commodities from year to year were essentially random and tended to cancel one another out over time, rather than concealing a general upward or downward trend. Furthermore, the prices of the different commodities bought by the priory varied independently of one another. It was therefore not generally the case that a year in which one type of goods was particularly expensive was a year in which

[91] Y. S. Brenner, 'The Inflation of Prices in Early Sixteenth Century England', *Economic History Review*, 2nd ser., 14 (1961), 226: S. V. Hopkins and E. H. Phelps-Brown, 'Seven Centuries of the Prices of Consumables', *Economica*, NS 23 (1956), 297–302.

high prices prevailed over the whole monastic shopping basket of goods, and this again tended to cancel out the effects of fluctuations over time.

As has been seen in the case studies presented here, the priory's response to such fluctuations in price varied between commodities. The level of need, strength of desire, and social implications of any given purchase all shaped the extent to which considerations of price were permitted to influence the priory's purchases of any particular commodity. The priory's grain purchases were characterised by a basic minimum need which was met regardless of price, coupled with an elastic degree of demand over and above that minimum when the price was right. For some other goods there was a more immediate correlation between price change and change in the amount bought by the priory. This was the case for two distinct types of commodity, both the very mundane and the very luxurious, and can be seen for example in the priory's purchases of hardyn and of sugar.

Other luxury goods which were highly associated with status and prestige were bought apparently regardless of price changes. This applied both to the priory's purchases of wine and of the livery cloths, which were bought in relatively constant quantities throughout this period whether or not the price rose or fell. Nevertheless, for both these commodities the priory appears to have been conscious of the prices paid for various qualities and types, and alert to subtle nuances in the social implications of such distinctions. Moreover, there is some evidence for both these commodities that the priory actively shopped around for the best deal and was prepared to switch suppliers or look outside the immediate area to achieve the best price, implying that the maintenance of a constant volume of supply in the face of fluctuating prices was a considered decision rather than a side effect of consumer inertia.

Overall, this analysis of the main factors influencing the priory's purchasing choices suggests that the obedientiaries were relatively sophisticated consumers. They were aware of the different varieties of goods available to them, and these were chosen taking into account both the absolute prevailing prices of goods and the relative costliness of one variety compared to another. The social implications of their choices were also considered, and the extent to which these and other factors were weighted in their final decisions varied from one commodity to another. They were also both willing and able to source goods in a variety of ways and from a variety of markets. The strategies and techniques used by the priory in the actual sourcing of the goods they had decided to buy, and the impact in return of these issues on the goods bought, are the focus of the next chapters.

4

Tenurial Purchasing

Purchasing the goods required by a large medieval household such as Durham Cathedral Priory was a major undertaking, requiring a range of decision-making and implementation strategies. Every transaction made involved at least four basic steps, at each of which decisions had to be made. First, it was necessary to decide what was wanted: how much of a particular commodity was needed, whether a specific quality or variety was required, and so on. Prevailing prices, availability, tradition, and the expectations of various interested parties all played a role in determining the answers to these questions, as has been seen in the previous chapter.

Secondly, it had to be decided from whom the commodity in question was to be sourced. The same factors of price, availability, tradition, and expectations were important here, too, but others may also have had a bearing on the decisions made. It is possible, for example, that some purchasing decisions may have been affected by the convenience of using a particular supplier, kinship or other ties, or even by a desire to manipulate the market in some way—for example, to foster competition or conversely to maintain or establish a monopoly. Thirdly, once goods had been contracted for, they had to be brought to the priory (or other place of consumption). Arranging and paying for the carriage of goods may have been separate from or included in the original transaction; if separate, further decisions had to be made. Transport arrangements and costs may also have impacted on the decision of who to buy from, and in particular of whether it was worth looking outside the immediate area for supplies. Finally, the goods had to be paid for. How and when this was done again varied a great deal; the priory had to decide between direct payment, payment through agents, or payment offset against debts owed to the priory by the supplier, and the date of payment appears also to have been a matter for negotiation.

Each transaction could involve any combination of decisions at each of the four stages, and examples of a wide variety of permutations can be found in the accounts, although certain decisions were much more likely to be taken for certain commodities, or for luxury as opposed to staple varieties. Cutting across these complexities, however, were two clearly distinct purchasing strategies: the 'tenurial' and the 'market' methods. Whilst there was some overlap between the commodities bought using these two methods, it was generally the case that local agricultural produce such as grain and livestock were bought via tenurial contacts, whilst imported and/or manufactured goods were bought via market networks.

This chapter addresses the first of the two patterns, the tenurial method of purchasing goods. Most of the basic foodstuffs purchased by the priory were acquired in this way, as were some locally manufactured goods such as coarse cloths and Weardale iron. These commodities were purchased primarily from tenants of the priory lands which lay scattered around Durham, within an area roughly bordered by the Tyne to the north, the Tees to the south, the Wear to the west, and the coast to the east. The priory's purchases of such goods from their own tenants meant that a close economic relationship existed between landlord and tenant, and this was mirrored in the accounting and payment system used for the purchases. That is to say, a two-way relationship of supply and payment existed between the priory and its tenants, the priory providing land for which the tenants owed rents, and the tenants supplying the priory with goods for which payment was owed by the prior.

The accounting system used by the priory acknowledged and made use of this interrelationship. Rents were accounted for in the income sections and goods were accounted for in the expenditure sections of the obedientiary accounts at their cash values; however, it is clear that these two cash payments were rarely actually made. Instead, the tenants of the priory supplied goods, the value of which was recorded against the rent owed by each individual. Debts in both directions were thus balanced against each other and often any surplus was carried forward into future accounting years. Theoretically, therefore, the system could have been run on an entirely cashless basis, although in practice discrepancies in either direction at the end of the accounting year were often made good by cash payments of the balance to or by the priory as appropriate.

In this chapter the extent to which certain goods were acquired by the priory in this way rather than via market transactions is analysed, and some of the implications of the use of this method of supply are discussed. Grain was primarily bought from tenants using this pattern of acquisition, and provides a useful case study. Meat, fish, and other commodities are also considered more briefly. The issue of the locations from which the priory sourced its purchases is then addressed, and this leads into the next chapter which considers the characteristics of the market method of acquiring goods.

GRAIN

The single most prominent commodity acquired by the priory by the tenurial method of supply was grain—wheat, barley, and oats. The grain acquired by the bursar came primarily from tenants of the priory, and the majority of this was paid to the priory as rent payments in kind, as are detailed in the various bursar's rent-books to have survived. These core supplies were supplemented by small amounts of grain bought by the bursar, and grain which came into the priory from a few tithes that were paid directly rather than being farmed. The grain acquired from the bursar was then passed to the granator, who often also accounted for an incrementum (an adjustment to compensate for differences in measurement), which the bursar makes no mention of.[1]

In order to investigate how many of the bursar's apparent grain purchases were in fact payments of grain made in kind as part payment of debts or rents owed to the priory, a full comparison was made of all the grain mentioned in the grain sections of the bursar's account and in the bursar's rental for 1495/6. This year falls in the middle of the period under consideration here, but more importantly

---

[1] An increment occurs in these accounts mainly in connection with wheat purchases, and occasionally for barley. It seems likely that an increment was recorded as and when the grain was measured into the granary, so that the amount received by the granator using the priory's standard measures could be harmonized with the amounts the bursar had contracted for and accounted for. It is clear that such differences in measurement were of only minimal significance, accounting for only 1.4% of the priory's grain.

the rental for the year has survived intact and has recently been edited and published.[2] There are a few relatively small discrepancies between the details listed in the account and the rental, some of which are clearly errors of little importance, and a small amount of additional grain was purchased by the bursar over and above that received from his tenants. Overall, however, the grain purchased by the bursar shows an almost exact match to that paid by tenants in lieu of money rents, clearly demonstrating that the overwhelming majority of the priory's grain was acquired in this manner. The details of grain purchases given in the bursar's account roll and the records of grain used to pay rents in kind listed in the rental match exactly in eleven cases and are substantially the same in four more. These four latter cases have small differences in names and so on between the two accounts, but the quantities and values of the grain involved are either identical or would be but for what are clearly scribal errors. There are also eleven entries in the bursar's grain accounts which do not quite tally with those recorded in the rental. The majority of these discrepancies are very minor indeed, and are probably simply errors. For example, in the case of Roger Morland of Pittington the bursar's account records that he provided 44 quarters of wheat for £8. 16s. 0d. and 35 quarters of oats for £2. 3s. 9d., whilst the rental has it that he paid the first sum with only 40 quarters of wheat (still worth £8. 16s. 0d.), and that the 35 quarters of oats were worth £2. 3s. 10d.[3] The only significant differences between the two accounts are due to the appearance in the bursar's account roll of grain which was not mentioned in the rental, appearances which presumably imply additional purchases made over and above the grain received in payment of rent.

There are three main examples of this happening. First, 5 quarters of wheat, 4 quarters of barley, and 12 quarters of oats were purchased from Richard Denom of Newhouse. The same person also appears in the rental, where he paid the large rent of £2. 13s. 4d.; the rental does not record how this was paid, only that it was owed, so it is possible (the value of the grain being less than this at £2. 7s. 0d.) that this was in fact a payment in kind.[4] It is not clear why this should

[2] Lomas and Piper (eds.), *Durham Cathedral Priory Rentals*. The rentals for 1507–10 have also survived for this period in the Durham archive, DCM B. Bk. H.

[3] The account is likely to be right rather than the rental, since the sum divides by 44 to give 4s. per quarter, whereas £8. 16s. 0d. does not easily divide by 40.

[4] Lomas and Piper (eds.), *Durham Cathedral Priory Rentals*, 171.

not be mentioned in the rental if it were the case, however: it cannot simply have come in too late to be included, since the grain must have been provided in the same accounting year to have been included in the bursar's accounts. The other two examples do seem definitely to have been direct sales. The grain acquired by rental payments from Billingham was supplemented by a further 20 quarters of wheat and 39 quarters of barley which are recorded in the bursar's accounts as having been bought from individuals who are not mentioned in the rental. Similarly, John Matho of Southwick's name appears only in the bursar's account (not also in the rental), where it is recorded that he sold the bursar 21 quarters 1 bushel of barley.

More surprisingly, some grain is listed only in the rental and not in the bursar's account. It is hard to explain why this should occur, since in general any grain entering the priory was accounted for by the bursar at its cash value whatever its provenance or mode of acquisition. Indeed, a failure to double-account in this way for such sums as were paid in kind to the bursar in settlement of rents owed to him would have meant that he would be personally liable for the apparent disappearance of the sums paid. It seems likely that some of these instances were the result of errors: the sums involved are small, and they come from areas which were supplying the bursar with other grain. Three occurrences are less easily explained away, however, since they come from people and/or areas not otherwise supplying grain to the priory. The rental lists 2 quarters of wheat paid by Thomas Hilton of Wardley, 21 quarters of barley paid by John Atkynson of Fulwell, and 20 quarters of barley paid by the widow of Richard Clifton, from the manor of Bewley, which are not accounted for in the bursar's account roll as purchases.[5] It is conceivable that these small quantities were simply overlooked by the bursar when he compiled his annual accounts, but they do present something of a puzzle.

Nevertheless, these quantities are minor in comparison to the large amount of grain purchased by the bursar in each year, and it can be seen that the vast majority of the grain which entered the priory did so as a result of the payment in kind by the priory's tenants. The next largest source of grain for the priory, tithes, was also predicated upon such tenurial relationships. Throughout the period under consideration here the tithes of Billingham, Wolviston, Bewley manor, Cowpen

---

[5] Lomas and Piper (eds.), *Durham Cathedral Priory Rentals*, 138, 150, 164.

Bewley, and Newton Bewley were received directly by the priory in grain. However, although the tithes of the other manors were generally farmed there was some variation from year to year, with certain tithes reverting to the priory as farms ended and being re-farmed in the following year or soon afterwards. For example, the years 1461/2 and 1463/4 saw particularly large numbers of manors rendering their tithes directly to the priory, including Monk Hesleden, Sheraton, Hutton Henry, and Aycliffe. Indeed, Aycliffe was in hand throughout the 1460s, but was farmed for the remainder of this period reverting to hand only briefly in 1485/6. Heighington and Walworth also rendered their tithes directly to the priory sporadically throughout this period; both were in hand in 1495/6, for example. This variation in the manors in hand in any one year naturally led to variations in the amount of grain received by the priory from directly paid tithes, from a low of just over 51 quarters in 1481 to a high of 287 quarters and 4 bushels in 1464. On average, however, the priory received 124 quarters and 4 bushels of grain annually from this source, 6 per cent of the total grain acquired by the priory in an average year.

In addition to these direct payments of tithes, the 1495/6 rental shows that even farmed tithes were occasionally paid partially in kind. For example the Aycliffe tithe, sold to George Popley for £9. 0s. 0d., was in fact paid in a variety of goods. Included in this mixed bag were 9 quarters and 5 bushels of barley, worth £1. 8s. 6d., a horse worth £1. 10s. 0d., and some cash payments.[6] Similarly the Nunstainton tithe, sold jointly to Thomas Foster, Thomas Hergyll, and William Tailor for £6. 13s. 4d., was paid partly in 8 quarters each of barley and oats.[7]

It is impossible to be precise in quantifying the proportion of the grain bought by the priory via market transactions. The accounts rarely specify whether purchases were made via tenurial networks or on the open market, although occasional references are made to purchases *in foro*, and there are other indications of market transactions which are discussed in full in Chapter 5. However, the 1495/6 rental includes the rent payments that were made in grain, and by a process of elimination it can be assumed that grain that was not accounted for here or from tithes, or that was listed as 'increment', was acquired as the result of market transactions. A comparison of the bursar's account for 1495/6 with the rental reveals a discrepancy

---

[6] Ibid. 194.   [7] Ibid. 193.

of 37 quarters and 3 bushels of grain which on this assumption was bought at market, just under 2 per cent of the total grain acquired by the priory that year.[8]

The year 1495/6 was a fairly average one, with 2,180 quarters and 4 bushels of grain being received by the granator. If the market purchases figure for this year calculated above is taken as normative, then the result is a picture of the priory's grain income in which roughly 91 per cent of the grain was acquired as the result of rent payments being made in kind, 6 per cent came from tithes, 2 per cent from market transactions, and 1 per cent from measuring increments which cannot be precisely allocated between these categories.

The payment of grain in lieu of rents which were expressed in cash terms was such a significant feature of the monastic economy that it seems probable it was in some sense designed or planned to the advantage of the monastery. Looked at from another angle, grain was such an important staple item of the medieval diet, supplying both the bread and the ale which formed the basis of the monks' sustenance, that it is hard to believe that the monastery would have taken no steps to safeguard its supplies. From both these points of view it would seem likely that some fixed arrangement, either legal or customary, underlay the tenurial system of supply. Surprisingly, however, no such pattern is discernible from the surviving rentals. In addition to the published rental from 1495/6, the bursar's rentals for the four years 1507–10 have survived in the priory archive. A comparison of the payments made by tenants who are recorded in all of these rentals shows that the way in which their rents were paid could and did vary considerably from year to year.

Table 4.1 shows the grain payments made by tenants of Cowpen Bewley, chosen because it was one of the places showing an exact match in the 1495/6 bursar's account/rental comparison, and because several tenants can be traced through all the surviving rentals.[9] The table includes all the tenants who paid some part of their

---

[8] The bursar's account for 1495/6 in fact includes 101 quarters 1 bushel more grain than is listed in the rental. However, in addition, and inexplicably, the rental lists a total of 64 quarters 6 bushels for which no counterpart can be found in the bursar's purchases. If these sums are offset against each other, a remainder of 37 quarters 3 bushels is left which it may be assumed was purchased by the priory.

[9] Lomas and Piper (eds.), *Durham Cathedral Priory Rentals*, 157–9 for 1495/6; DCM B. Bk. H, fos. 28^r–29^v (1507/8), 97^r–98^v (1508/9), 168^r–169^v (1509/10), 232^r–233^v (1510/11).

TABLE 4.1. Rental payments made in grain by tenants of Cowpen Bewley, 1495–1510

	1495/6	1507/8	1508/9	1509/10	1510/11
Robert Clyfton	10 q. wheat (£2)	6 q. wheat (£2)	2 q. wheat (10s. 8d.)	12 q. wheat (£2. 8s.)	none
William Clyfton	6 q. wheat (£1. 4s.)	4 q. wheat (£1. 6s. 8d.)	4 q. wheat (£1. 1s. 4d.)	8 q. wheat (£1. 12s.) 2 q. barley (5s. 4d.)	none
Robert Shoroton*	2 q. 4b. wheat (10s.)	6 q. wheat (£2) 2 q. barley (8s.)	8 q. wheat (£2. 2s. 8d.)	12 q. wheat (£2. 8s.) 4 q. barley (12s.)	4 q. barley (12s.)
Edward Dawson	2 q. wheat (8s.)	2 q. wheat (8s. 4d.) 1 q. barley (4s.)	6 q. wheat (£1. 12s. 0d.)	10 q. wheat (£2) 4 q. barley (12s.)	4 q. barley (12s.)
William Lawe junior	4 q. wheat (16s.)	2 q. wheat (13s. 4d.)	2 q. wheat (10s. 8d.)	2 q. wheat (8s.) 2 q. barley (6s.)	2 q. barley (4s. 3d.)
William White**	5 q. wheat (£1)	4 q. wheat (£1. 6s. 8d.)	7 q. wheat (£1. 17s. 4d.) 2 q. barley (10s.)	12 q. wheat (£2. 8s.) 4 q. barley (12s.)	2 q. barley (6s. 8d.)

Note: The value assigned in the accounts to the payments in kind is shown in parentheses.
* Robert Shoroton is named in 1495/6, his widow in 1507/8, his widow and her son together in 1508/9 and 1509/10, and the son only in 1510/11.
** William White is named in 1495/6 and 1507/8, and Alice White, probably his widow, from 1508/9 onwards.

rent in grain in 1495/6 and whose tenancies were still included, either in the same name or in that of a recognizable close relation, in each of the 1507–10 rentals. Both the quantity and the value of the grain paid is given, as clearly either element could have been fixed by the priory. Most of those included below paid a substantial amount of their rent in grain each year, presumably reflecting their farming interests; but even this aspect of their payments was not fixed, with both Robert and William Clyfton paying none of their rent using grain in 1510/11.

The variety and haphazard nature of the payments shown here makes it clear that the way rents were paid was by no means frozen or fixed from year to year. In the light of this unexpected finding it is interesting to speculate whether the priory or the tenants had the upper hand in choosing how to make up the rental payments. If the priory specified this, one would expect to find more rents paid in grain when prices were high (if the intention was to minimize expenditure), or conversely when prices were low (if the intention was to maximize stores where possible). Similar alternatives might motivate tenants' decisions if they had the choice; in either case, one would expect there to be a strong correlation between price and the amount of rent paid in grain. In fact there is no such thing; rather, the amount of grain used by the tenants of Cowpen Bewley to pay their rents varied independently of the prevailing price. This may be seen particularly clearly in the different amounts of wheat rendered in the years in which the price was identical, 1495/6 and 1509/10. Such variation would suggest that the way in which rents were paid was a matter for the tenants to decide, and that their decision was based on their individual circumstances in each year rather than being a matter of policy. If this were indeed the case, it would in turn imply that the relationship between the priory and its tenants was cordial and based on a high degree of mutual trust and understanding.

It has been suggested that grain and other goods were used in lieu of currency in the later middle ages due to a severe shortage of circulating coinage, especially small change. However, this theory does not suffice to explain the widespread use of payments in kind found at Durham. In the first place, the chronology is wrong. The priory accounts show the use of payments in kind flourishing in the years for which rentals have survived, 1495/6 and 1507–11, whereas the European 'bullion famine' of the mid fifteenth century was at its height in the years 1457–64, with the development of new sources of silver rapidly righting the shortage across Europe from the early

1470s.[10] Meanwhile in England Edward IV's debasement of the coinage in 1464/5 (the only example of it in England in the period) led to an increase in production in English mint outputs between 1465 and 1480.[11] Secondly, the importance of rent payments in kind to the provisioning of the priory should not be allowed to obscure the fact that such payments were not the primary means by which the priory's tenants paid their rents. In the 1495/6 rental, 226 rents were paid entirely and 165 partially in cash, whilst 138 rents were paid entirely and 165 partially by goods or other non-cash means.[12] It is possible that such a pattern would have been reversed in earlier decades when the currency shortage was at its height. Indeed, Spufford suggests that the end of the shortage in 1465 led to a major shift in the nature of the medieval economy, being the turning point between a host of changes including a shift from deflation to inflation and 'a tendency to pay rents increasingly in kind . . . and a tendency to pay rents once again in cash; between an increasing resort to barter and a decreasing use of direct exchange of goods'.[13] It is unfortunate that the bursar's rentals do not exist from earlier in the century to enable this suggestion to be tested. Whilst no statistical comparison of the 1495/6 rental with those from two decades later has been made here, there was no discernible drift towards cash and away from commodity payments over these years.

MEAT, FISH, AND OTHER COMMODITIES

Grain was by far the most important of the commodities in which rent was paid, but other commodities, notably meat and fish, were also prominent in the rentals. In 1495/6, 91 tenants paid their rent partially or entirely in livestock, while fish was used by a total of 72 tenants, compared with 115 tenants who paid their rents using an element of grain.[14] However, unlike the grain rents the meat, fish, and sundries received by the priory in this way did not account for

---

[10] P. Spufford, *Money and its Use in Medieval Europe* (Cambridge, 1988), 359–63.

[11] J. H. A. Munro, *Bullion Flows and Monetary Policies in England and the Low Countries, 1350–1500* (Aldershot, 1992), 114, 117.

[12] R. A. Lomas, 'A Priory and its Tenants', in Richard Britnell (ed.), *Daily Life in the Late Middle Ages*, (Stroud, 1998), 117–19.

[13] Spufford, *Money*, 377.

[14] Lomas, 'Priory and its Tenants', 118–19; Lomas and Piper (eds.), *Durham Cathedral Priory Rentals*, 145–9.

virtually all of its requirements in these categories. A comparison of the 1495/6 rental payments made in meat, fish, honey, oil, and so on with the purchases of such commodities recorded in the bursar/cellarer indenture for that year shows that only around half of the total amounts of these goods bought by the priory were acquired in this way.

A total of 55 place names are mentioned in the bursar/cellarer indenture as supplying meat, fish, and sundry comestibles to the priory in 1495/6, and most of these places also appear in the 1495/6 bursar's rental. However, 11 places from which the priory sourced such goods do not appear in the rental at all, whilst the identification of a further 4 is uncertain. Of the 40 places common to both sources, all but 2, Farne and Holy Island, have payments in kind made to the priory listed in the rental; and of the 38 places for which such payments are recorded, 23 have at least some of their payments made in commodities that are also listed in the indenture as having been bought from them, while the remaining 15 have none of these commodities mentioned in the rental. In other words, a total of only 23 out of the 55 places recorded in the bursar/cellarer indenture as supplying foodstuffs other than grain to the priory had at least some overlap between their rents and their sales to the priory, 45 per cent, in striking contrast to the near-exact correspondence between the two seen for grain.

Only a single manor, Burdon, shows an exact correspondence between the goods received by the priory listed in the rental and the goods bought by the priory from that place as recorded in the bursar/cellarer indenture. The acquisition of three capons from Norman Maynerd at a value of 9d. is noted in both documents, whilst no other goods were recorded as coming from Burdon and no other rental payments from that place were made in kind.[15] Slightly less rare was the situation at Chilton, where the rental entries correspond exactly with entries in the bursar/cellarer indenture, but where a number of other goods not noted in the rental were also acquired from the village, presumably under market conditions. The goods other than grain paid in the rental by Chilton tenants comprised an ox worth 8s. 0d. from William Maltby and an ox and a cow, worth a total of 16s. 4d., from Thomas Kay.[16] The bursar/cellarer indenture, meanwhile, notes these acquisitions alongside the additional purchases of ten

---

[15] Lomas and Piper (eds.), *Durham Cathedral Priory Rentals*, 168–9.
[16] Ibid. 175–6.

hens and twelve piglets from William Maltby, a calf from Thomas Kay, and twenty piglets from a Thomas Lax, whose name does not appear in the rental. This pattern also occurred at Monk Hesleden and at Newton Ketton.[17]

More commonly, there was a degree of correspondence but with some additional items in the rental or in both the rental and the indenture. From Cowpen Bewley, for example, the bursar/cellarer indenture noted only the purchase of £1. 8s. od. worth of cockles and mussels, whilst the rental recorded receipt of this item, but also of six pigs, worth a total of 13s. od., from two other tenants.[18] Similarly, the indenture records only eight gallons of honey, worth 6s. 8d., from Wardley in Jarrow, whilst the rental notes that Thomas Hilton paid his rent using this, together with forty ewes, forty lambs, and three cows.[19] In both cases, the additional items mentioned in the rental but not in the bursar/cellarer indenture are livestock, and the discrepancy between the two documents suggests that these animals were received as breeding stock for the priory's farms rather than either as dead meat or as animals intended for immediate slaughter and consumption. A similar situation applied at several other places, notably at Aycliffe, Billingham, East Merrington, Ferryhill, Newton Bewley, and Westerton, with the addition of several items which appeared only in the bursar/cellarer indenture implying that these were bought via normal market transactions.[20] In addition, however, some fish appears in the rental without being listed in the bursar/cellarer indenture, which is highly unlikely to have been breeding stock. For example, George Williamson of Gateshead used several hundred sparling as part payment of his rent in 1495/6, yet no fish at all is mentioned in the indenture in connection either with Gateshead or with a supplier named George Williamson. Similarly, some 'surplus' fish occurs in the rental from Harton, Nether Heworth, and (especially) South Shields. It is possible that this fish, otherwise unaccounted for in the bursar/cellarer indenture, might be referred to in the mention of payments to fish purveyors in that document, although the quantities involved do not seem large enough to account for the size of these puzzling payments, and there is no suggestion in the rental that this 'surplus' fish paid towards rents was acquired differently or via particular agents.

[17] Ibid. 156–7, 170.   [18] Ibid. 157–9.
[19] Ibid. 138–9.   [20] Ibid. 162–8, 172–82.

There were also some places for which there is only a small degree of overlap, or even very little in common between the goods or live-stock received as rent payments and the goods bought by the cellarer for the priory's consumption. This situation occurred both at places that were of only minor importance and at places that were major suppliers of the priory. An example of the former was Aldin Grange in Durham, from which a boar worth 9s. 0d. and eighteen lambs worth a total of 15s. 0d. were received as part payment of William Cliff's rent in 1495/6.[21] In the bursar/cellarer indenture for that year the boar is recorded and the lambs are not, suggesting that they were intended to be used as breeding stock, but in addition the cellarer purchased twelve ewes and two oxen from William Cliff. At Coatsay Moor, part of Heighington, there was no point of comparison at all between the goods bought by the cellarer in 1495/6—piglets, capons, geese, and hens—and the single cow received as rent.[22] Even the suppliers of these goods were different, the cow being used as pay-ment by one Thomas Denom from whom no goods were sourced by the cellarer, although a John Denom of Coatsay Moor does appear in the indenture supplying capons, hens, and piglets that year. At East Rainton, an important supplier of the priory, there was again no match between the goods supplied to the priory as recorded in the two documents; the bursar/cellarer indenture recorded the purchase of capons, hens, piglets, and calves from there, whilst only cows are recorded as having been used in part payment of the East Rainton rents.[23] In this case, however, the individuals named in the two sources do coincide.

SOURCES OF SUPPLY

An analysis of the locations at which the priory's purchases were made, or of the geographic origin of the goods bought by the priory, is hampered by two things. First, the distinction, if any, between where an item was bought and its ultimate origin is not made in the accounts; where a location is given, it is usually indirectly associated with the commodity in question, stating that the item was bought 'from [the supplier's name] of [place name]'. Very occasionally it is

---

[21] Lomas and Piper (eds.), *Durham Cathedral Priory Rentals*, 183.
[22] Ibid. 171.   [23] Ibid. 151–2.

explicitly stated that the purchase was made 'at [place name]', usually instead of giving a supplier's name; and sometimes, usually with imported goods, the description of the commodity involved includes mention of its place of origin. Examples of the latter include Bay salt, Flemish cloth, and the distinction between Spanish and Weardale iron.[24] Of the 3,345 transactions analysed in this study, 1,632 have a place associated with them in the accounts. These include 87 transactions made with office-holders who are identified by the place with which their office was associated, such as 'the master of Farne', or 'the vicar of Easington'; 44 transactions involving 'the tenants of [place name]'; and 59 transactions which are described as having taken place 'at [place name]'. The remaining 1,442 transactions for which a place name is given have a named supplier also given, and the location is mentioned in connection with that individual. It follows that an analysis of the locations from which the priory acquired goods can only discuss around half of all transactions (49 per cent), although for some commodities proportionally more information is available.

Looking at the information by value, rather than by number of transactions, however, immediately changes the emphasis to be placed on unstated locations. Only 29 per cent of the total amount spent by the priory in these transactions was spent at an unspecified place. The largest shares of the amount spent by the priory went to York (21 per cent) and Leeds (14 per cent), and these amounts were almost entirely accounted for by the high-value livery cloth purchases made at the towns over this period. Other than these, only five other places had more than a 1 per cent share of the priory's expenditure: Shields (3 per cent), the Raintons (East and West jointly, 2 per cent), West Merrington (3 per cent in its own right, 4 per cent being spent with the Merringtons in total), Jarrow (1 per cent), and Durham itself (2 per cent). The other 106 places named in these accounts each received only a tiny share of the priory's expenditure.

These results, shown in Fig. 4.1, are clearly skewed by the inclusion of the high-value cloth purchases made at major marketplaces, which themselves accounted for over half of the spending analysed in this study. When these purchases are excluded from the analysis, four

---

[24] In the case of iron these terms may not have been intended as an exact description of origin, but rather as a means of making the distinction between the local and imported product (Threlfall-Holmes, 'Late Medieval Iron Production', 111).

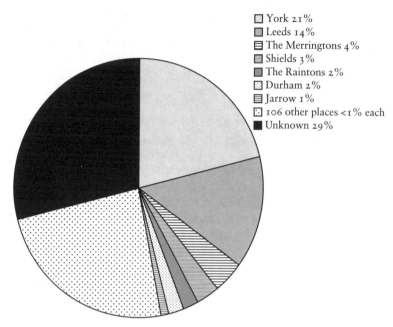

York 21%
Leeds 14%
The Merringtons 4%
Shields 3%
The Raintons 2%
Durham 2%
Jarrow 1%
106 other places <1% each
Unknown 29%

Fig. 4.1. Locations of suppliers to the priory, according to expenditure, 1460–1520

Note: Total percentage = 101 due to rounding.

places (Halifax, Leeds, London, and Yorkshire) disappear from the list of locations supplying goods to the priory, although York remains, supplying a small amount of fish. With cloth purchases excluded from the data, 37 per cent of expenditure was made at an unstated place, a proportion just low enough to make further investigation worthwhile. Overall, the picture remains similar, but the places which were notable before now stand out more prominently: 9 per cent was spent at the Merringtons (5 per cent at West Merrington), 6 per cent at Shields, 3 per cent at the Raintons, 3 per cent at Durham, and 2 per cent at Jarrow. A further eight places took between 1 and 2 per cent of the priory's expenditure each (Aycliffe, Billingham, Esh, Ferryhill, Hartlepool, Newton Ketton, Sunderland, and Southwick), leaving each of the ninety-six other places mentioned in the accounts still with less than 1 per cent of the priory's spending.

As the effect of the removal of the cloth purchases from this analysis demonstrates, there was a clear distinction between the commodities purchased primarily via market transactions and those acquired mainly or in significant proportion via the priory's residual tenurial networks and tenurial relationships. Purchases of the former were characterized by large orders being made at the main towns of the region; the sources of supply for goods bought primarily via market transactions are discussed in Chapter 5. In contrast, local agricultural produce was acquired from a wide variety of suppliers scattered across the region of the priory's influence, and this pattern applied to purchases of such commodities as grain and livestock whether the particular transaction under consideration was in fact a purchase made under market conditions or a rent or other payment made to the priory in kind. In other words, the distinction to be made when considering the geographical distribution of supply is between types of goods rather than strictly between the way in which an individual transaction was made. Agricultural produce such as grain and livestock, of which roughly half was purchased and half acquired in lieu of monetary payments owed to the priory, was almost all sourced from the Tyne/Tees region, whereas imported and manufactured goods (as will be seen in the next chapter) were almost all sourced from towns even in the few cases where such goods were supplied on the tenurial basis.

The following analysis considers the total amount spent on each commodity for each place name given in the accounts.[25] The categories into which the purchases have been divided for the purposes of this analysis are grain, poultry, pigs, cattle, sheep, herring, dogdraves, salmon, miscellaneous fish (a category which includes unspecified fish, various freshwater fish, eels, seals, shellfish), and miscellaneous other foodstuffs (butter, fat, green peas, etc.). This data shows the geographical distribution of the various types of agricultural produce and fish acquired by the priory. It is notable that each type of produce was sourced from a large number of places, and that although slightly different areas can be seen supplying different products there is no evidence of strong specialization except in the case of coastal towns supplying fish.

---

[25] For grain this analysis has been done for 1495/6, whilst for the commodities recorded in the bursar/cellarer indentures the sample years 1465/6, 1467/8, 1474/5, 1485/6, 1495/6, 1504/5, and 1515/16 have been taken.

Virtually all of the grain acquired by the bursar is associated with a location in these accounts, a fact which emphasizes the close connection between the priory's grain supply and tenurial relationships. As might be expected, the grain acquired by the priory came from a wide range of places within the area defined to the north by the river Wear and to the south by the river Tees (see Fig. 4.2). Grain was not acquired from the priory's more distant manors such as those on the Tyne or in Weardale or Derwentdale, but significant quantities were acquired from as far afield as the area around Billingham, which lies twenty-six miles from Durham as the crow flies and rather more by road. No single place dominated the priory's grain supplies, but Ferryhill was the most prominent, supplying 9.5 per cent of all the grain purchased by the bursar. This was closely followed by Pittington (9.4 per cent), Billingham (8.1 per cent), Newton Bewley (7.8 per cent), and Wolviston (7.6 per cent). East and West Rainton supplied 8.5 per cent, split roughly equally between them, whilst the three Merringtons supplied a total of 7.6 per cent, with the majority (4.7 per cent) coming from East or Kirk Merrington. Slightly less was supplied by Monk Hesleden (5.8 per cent), Dalton (3.1 per cent), and Aycliffe (2.8 per cent), whilst the remaining places each supplied under 2 per cent of the priory's requirements.

The first thing to note in looking at the data for produce other than grain is that a great many acquisitions were made without the location being specified in the account. It is perhaps more surprising that in many cases this unknown classification is not an overwhelmingly large proportion of the total number of transactions. Rather in several cases, notably for fish and for poultry, well over half or two-thirds of acquisitions can be associated with a place name. The categories for which the majority of the place names are unknown, however, can clearly have few conclusions about location drawn from them.

With the exceptions of cloth and grain, poultry is by far the most clearly 'located' class of goods bought by the priory, only 12 per cent of the total value of this category being spent at unspecified locations. For cattle the figure is 24 per cent, for pigs 41 per cent, whilst 77 per cent of the amount the priory spent on sheep has no place name associated with it in the accounts. Of the fish bought by the priory, 26 per cent of purchases of dogdraves are unlocated, as are 33 per cent of salmon. The figure for miscellaneous fish is 43 per cent of the value of transactions, whilst for herring it is 62 per cent. Other miscellaneous

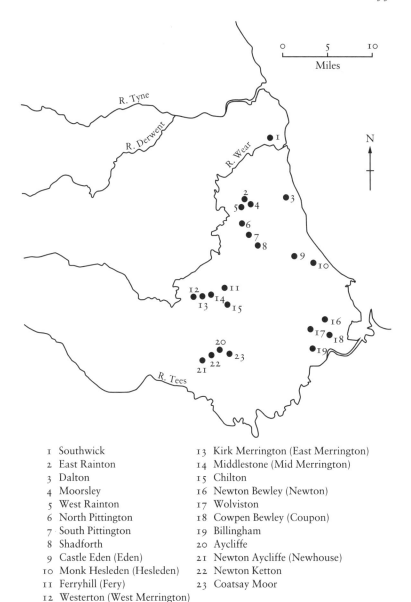

1 Southwick	13 Kirk Merrington (East Merrington)
2 East Rainton	14 Middlestone (Mid Merrington)
3 Dalton	15 Chilton
4 Moorsley	16 Newton Bewley (Newton)
5 West Rainton	17 Wolviston
6 North Pittington	18 Cowpen Bewley (Coupon)
7 South Pittington	19 Billingham
8 Shadforth	20 Aycliffe
9 Castle Eden (Eden)	21 Newton Aycliffe (Newhouse)
10 Monk Hesleden (Hesleden)	22 Newton Ketton
11 Ferryhill (Fery)	23 Coatsay Moor
12 Westerton (West Merrington)	

FIG. 4.2. Map showing the distribution of the priory's grain purchases in 1495/6

Note: Modern place name given, followed by name in accounts if different.

foodstuffs have no location associated with their purchase for 70 per cent of cases.

An analysis of the place names that are mentioned in association with purchases of poultry reveals no clear preference for any one location, but rather a succession of small purchases being made in a total of forty-six different places. Some of these form groups of villages which can reasonably be counted together, notably the Merringtons (East, Mid, and West Merrington, now known respectively as Kirk Merrington, Middlestone, and Westerton) and the Raintons (East and West). These two groupings received 41 per cent of the priory's total poultry expenditure between them, a total of 21 per cent being spent at the Merringtons and 20 per cent at the Raintons. The priory's remaining poultry purchases were widely distributed over forty-one other places, of which the most prominent were Pittington (9 per cent), Easington (5 per cent), Aycliffe (4 per cent), Billingham (4 per cent), and Heighington (3 per cent).

When these places are plotted on a map of the area (Fig. 4.3) a tendency for poultry suppliers to be grouped to the west of the region may be seen. However, it is clear that poultry was sourced widely and was not the special preserve of any one area. Further analysis at the more detailed commodity level reveals a similar picture. There are no great centres of specialism supplying all or most of the priory's requirements for any one commodity, although some villages do appear to be supplying only a small range of goods. For example Heighington supplied only geese to the priory in these years, so may perhaps be considered a goose specialist; but the 108 geese supplied accounted for only 6 per cent of the priory's total geese acquisitions, being outweighed by transactions involving several other villages. In particular, 366 geese were acquired from the Merringtons and 495 from the Raintons. It seems more likely that Heighington was simply a small supplier of the priory in general, and maybe a small village with a not very mixed economy, rather than a specialist in any significant sense of the word. Similarly, it does not appear to have been the case that the more prominent Merringtons and Raintons were poultry specialists, rather that they were major suppliers of the priory in general.

A similar picture of general sourcing of livestock from a wide variety of places with no strong locational bias may be seen for the priory's purchases of pigs and cattle. In the sample years looked at here, cattle for which a location was given in the accounts were

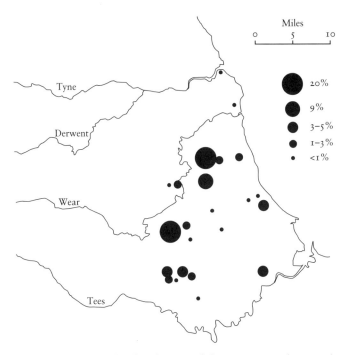

FIG. 4.3. Map showing the distribution of the priory's poultry purchases, 1465–1515

Note: Omitted from the map as either outside the mapped area or invisible since contiguous with another mapped place are Eastrington, East Yorkshire, and St Margaret's Chapel (all 3–5%) and Wiralshire and St Oswald's Church (both <1%). A location is unstated in the accounts for 12% of poultry purchases.

supplied from a total of sixty-six places, and these transactions accounted for 76 per cent of the total amount spent on cattle by the priory in these years. The place of purchase was unstated for a further 23 per cent, whilst the remaining 1 per cent was specified only to have been spent *in foro*; perhaps Durham market is implied. The sources of cattle were even less concentrated than was the case for poultry, only three places providing more than 3 per cent of the total: the Merringtons (19 per cent), the Raintons (5 per cent), and Durham itself (7 per cent). A further five places provided between 2 and 3 per cent of the priory's requirements (Ferryhill, Newton Ketton, Esh, Aycliffe, and Billingham), with the remaining fifty-eight places supplying under 2 per cent each, and in most cases well under 1 per cent.

Pigs were acquired from forty-six specified locations, accounting for 62 per cent of the total value of pig transactions between them, while 37 per cent of transactions had no location given and again 1 per cent were purchased *in foro*. The priory's pig sources show a similar low level of concentration to that found for cattle; only seven places provided more than 2 per cent each of the priory's needs. As usual, the Merringtons and Raintons predominated, with 12 per cent and 8 per cent of the total value of pigs acquired by the priory being accounted for by supplies from those two areas respectively.

Although sheep have so few locations given that an analysis would be misleading, it may be noted that 3 per cent was specified to have been spent *in patria* and none *in foro*, in marked contrast to the terminology used for cattle and pigs alike. Whether this reflects a different nature of transaction is unclear, but it may simply have been the case that sheep tended not to be brought to market but were sold from the field. It may well also be the case that the high level of unlocated transactions found here indicates that a much higher proportion of the sheep acquired by the priory were purchased in market transactions rather than being supplied via tenurial links, since it would be more likely that place names would be specified in the accounts when they were intimately bound up with the transaction, as was the case when goods were supplied by tenants in lieu of rents.

Even fish, a class of goods which might have been expected to have been very much more localized than livestock, were supplied from thirty-two stated places, in addition to the 41 per cent overall which was of unstated origin. There was some degree of clustering, with 19 per cent of the fish acquired by the priory in these years coming from South Shields, 7 per cent from Jarrow, 6 per cent from Hartlepool, and 3 per cent each from Holy Island, Southwick, and Sunderland. However, a greater degree of geographic specialism emerges if individual fish types are looked at instead of the class of fish as a whole. Dogdraves, a type of cod which formed one of the staple ingredients of the fish part of the monks' diet and which accounted for 37 per cent of the amount spent on fish by the priory, were unsurprisingly all supplied from the coast, primarily from South Shields. There were also many fewer different places listed in association with these acquisitions than was the case for meat. In all, 26 per cent by value of the dogdraves acquired by the priory in this period were unlocated, 39 per cent were from Shields, 10 per cent each from Jarrow and from Hartlepool, and the remainder from only seven other locations

(Beadnell, Farne, Harton, Holy Island, Wearmouth, and Westoe). Notable here are the much more northerly Holy Island, Farne, and Beadnell, especially Beadnell which was not a place belonging to the priory. The distribution of supplies between these sources was not static over the seven years looked at here. For example, the appearance of Beadnell in these accounts was almost entirely accounted for by the 600 dogdraves supplied from there in 1467/8, whilst Hartlepool appears only twice, providing 180 dogdraves in 1467/8 and 740 in 1474/5. Whilst the fact that a quarter of the dogdraves supplied do not have any location mentioned in the accounts prevents any firm conclusions about the changing location of supplies being drawn, it would seem likely that the South Shields fish formed the bulk of the priory's supply and that this supply was supplemented as necessary by purchases or ad hoc rental payments from elsewhere.

The priory's herring supplies were characterized by an even smaller number of sources, although unfortunately a much larger proportion of these acquisitions are unlocated: 56 per cent in the case of white herring and 72 per cent for red herring. As has been noted for sheep, it is possible that this indicates a higher proportion of market purchases operating here. Of the remaining 44 per cent of white herring supplies with which a location is associated, just over two-thirds, or 30 per cent of the total, came from South Shields. This represents 45 barrels out of a total of 148.5 barrels acquired over the period. Much smaller amounts came from four other places: 10 barrels from Jarrow, 6 from Hartlepool, and 2 each from Newcastle and Harton. Of the 28 per cent of red herring for which a location is given, supplies from South Shields again predominated although by a far smaller margin, accounting for just under a third of this proportion. Again, only four other place names are mentioned: Sunderland, Jarrow, Hartlepool, and Harton.

Turning to salmon, which formed a substantial but not staple part of the monks' fish diet, we find the pattern somewhere between those seen so far for the staple varieties of fish, that is for dogdraves and herring, and for meat. The proportion of the priory's salmon which is unassociated with any place name is not prohibitively high, at 33 per cent. The general picture is of several small acquisitions from a total of sixteen different places. Of these, four or five bear a larger part, with the most prominent being Southwick, supplies from which accounted for 17 per cent by value of the salmon acquired by the priory in this period. Southwick is followed in importance by

Berwick and Sunderland (8 per cent each), Holy Island (7 per cent), Gateshead and Shoreswood (6 per cent each), and Norham (5 per cent). Lesser amounts were spent at the other places mentioned: Westoe, Monkwearmouth, Simonside (in Jarrow), Chester-le-Street, Fulwell, Ryton, Newcastle, Morpeth, and 'Marom' (unidentified).

It can be noted that the priory's salmon was sourced from a rather wider catchment area than other fish or meat purchases. Both Shoreswood and Norham are in Northumberland, and particularly notable in this context is the 8 per cent of the total expenditure on salmon by the priory in this period which was spent at Berwick. When a more detailed analysis is carried out, distinguishing between different types of salmon, it can be seen that all the salmon coming from Berwick and Holy Island was salt salmon (which accounted for 85 per cent of the total salmon supplied to the priory, the rest being fresh). It is tempting to draw the conclusion that salt salmon— generally described as being bought by the barrel, which seem to have contained an average of twenty-eight fish each—was more susceptible to long-distance carriage, but it should also be remembered that since salt salmon predominated in the priory's supply, it might be expected similarly to dominate that sourced from outside the immediate locality. Fresh salmon certainly came from as far afield as Morpeth, where four were bought in 1467. Others came from Shoreswood, Ryton, Cornhill, and Sunderland, but the majority of the salmon specified to have been fresh is not associated with a location in the accounts. It might be speculated that it was locally caught, perhaps in the priory's fish-weirs on the river Wear below the cathedral.

Miscellaneous other fish, including shellfish and freshwater fish, accounted for the remainder of the amount spent on fish by the priory. Only thirteen places are mentioned in connection with the supply of such goods, whilst 43 per cent of these transactions had no place name specified in the accounts. The main places from which such miscellaneous fish were supplied were Cowpen Bewley (16 per cent) and Farne (15 per cent). Cowpen Bewley was the major supplier of cockles and mussels to the priory. One cockle and mussel transaction is recorded in each of the sampled bursar/cellarer indentures, and on only one occasion, in 1504/5, was this commodity acquired not from Cowpen Bewley but from nearby Billingham instead. The miscellaneous fish supplied by Farne over this period consisted of a total of nineteen seals and dolphins, whilst the only other transaction in which Farne participated in these years was the supply of 360 dog-draves to the priory in 1467/8. In addition to the seals and dolphins specified to have been from Farne, 26½ other seals and dolphins were acquired by the priory in these years. Of these, 23½ were of unstated origin, two came from Beadnell, and one from Wearmouth.

Whilst it was to be expected that the priory would consume a greater proportion of fresh fish than it might otherwise have done due to its location on a river and near the coast, preserved forms of fish were also acquired in large numbers. Although the number of entries for such goods for which a location is specified is severely limited, there is some evidence to suggest that these were predominantly sourced from the major market towns, and were probably bought via market transactions rather than using the tenurial model. Eels were normally bought salted, although fresh eels also frequently appear in the priory accounts, but virtually all eel purchases have no place name given in the accounts. The only two entries which do include a location are for purchases from Hull and Newcastle respectively. Similarly, of the ten stockfish (dried cod) transactions recorded in these accounts, only three have a location specified and these relate to transactions at Hull, York, and Newcastle respectively. The latter was the only purchase of fish made at York in these years, whilst the only other fish supplied by Hull was a barrel of sturgeon, and by Newcastle two barrels of salted herring, again preserved forms of fish.

Finally, of the miscellaneous other foodstuffs bought by the priory over this period only two, honey and oil, have locations associated with them in the accounts. The first, honey, was 64 per cent un-specified, whilst a further 21 per cent of purchases were noted only to have been made *in patria*. Locations given for the remaining 15 per cent of purchases were 'Caldronley' (unidentified), Hebburn, Beaurepaire, Consett, Durham, Follingsby (in Jarrow), Holmeside (near Edmondsley), Ludworth, Muggleswick, Newton Bewley, Wardley, and West Rainton. The pattern, insofar as it can be ascer-tained from such a small sample, was therefore for honey to come in small parcels from widely dispersed priory lands. Clearly, however, the two-thirds of the honey acquired by the priory for which no loca-tion was specified may have followed an entirely different pattern, and may have been the result of market transactions. It should be noted that only a single instance of honey being used to pay rent occurs in the 1495/6 rental, involving 8 gallons supplied by Thomas

Hilton of Wardley (in Jarrow).[26] The picture for oil appears to have been rather different. Just over a quarter of oil purchases had no location specified in the accounts, whilst one barrel, representing around 5 per cent of the priory's oil purchases, was acquired from Nether Heworth. The remainder was bought at the region's sizeable towns (Gateshead, Hull, Newcastle, and Durham itself) indicating that the commodity was bought primarily by market transactions.

CONCLUSION

The tenurial system of purchasing, then, was used primarily for the staple foods which resulted from local agriculture and fishing, rather than for imported, manufactured, or processed goods, or for high-value goods bought only occasionally such as freshwater fish. It was most prevalent for grain, almost all of which was supplied to the priory or sourced by the priory in this manner. Cattle, sheep, pigs, poultry, and some seafood such as dogdraves, cockles, and mussels were also sourced substantially from the priory's tenants, though for most of these goods only around half were bought using this method, that is were paid for by the priory by being offset against rents owed, whilst the rest was bought from the same individuals but on the market principle.

The tendency of the priory to buy such goods from its tenants is not in itself surprising, since much of the surrounding area was owned by the priory and so simple availability would have forced some such pattern even if relations between the priory and its tenants had been exceptionally bad. However, the interrelationship between priory and tenants seen here was exceptionally close. In the first place, the extent to which such goods were bought almost exclusively from tenants does suggest a closer relationship than mere expediency would necessarily demand. More importantly, the evidence seen here shows that such a relationship was actually designed into the structural framework of the priory's purchasing and accounting systems. Finally, the variation seen in the ways in which tenants' rental payments were paid from year to year and the lack of any clear pattern in such changes suggest that neither party to this arrangement was abusing the system. That is to say, the priory does not appear to have

---

[26] Lomas and Piper (eds.), *Durham Cathedral Priory Rentals*, 138.

used its influence to insist upon goods when prices were high and cash when prices were low, and neither do the tenants seem to have been attempting the reverse. It is not possible to ascertain from the blunt lists in the rentals exactly what negotiations or decisions led to the payments that were made, but it would appear that the tenants had considerable freedom of choice as to how to pay their rents and that the priory may have indicated its preferences from time to time but either did not or could not enforce compliance. Such a system must have been based upon goodwill and personal relationships, and that it was still in place at this period suggests that it worked.

Nevertheless there was a limit to how useful this system could be. The market was still needed throughout the priory's life both to supply the goods that tenants could not or did not produce, or to purchase top-up supplies of commodities that were primarily supplied via the tenurial system. Such supplementary supplies were normally needed to some extent from year to year because of natural fluctuations in the exact amounts of any one commodity rendered by tenants in a system which did not strictly regulate the goods owed by each individual, but the market was also a safety net which could be used to acquire a supply of goods from outside the region when local conditions or disease caused supply failure on the priory's lands. This issue of inter-regional trade and the related question of regional price and supply variations will be looked at in the next chapter on the market system of supply, which also addresses more general thematic questions such as transport and the carriage of goods.

5

Market Purchasing

INTRODUCTION

Whilst many goods were acquired by the priory via the system based on tenurial relationships described in the previous chapter, most imported and manufactured goods were bought on the open market. In addition, market transactions were used when necessary as a method of topping up supplies of the local agricultural produce acquired primarily from the priory's tenants in lieu of rent payments. There is thus no clear dividing line between either the goods or the individual suppliers involved in these two methods of supply; the same tenant might supply the priory with two pigs in lieu of rent and sell another to the priory in a market transaction. Nevertheless, the two strategies of acquisition are themselves distinct, and certain goods and suppliers tended to be more closely associated with one or the other. The clearest difference between the two lies in the method of payment used by the priory. The complex double accounting used in the payment of rents in kind by tenants is mirrored in the equally complex web of payments, agents, and credit used by the priory when purchasing on the open market, although the extent and details of the latter are much less clearly indicated in these accounts. In addition, the locations at which market purchases were made were clearly different from those from which tenurial payments in kind came.

This chapter takes a thematic rather than a commodity-based approach, examining certain key features of the priory's market purchasing strategies using evidence drawn from the purchase of a wide range of goods. The role of purchasing agents, methods of payment, credit, the markets from which the priory bought goods, and transport issues are all addressed in turn, with both changes over time and geographic or regional differences being identified and discussed. In the first place, however, it is important to look at the priory's use of the market in relation to the staple agricultural goods which were supplied primarily via the priory's network of tenurial relationships.

The first part of this chapter takes the form of a detailed analysis of the grain purchases made by the priory on the open market, a study which emphasizes the importance to the medieval market of regional variations in supply and demand.

MARKET PURCHASES OF GRAIN AND
THE REGIONALITY OF GRAIN PRICES

The majority of the grain acquired by the bursar each year was received in lieu of rents from priory tenants, as has been seen in Chapter 4. In addition, however, some grain was bought on the open market in most years. This was usually only a small amount, but occasionally more significant quantities were purchased. Although the information relating to the rent-book is available for only very few years, the accounts of the bursar's grain purchases survive for most years, and these suggest that the pattern of purchases seen in the years for which these can be compared with the rentals was typical. Most of the examples of purchases of grain that were market transactions refer to grain bought *in patria* or *in villa et patria*. These purchases tended to be of fairly small amounts, certainly less than that coming in from tenants as rent payments: the impression given is of top-up supplies being purchased. This interpretation is given further credence by the fact that these purchases were very often made at a higher price per quarter than the mode price in operation in the relevant year – such purchases may well represent additional purchases made towards the end of the year. For example, in 1514/15 the bursar bought 77 quarters 3 bushels of wheat and 71 quarters of barley from various unspecified suppliers in the countryside, roughly 10 per cent and 8 per cent respectively of the total amount of each grain bought that year. In both cases the price paid for this grain was higher than the year's mode price for each variety. The wheat was bought for 8s. 0d. a quarter, compared to the mode price of 5s. 4d. (an increase of 50 per cent), and the barley for 5s. 0d. as against the mode price of 4s. 0d. (an increase of 25 per cent).[1]

---

[1] Other examples of such purchases in the bursar's accounts are oats being bought *in patria* in 1515/16, *in foro* in 1482/3, and *in foro et patria* in 1512/13; barley being bought *in patria* in 1514/15; and wheat being bought *in patria* in 1515/16 and 1520/1, and *in villa et patria* in 1512/13 and 1513/14. In each case the price(s) paid were higher than the mode price in the relevant year.

In addition to such *in villa* or *in patria* purchases, other transactions in the bursar's accounts also appear to represent market transactions rather than tenurial renderings. There are often a handful of entries in a year that are charged at a higher price than the mode price for that year, and it may well be that these too represent top-up purchases of grain later in the season. This cannot be proven, but it is worth noting that such entries tend to be grouped together in the accounts, and are often towards the end of each section. Furthermore, some of the individuals named as the suppliers in these entries were clearly not tenants of the priory. For example, just under 25 quarters of barley were bought from the suffragan bishop in 1513/14, whilst the names of Newcastle merchants are given on three occasions. In 1505/6, the wheat purchases section of the bursar's account includes 5 quarters 6 bushels of wheat from Alan Harding of Newcastle, and 4 quarters of rye from Edward Baxter. Edward is not identified in the account as being from Newcastle, but was probably the same Edward Baxter who was a prominent Newcastle merchant in this period.[2] In 1520/1, the bursar purchased 80 quarters of wheat from John Brandling and John Tailor, whom he specifically described as being 'merchants of Newcastle' in the entry. Both wheat purchases in these two years were charged at a price higher than the mode price for their years; in 1505/6 Alan Harding was paid 9s. 4d. the quarter compared to the mode price of 8s. 0d., and in 1520/1 the prices were 9s. 4¼d. and 5s. 4d. respectively.

As can be seen from these dates, there was a marked increase in the incidence of identifiable market transactions in the second half of this period. This goes alongside a similar increase in the amount of price variation in each year.[3] There is of course a danger of entering into a circular argument here, since one of the features by which such transactions have been identified is their tendency to have different, normally higher, prices than the mode price: however, other distinguishing features such as the terms used in the entries are also used to mark out likely market transactions. It seems likely, therefore, that the increase in the amount of price variation is to some extent a factor of the increase in market transactions, rather than the latter being an illusory effect of the former.

[2] M. Threlfall-Holmes, 'The Import Merchants of Newcastle upon Tyne, 1464–1520: Some Evidence from Durham Cathedral Priory', *Northern History*, 40 (2003), 79; C. M. Fraser, 'The Early Hostmen of Newcastle-upon-Tyne', *Archaeologia Aeliana*, 5th ser., 12 (1984), 169–70.
[3] See Ch. 4.

The striking exception to this pattern of occasional small top-up purchases being made from local merchants or other suppliers, and by far the starkest example of the reality of market conditions operating in the priory's supply, comes in 1482/3. In this year prices were at their highest in this period, with wheat costing 13s. 4d. and barley 8s. 0d. per quarter, both at least twice their average modal prices over this period of 6s. 0d. and 4s. 0d. respectively. In this year, the bursar bought a very substantial amount of grain from outside the region – 531 quarters of barley, at the much lower price of 5s. 6½d. per quarter, *in partibus Australibus*, in other words 'from Southern parts'. This purchase, unique in the period, accounted for well over three-quarters of the barley acquired by the bursar that year, and for 71 per cent of the total amount spent by him on barley. It is notable that no carriage charge relating to this grain appears in the account, suggesting either that the much lower cost of the southern grain included the cost of its transport to Durham, or that it was collected by the priory and that this cost was not specifically accounted for.

The only other example in this period of grain being bought from outside the immediate region is much smaller in scale, when in 1507/8 the bursar purchased 4 quarters of peas and beans at Hartlepool. Though clearly of much less importance, this purchase in fact came about in very similar circumstances to the 1482/3 barley purchase. The price paid at Hartlepool was 4s. 0d. per quarter, whilst the mode price being paid by the bursar around Durham was 6s. 8d. per quarter, only the second highest price recorded for peas and beans in this period and 188 per cent of the average mode price, 3s. 8d. (the highest peas and beans price, 8s. 0d., came in the very bad year 1482/3). A similar situation, in which grain shortages explicitly forced the priory to purchase grain on the open market to supplement supplies acquired from tenants, would appear to have occurred just prior to 1438/9, although it is not clear in this instance whether the grain in question was imported from outside the immediate region. In that year the priory agreed a schedule of debt repayment with William Hoton of Hardwick, which included the sum of £23. 16s. 4d. owed to him by the priory for grain which he had bought for them. The schedule stated that, 'considering the serious burdens incumbent on the monastery this year, [including] purchasing grains at an excessive price', the total debt would be paid off over the following three years.[4]

---

[4] DCM Reg. Parv. II, fos. 100ᵛ–101ʳ.

Since grain was a staple food of (largely) uniform quality it is an ideal candidate for a study of price regionality. Much study of grain prices in England has been based upon the figures compiled by Thorold Rogers at the end of the nineteenth century, and this collection of evidence remains important although some more recent studies take a wider range of evidence into account.[5] However, several criticisms have been made of the quality of Rogers' evidence. Of particular relevance to the questions under consideration here, concerning regionalism and the typicality of the Durham price series, is a point made by Lutz: that Rogers' price series seriously under-represent the north and the west of England, being dominated by prices from the south-east region.[6] Lutz has compiled separate decennial averages for each of these three regions using the figures given by Rogers, and these demonstrate that grain prices could vary dramatically between regions, not only absolutely over time but also relatively. For example, the average decennial price of grain was higher in the north than in the south-east of England in four out of the six decades looked at here, but lower in the other two.[7]

These problems with Rogers' data were noted by Gras when he used the grain prices for his detailed study of the grain trade in England. He added data from Winchester, but other than that used Rogers' figures as they stood, notwithstanding these issues. Gras concluded that 'an empirical study of the price materials of Rogers indicates the existence of local market areas, that is, districts having a strong tendency towards a differential price level', and he mapped fifteen of these areas onto England.[8] Durham and its environs he classified as area thirteen, with the third highest grain price levels after East Essex and Battle. The cheapest grain was to be found in a broad band between the Upper Severn region, Bristol, and East

[5] Rogers, *History of Agriculture and Prices*. Important studies based on Rogers' figures include Gras, *Evolution of the English Corn Market*, and W. Abel, *Agricultural Fluctuations in Europe*, trans. O. Ordish (London, 1980). More widely based studies include W. G. Hoskins, 'Harvest Fluctuations and English Economic History, 1480–1619', *Agricultural History Review*, 12 (1964); P. Bowden, 'Agricultural Prices, Farm Profits and Rents', in J. Thirsk, ed., *The Agrarian History of England and Wales*, iv: *1500–1640* (Cambridge, 1967), 593–695; and D. L. Farmer, 'Prices and Wages 1350–1500', in E. Miller (ed.), *The Agrarian History of England and Wales*, iii: *1348–1500* (Cambridge, 1991), 431–525.

[6] H. L. Lutz, 'Inaccuracies in Rogers' History of Prices', *Quarterly Journal of Economics*, 23 (1909), 356–7.

[7] Ibid. 357.   [8] Gras, *Evolution of the English Corn Market*, 38–9, 42, 47.

Anglia, with higher prices in the south-west, north (Durham and York), and extreme south-east.[9] The picture of regionalism thus drawn is one which it is tempting to take at face value, but Gras's figures have been trenchantly criticized. Kneisel pointed out that evidence for most areas for most years was lacking, and that Gras's results were counter-intuitive since they ignored river corridors which would be expected to produce more consistent grain prices than areas joined only by proximity over land, since transport costs could easily account for the relatively small price differences found between Gras's regions. Kneisel concluded that the regionalism drawn by Gras was illusory, apparently 'formed more or less arbitrarily by drawing neat circles round contiguous areas on the map'.[10] Nevertheless, other historians have also identified Durham as a region of high cereal prices. Bowden points out that prices and wages could and did vary significantly from area to area as a result of factors independent of actual harvest quality in a particular year, such as the demand for labour and the geography and climate, and that wheat was expensive in the Durham region since conditions there favoured pastoral husbandry and spring-sown crops instead.[11] Farmer adds that barley as well as wheat was relatively expensive in this region, but that in contrast oats were relatively cheap.[12]

A coherent source of price data for the period after 1480 comes from Hoskins's analysis of harvest fluctuations in the long sixteenth century. Hoskins used evidence primarily from Winchester, Exeter, and Lincoln, with some prices also coming from Norwich and London, to give information on a total of 140 harvests. These were classified by price: the harvest in years in which prices were within 10 per cent of the average for the period was designated average; when prices were between 10 per cent and 30 per cent higher than average the harvest was described as deficient, or bad when prices were more than 30 per cent higher than the average; when prices were between 10 per cent and 30 per cent lower than average the harvest was described as good, and when prices were more than 30 per cent lower than the average the harvest was classified as abundant.[13]

[9] Ibid. 47.
[10] E. Kneisel, 'The Evolution of the English Corn Market', *Journal of Economic History*, 14 (1954), 46–52.
[11] Bowden, 'Agricultural Prices', 609–16.
[12] Farmer, 'Prices and Wages', 447.
[13] Hoskins, 'Harvest Fluctuations', 29–30.

Overall, Hoskins found that the 1480s were a period of bad harvests, with prices in the three consecutive years 1481–3 all being higher than 30 per cent above the average, and the harvest of 1482 being particularly bad, especially in the eastern counties. The 1490s, on the other hand, saw a series of particularly bountiful harvests: according to the classification outlined above, those for 1492–3 were good, 1494–5 abundant, 1496–8 average, and 1499 good. The sixteenth century began badly, but harvests picked up in the latter half of the first decade, with the price in 1509 being the lowest in two hundred years and 1510 also being an abundant year. Overall, the second decade of the sixteenth century was slightly better than average, with harvests average or good from 1513 to 1518, but that of 1519 was deficient and 1520 saw dearth, with prices 53.9 per cent higher than the average.[14] Again, regional differences could be striking: the years 1487, 1504, and 1515 saw average prices overall but a bad harvest in the west, for example.[15] Some confirmatory evidence for the years pre-1480 is provided by Stratton and Brown.[16]

All the information for grain prices and harvest qualities across England in this period can be compared with the figures derived from the Durham bursar's accounts. Wheat prices, the standard measure used in most of the studies referred to above, will be used as the measure of comparison. At the highest level of abstraction, decennial averages for Durham can be compared with those given for England as a whole by Abel (using Rogers' figures which are weighted towards the south-east). This comparison is tabulated in Table 5.1. To make the figures comparable, indices are given, where 100 represents the average of each series for this period, so that the relative changes in each decade are compared, rather than absolute prices.

It can be seen from the table that the proportional movements in grain prices were generally similar, with less than 6 per cent difference between the two in four out of the six decades examined. However, in the two decades in which grain prices were notably higher in England as a whole the regional difference was striking. In 1481–90, when grain prices were 11 per cent higher than the average in England as a whole, the priory paid 34 per cent more than the average. By contrast the priory paid 10 per cent less than average in

[14] Hoskins, 'Harvest Fluctuations', 31–3.   [15] Ibid. 44.
[16] J. M. Stratton and J. H. Brown, *Agricultural Records, A.D. 220–1977*, ed. R. Whitlock (2nd edn., London, 1978), 36.

TABLE 5.1.   Grain price indices at Durham compared with those for England overall, 1461–1520

Years	England	Durham	Difference (%)
1461–70	92	98	6
1471–80	94	93	1
1481–90	111	134	23
1491–1500	89	86	3
1501–10	95	98	3
1511–20	118	90	28

Note: The indices used in the table are based on the average grain price in each region for the period. For the England figures (which are calculated from those given in Abel, *Agricultural Fluctuations*, 304), 100 = 22.6 grains of silver per 100 kg of wheat. For the Durham figures, 100 = 5.88*d*. per quarter of wheat. These bases are different in order to factor out regional variations in absolute grain prices, so that only differences in the size or direction of grain price fluctuations are shown here.

the last decade of the period, when prices overall in England were 18 per cent higher than average. Clearly, therefore, prices in the Durham region were subject to fluctuations and local conditions which could operate quite independently of those affecting the rest of the country.

More detail of how the Durham prices varied with or apart from the average for the country as a whole may be gained by examining individually the years in which particularly high or low prices were current. Using Hoskins's methodology and designating bad or good harvests to be those in which the price rose or fell by more than 30 per cent of the average for this period, Durham may be said to have enjoyed particularly good harvests in 1473/4, 1494/5, 1495/6, 1498/9, 1499/1500, 1509/10, and 1510/11. Bad harvests occurred in 1465/6, 1470/1, 1481/2, 1482/3, 1486/7, 1488/9, and 1505/6. Those of 1481–2 were especially disastrous, the prices in these years rising to 168 per cent and 224 per cent of the average for this period.

A comparison of the harvest qualities calculated for the Durham region with those calculated for the rest of the country by Hoskins (Table 5.2) shows that, overall, Durham harvests tended to be slightly worse than those elsewhere. In particular, the dearth of the early 1480s seems to have been even more disastrous in the north than in the rest of England, starting earlier and affecting prices more severely; elsewhere, dearth hit only in 1482/3, when prices rose to

TABLE 5.2. Comparison of harvest qualities for Durham and
England overall, 1460–1520

Year	England	Durham	Year	England	Durham
1460			1490	Deficient	
1461			1491	Average	
1462		Good	1492	Good	Good
1463			1493	Good	Good
1464			1494	Abundant	Abundant
1465		Bad	1495	Abundant	Abundant
1466		Good	1496	Average	Bad
1467		Deficient	1497	Average	Bad
1468		Deficient	1498	Average	Abundant
1469		Deficient	1499	Good	Abundant
1470		Bad	1500	Deficient	Average
1471		Deficient	1501	Bad	Good
1472		Good	1502	Bad	
1473		Abundant	1503	Deficient	Deficient
1474		Good	1504	Average	Deficient
1475		Good	1505	Average	Bad
1476		Average	1506	Good	Good
1477			1507	Average	Deficient
1478		Average	1508	Good	Good
1479		Good	1509	Abundant	Abundant
1480	Average	Deficient	1510	Abundant	Abundant
1481	Bad	Dearth	1511	Average	Good
1482	Dearth	Dearth	1512	Deficient	Good
1483	Bad		1513	Average	Good
1484	Average	Good	1514	Good	Good
1485	Good	Good	1515	Average	Good
1486	Average	Bad	1516	Good	
1487	Average	Average	1517	Good	
1488	Average	Bad	1518	Good	
1489	Average		1519	Deficient	
			1520	Dearth	Good

Source: England harvest qualities after 1480 taken from Hoskins, 'Harvest
Fluctuations', 44. Durham harvest qualities are calculated using the same
methodology.

175 per cent of their average level, whereas Durham saw very bad harvests in the previous two years also, and prices peaked at 224 per cent of the average. However, Durham did do better in certain other years, and especially in the early sixteenth century when Durham prices were proportionally lower than those elsewhere in 1498–9 and 1511–20, and were notably good in 1520/1, a year which saw dearth elsewhere. Some regionality in grain prices was clearly present, therefore, but in a more dynamic fashion than suggested by Gras. Whilst prices overall do seem to have been somewhat higher in the north, this was not a static pattern but varied as harvests varied from region to region and from year to year.

It is clear that, whilst the bursar made small additional purchases of grain in most years to supplement that supplied by tenants in part payment of their rents, large-scale market purchases were an eventuality reserved for years of dearth. The situation in 1482/3, when grain had to be purchased in southern England to make good the shortfall felt in the Durham region, was unique as far as the priory was concerned in this period and perhaps in the century. That the price in southern England was so much lower than in the north that buying outside the region was both necessary and worthwhile is particularly interesting, as is the fact that this was such an unusual event.

MARKETS

The above discussion on the regionality of grain prices, whilst specific to grain, is nevertheless indicative of the variations of demand, supply, and pricing in different areas that could apply to all kinds of commodities in this period. Despite these differences, however, it is clear that the priory sourced grain from outside the immediate region only in exceptional circumstances, being largely self-sufficient in all but exceptionally bad years. It might be expected, however, that other commodities such as luxuries and imported or manufactured goods would be sourced from a wider area, perhaps including the major fairs and certainly including London. In fact, whilst to some extent this was the case in an earlier period, one of the major long-term changes that these accounts reveal is the increasing proportion of the priory's business that went to Newcastle merchants over the medieval period, to the extent that the immediate north-east region supplied virtually all the priory's requirements by the beginning of the sixteenth century, with Newcastle assuming an increasingly dominant role within the region.

This may be illustrated by the history of the priory's wine purchases. Margaret Bonney has shown that in the thirteenth and fourteenth centuries, local middlemen supplied the priory with wine which they probably purchased in turn from London wholesalers. By the mid fourteenth century, the emphasis had shifted to the great fairs of Durham, Darlington, and Boston, and by the late fourteenth century to the merchants of Durham, Newcastle, Hartlepool, Darlington, York, and Hull. As early as the first years of the fifteenth century, the majority of the priory's wine came from Newcastle.[17] The evidence from the fifteenth century indicates that this trend towards Newcastle continued over the century, with Newcastle merchants claiming an increasing share of the priory's business.

Of the £2,255. 11s. 0d. that the bursar's office is recorded as spending on wine over the forty-seven years for which totals survive in the period looked at here, 94 per cent was paid to Newcastle merchants, nearly 6 per cent to the merchants of Hull, and negligible amounts to merchants of York (£36. 3s. 4d.), London (£17. 0s. 6d.), and Durham (£9. 6s. 8d.). The proportion of the priory's trade that was given to York, in particular, had declined noticeably since the first half of the century, when 11 per cent of the bursar's wine had come from that city.[18] This reflects the decreasing numbers of York merchants participating in overseas trade over the fifteenth century,[19] an important feature of the recession that lasted there from c.1420 to the early decades of the sixteenth century. The pattern of the priory's purchases from York merchants suggests that the increasing focus on Newcastle suppliers was a response, rather than a contribution, to this decline; there was no sudden abandonment of the York market (indeed in 1471/2, 49 per cent of the bursar's wine purchases were made there). In the first half of the fifteenth century, the bursar had occasionally purchased wine not simply at the four towns used in the second half of the century, but also from South Shields and Hartlepool; by the sixteenth century, no wine was bought from even

---

[17] Bonney, *Lordship and the Urban Community*, 169–74. For the wide range of luxury goods available in Durham in the late 13th and 14th cent., see also Fraser, 'Pattern of Trade', 46, 50.

[18] Morimoto, 'Demand and Purchases', 101.

[19] J. I. Kermode, 'Merchants, Overseas Trade and Urban Decline: York, Beverley and Hull, c.1380–1500', *Northern History*, 23 (1987), 51–73.

Hull, York, or Durham merchants. Apart from the purchase of a butt of malmsey from London in 1500/1 and 1506/7, Newcastle merchants supplied all of the priory's wine after 1497/8, even the luxury wines such as malmsey which have generally been considered to have been the preserve of London merchants.[20]

A different pattern may be seen for the priory's purchases of livery cloths, although the north-east as a whole still predominates. For most of the cloth purchases recorded in these accounts no indication of location is given, except the negative evidence of silence which might be taken to imply cloth of local manufacture and/or supply. However, most of the purchases were also of small importance in terms of the quantity or value involved. In contrast, the livery cloths bought by the bursar were of very high value and represented a high proportion of the priory's total expenditure on cloth in each year. The account entries recording these purchases are accompanied in almost every year by an item of expenditure for the carrying of that cloth from the home town of the cloth merchant (or the place where the cloth was bought if different) to Durham. This makes it clear that these transactions were in fact carried out in the town mentioned, and thus implies that the merchants were residents of the towns associated with them in the accounts, rather than being Durham- or Newcastle-based tradesmen originally hailing from elsewhere. More importantly, the existence of these carriage charges in the bursar's accounts confirms that it is valid to trace the movement of the priory's cloth purchasing by reference to the place names.

From 1465/6 up to and including 1482/3, the cloth purchased for liveries by the bursar was bought in York. In 1484/5, this cloth was bought in Halifax, and this was followed by three years (out of seven, four being missing) in which purchases were made in London. It should be noted that on one of these occasions the merchant supplying the cloth was specified to be a Colchester man selling in London, the locality of the sale being confirmed by the entry for carriage from London to Durham. From 1492/3 until 1505/6, purchases were made in Leeds, whilst from 1505/6 to 1515/16 (when the account series is broken off) the priory's livery cloth was bought in Durham itself.

---

[20] Newcastle was the centre of the wine trade for the northern region by the 16th cent., sending wine throughout Northumberland and even on occasion into Scotland (A. L. Simon, *The History of the Wine Trade in England*, 2 vols. (London, 1906–7), ii. 122–3).

The changing location of the bursar's main cloth purchases thus mirrors the trend traced by several historians of the medieval textile industry for the focus of cloth-making activity to move from York itself to the West Riding towns over this period.[21] It is interesting to note in this context that the (remarkably abrupt) changeover found in these accounts was punctuated by an interval of purchasing in London, suggesting that York became an unsatisfactory source of supply before an alternative source in the West Riding had become established. It is also interesting that towards the end of the period cloth was purchased in Durham. It would seem likely that the cloth was bought from a middleman, and that William Middley was a Durham merchant who sourced it from the West Riding, since we have no record of any large-scale woollen cloth industry in the Durham area in this period.

The pattern for these high-value cloths is rather different from that for wine, since the goods were mainly being bought directly from their place of manufacture rather than from their place of import. Two things remain consistent for both commodities, however, and for the priory's supply as a whole. First, London, whilst occasionally occurring in these accounts, plays only a minor and fleeting part in supplying the priory. Of all the purchases made by the priory over the period, London is mentioned in connection with only a few. In addition to the wine discussed above, the bursar made three purchases of linen there in these years, buying 41 ells of Holland cloth in 1468/9 and 54 ells of Flemish cloth in 1478/9 in London, and purchasing a further 30 ells of unspecified linen from Thomas Ayer of London in 1494/5. No other mentions of London are to be found amongst the goods looked at here; the majority of the goods purchased by the priory came directly from suppliers based in the north-east. Although some goods (such as spices) may well have been purchased in London by middlemen and then brought to the north-east to be retailed there, this was not the general pattern as the number and variety of imports into Newcastle implies.

Secondly, it is notable that the area from which the goods bought by the priory were sourced shrank over this period. For wine the

---

[21] This has become virtually a truism in recent discussions on the subject. H. Heaton, *The Yorkshire Woollen and Worsted Industries, from the Earliest Times up to the Industrial Revolution* (2nd edn., Oxford, 1965), 45–7, gives a clear account of the change.

focus shifted increasingly to Newcastle at the expense both of London and of other regional centres such as York, Hull, and even Durham itself. For cloth, though the most significant development is the shift in manufacturing activity from York to the West Riding implied by the priory's changing purchases at the end of the fifteenth century, it is also notable that the priory chose to buy such cloth from a Durham merchant after 1505/6. These two trends, purchases moving away from London and increasingly focusing on the priory's immediate locality (including Newcastle), were common to all the goods purchased by the priory on the open market. Purchases from London, Boston, Lincoln, and so on were by no means uncommon in the fourteenth and earlier fifteenth century obedientiary accounts, but of these only London appears in the accounts from this period and then only rarely.[22]

THE USE OF AGENTS

When purchases were made from a distance, the priory used agents to choose, purchase, and pay for goods, and to transmit them back to the priory. Agents were also used in transactions nearer to home, such as in Newcastle. Although no explicit statements exist in the priory records about the way in which or the extent to which such agents were used, the obedientiary accounts give tantalizing glimpses of a comprehensive system of purchasing agents employed by the priory. As has been seen, the obedientiaries were burdened with a wide range of responsibilities, and it would appear that agents were used to save the obedientiary the time which he would otherwise have to spend in finding and bargaining for goods.

Most of the references to agents in the priory records concern the payment of the expenses incurred by the agents, and it is clear from these entries that they could be involved at all steps of the procurement process. In particular, there is substantial evidence for the use of agents in the wine-buying process. For example, in 1495/6 the bursar's necessary expenses included an item of 3s. paid to William Wright and to Richard Wren for their expenses at Newcastle for the purchase and delivery of wine on various occasions. Similarly, in

---

[22] Bonney, *Lordship and the Urban Community*, 169–74. Several examples of such purchases are to be found in Fowler (ed.), *Account Rolls*.

1487/8 a payment of 14s. for the expenses of William Wright and Richard Simpson 'at Newcastle and Hull' is recorded. Agents such as these were clearly involved in all stages of the wine-purchasing process; an entry in the bursar's necessary expenses for 1535/6 records that Robert Whitehead was paid 2s. 7d. expenses for choosing wine at Newcastle.[23] As the above examples show, they arranged both the actual purchase and the delivery of the wine to the priory, and perhaps travelled between the different ports to ensure that the priory paid the best prices for its goods. Some of these men were evidently employed on a regular basis, as the bursar's account for 1488/9 includes in the wine purchases for that year the cost of five tuns and one pipe of red wine bought from William Wright and Richard Simpson, with their expenses. William Wright can be seen to have been associated with wine purchasing for the priory for at least eight years, and both he and Richard Simpson appear to have been wine merchants in their own right as well as agents employed by the priory. In general, however, the role of such agents seems to have been solely a facilitative one. None of their names appear in the Newcastle customs accounts as importers, and none other than the two mentioned above appear in the priory records as suppliers in their own right.

Agents like these were apparently not used in buying some other goods which might have been expected to be similar; no mention of such activity is to be found in connection with spice or imported iron purchases, for example. It is possible that the purchase of wine presented special difficulties for which agents were particularly valuable. In particular, that only two consignments of wine were shipped to England each year, and that such wine was frequently sold from the boat as soon as it was docked, may well have meant that speed and being on the spot were uniquely important in this case. The large quantities in which wine was bought might also have warranted the use of agents. However, it can be seen that agents were used by the priory not only for the purchase of wine, but also for other high-volume, high-value, or perishable commodities. A surviving example of letters patent given to such an agent by the prior demonstrates the wide-ranging role that he fulfilled. This example comes from a slightly earlier period, being dated from Durham on 1 September 1410. John, the prior of Durham, states that he has appointed John

[23] Fowler (ed.), *Account Rolls*, iii, 696.

de Hyndley as his attorney 'to supply and purchase for the prior's use all necessary grain and victuals as provisions for him and the church of Durham wherever, as seems most advantageous, the aforesaid attorney may travel in England'. The letter goes on to give John de Hyndley permission to do whatever he chooses in the prior's name, and calls upon all those who might come across him to let him travel freely and without toll.[24] Other examples of the use of agents occur in connection with the purchase of high-value cloth for vestments, or when large quantities of fresh fish were required for a feast.[25]

Such examples suggest a class of men who were professional agents, but more informal contacts could also be used in this way. Several other documents suggest that a similar means of purchasing used by the priory was to ask an employee, friend, or acquaintance who was away on business to purchase items for the priory's use. For example, a letter dated 13 June 1456 survives from William, prior of Durham, to an unknown addressee, apparently in London on business unconnected with the priory, which includes a request that the recipient of the letter provide two hogsheads of the best malmsey that may be bought in London and arrange to send them, as his own goods, to his own place in Newcastle upon Tyne. The prior promises that his correspondent shall be fully reimbursed.[26] It is clearly expected that the request will be complied with, and the impression is given that such informal arrangements, based on personal relationships and making use of circumstances as they arise, were usual.

PAYMENT FOR GOODS

Payments for goods were also on occasion mediated through agents and other individuals. This implies that payment was made at a later date than that on which the purchase was contracted for, a common form of credit (discussed further in the next section). The bursar's household book for 1531/2, for example, records that three hogsheads of wine were purchased from Master Lawson, through John Bukley, and were paid for through an unnamed servant, whilst a further three hogsheads were bought directly from a Thomas Potts,

---

[24] DCM Reg. Parv. II, fo. 12ᵛ.
[25] See the discussion of vestments in Ch. 3, and the section on transport below.
[26] DCM Reg. Parv. III, fo. 84ʳ.

but were paid for through Nicholas Newsham.[27] The complex web of payment systems used by the priory also incorporated merchants. There are two examples (both probably from the mid 1450s) of the priory using William Bird, a well-known merchant of Newcastle, as an agent in money transfers and the use of promissory notes. The first, an undated letter from William, prior of Durham, to an unknown addressee, asks for a loan or gift of money of at least £1. 13s. 4d., and that this sum be paid to William Bird, merchant of Newcastle upon Tyne, bearer of the request.[28] The second example specifies neither the author nor the addressee, but indicates a complexity of payments which must have been common enough. The letter informs the recipient that William Bird, bearer of the letter, will satisfy him for the full payment of £39. 13s. 4d., which sum it is trusted he has already paid to a merchant of London for a bull lately granted at Rome.[29]

It is noted in an aside at the end of the letter that the last time the author wrote to the recipient he had thought that Robert Rodes would be going to London soon, but he is now not sure whether he will be going or not, so William is being used as an agent instead, and this exemplifies the ad hoc nature of such arrangements. It is also clear that the priory relied greatly upon the discretion of the agents who were used in such transactions. Robert Rodes, who was the prior's steward, was very often used as an agent by the priory, and was trusted with large sums of money. He corresponded with the priory for specific instructions and sent samples for approval, but his own judgement was clearly relied upon a great deal, as has been seen.[30] The amount of detail contained within the surviving evidence is necessarily limited because of this, as much was left to the agent's discretion or was entrusted to verbal messages delivered by the bearer of a letter rather than to the letter itself. An explicit example of this is a letter written on 16 March 1456 to a Mr Robert Rock, vicar of St Lawrence in London, which asks him to provide cloth of gold at prices and qualities most approximating what the priory has had before, but to wait until Robert Rodes comes to London with further instructions, which will hopefully be by Easter.[31]

[27] Raine (ed.), *Durham Household Book*, 49.
[28] DCM Reg. Parv. III, fos. 87ᵛ–88ʳ.   [29] DCM Reg. Parv. III, fo. 88ʳ⁻ᵛ.
[30] See the discussion of vestment purchases in Ch. 3.
[31] DCM Reg. Parv. III, fo. 88ᵛ.

CREDIT

It is clear from the evidence of the bursar's household books that the priory did buy goods on credit in this period, although the majority of the entries do not make clear what period of credit was involved.[32] For example, the purchases of wine for 1531/2 are recorded without the date of each purchase being given; but each entry is followed by details of how and when payment was made, implying that this was some time after delivery.[33] These settlement dates vary considerably, which may simply be a function of wine being bought at intervals throughout the year, or may indicate differing credit periods extended to the monks by the different merchants. Unfortunately, since no dates are given for the original transactions, it is not possible to calculate the length of a typical credit period or to ascertain whether this was paid for by an increase in the original price of the wine.

However, there are some—very rare—examples in the household books of the dates of both purchase and settlement being given, and these make it certain that credit transactions did occur, and that the periods of credit were not uniform. In 1532/3, the bursar purchased a total of 15 lbs of sugar from a Master Swynburne on 6 and 9 July 1532. This was paid for on 1 December 1532, five months later.[34] On 23 December 1533, the bursar bought four bushels of salt, worth 3s. 4d., which was paid for on 14 January 1534, just over three weeks later.[35] Other goods were paid for in two or more instalments. In the household book for 1533/4, for example, the bursar records the purchase of 140 sheep, costing £16. The date of purchase is not given, but credit was certainly involved since 66s. 8d. was paid on 21 May in part payment, while the balance was paid on the Feast of St John the Baptist, 24 June.[36] It seems probable that the first payment date was the date of the transaction, in which case just over a month of credit was given in this instance.

When a man of some substance was used as an agent, very large debts could accumulate in the other direction, that is to say could be

---

[32] Fraser, 'Pattern of Trade', 50–1, lists several examples of high-value credit transactions appearing in the obedientiary accounts in previous centuries.

[33] Raine (ed.), *Durham Household Book*, 49. A typical entry reads: 'And from Thomas Johnson, 3 hogsheads of wine, £5. 15s. 0d. Settled in the account between us on the 21st of May, 1532.'

[34] Ibid. 216.   [35] Ibid. 255.   [36] Ibid. 305.

owed by the priory to the agent who had already paid the original supplier. These men may well have given the priory credit as a form of gift or loan: they were sometimes the same individuals to whom the prior might apply for cash sums when extra money was required. An example of this situation comes from 1439, when a schedule of debt repayment was drawn up between the prior and William Hoton of Hardwick. It was recorded that the priory owed William a total of £60, and it was agreed that this sum was to be repaid at the rate of £20 per year for the next three years.[37] It was unclear whether interest was being charged for this agreement, ostensibly made by William 'out of love for St. Cuthbert, the prior and convent'. No interest or fee is mentioned in the schedule, but it is notable that the round sum of £60 which is declared to be the total owed by the priory is significantly more than the sum of the amounts listed as contributing to the total. The schedule lists the sums owing as £9. 10s. 0d. of arrears of William's annual fees, £4. 0s. 0d. which he paid to third parties, £15. 7s. 4d. as repayment of a loan, and a total of £23. 16s. 0d. which he paid to various merchants for grain bought for the priory. This comes to a total of £52. 13s. 4d., £7. 6s. 8d. less than the sum to be repaid by the priory. Whilst this could simply be a mathematical error, it seems unlikely that the priory would make an error of this magnitude concerning a debt they had to repay, and similarly unlikely that an error would result in such a round number. It seems more likely that this represented a charge for credit.

Whilst it is impossible to calculate whether there was any cost associated with most credit transactions, the related question of whether the priory bought at preferential prices can be clearly answered in the negative. Dobson has already ascertained that the prices paid by the priory in the first half of the fifteenth century were the market prices.[38] A comparison of the purchases made by the obedientiaries in the period under consideration with entries in the Newcastle chamberlain's accounts makes it clear that the prices paid by the priory were in line with the terms offered to other customers.[39]

It should also be noted that not all goods bought via market transactions were acquired through straightforward cash transactions. Just as the transactions made by the priory with tenants often

---

[37] DCM Reg. Parv. III, fos. 100ᵛ–101ʳ.
[38] Dobson, *Durham Cathedral Priory*, 206.
[39] See the discussion of wine purchasing in Ch. 3.

resulted in the offsetting of an obligation of the tenant (such as a rent payment) against a payment due to the tenant from the priory for goods supplied, so too market transactions with individuals who owed money to the priory could result in similar paper accounting, with only the balance paid in cash. One example of a combined payment of this nature occurs in the household book for 1531/2, when four hogsheads of wine were bought from John Saunderson for £7. 13s. 4d., of which 30s. was paid in tithes, and £6. 13s. 4d. in cash.[40]

TRANSPORT

The final stage of these market transactions, when the goods had been chosen, a bargain made and payment, if not made, at least pencilled in, was for the goods to be transported to the priory from the place of sale. Calculating the costs, methods, and responsibility for the transport of the goods bought by the priory is difficult, primarily due to a lack of data. With some notable exceptions such as wine and livery cloth, the obedientiary accounts rarely mention carriage costs and even more rarely is it possible to identify the particular transaction to which a carriage cost relates, the amount of a commodity carried and the start and end points of the journey involved. In itself, this omission is suggestive. It may imply that in most cases the goods bought by the priory were brought to the priory by the vendor without a separate charge being made for this service. However, at least for the items that were bought as the result of a market rather than a tenurial transaction, this seems not to have been the case, since in a list of similar goods bought one transaction might specify the inclusion of carriage whilst this remains unmentioned for similar transactions. It appears that in general goods were brought back either by a priory official whose expenses in going to make the transaction had already been paid, resulting in no additional charge, or that goods were brought to Durham by specialist carriers who were paid for their service on an annual or day-rate basis, rather than job by job.

The impression of an annual contract or payment for carrying services is given by the inclusion of a lump sum for carriage in the

[40] Raine, *Durham Household Book*, 49.

bursar's necessary expenses each year. Around £1 is usually accounted for under this heading in a single undifferentiated payment for the carriage of wine, iron, herring, salmon, and other miscellaneous and unstated goods from Newcastle, South Shields, Sunderland, and elsewhere. For example, in 1465/6 the bursar's necessary expenses included 12s. 4½d. 'paid to Robert Blake, William Falker and Thomas Young for their expenses with cart-hire at Newcastle, Shields, Sunderland and elsewhere for carriage of iron, salmon, herring and other necessaries in the period of this account', and a further 7s. 6d. was paid to the porters of Newcastle for carrying wine, iron, herring, salmon, and other unspecified goods.

The infrequency with which carriage costs other than these appear in the accounts suggests that goods were normally carried by pre-arranged contract or by priory agents or officials in the case of non-bulky goods. The bursar's necessary expenses frequently include payments to individuals for procuring goods, and it seems likely that these expenses included the cost of bringing the goods back to the priory. For example, in 1495/6 the bursar paid 2s. 8d. for the expenses of John Youle 'riding to York for eels, pike, tench and roach for the feast of St. Cuthbert in March', and 1s. 6d. for the expenses of Antony Elison 'riding to Benwell, Ovingham and Ryton [all on the river Tyne just to the west of Newcastle] for fresh salmon for the same feast'. Goods bought on the tenurial pattern, which included bulky commodities such as grain and livestock, can only be assumed to have included carriage in the bargain as carrying costs are never mentioned and must surely have been considerable. It is possible that the goods paid in lieu of rent were physically taken to the exchequer of the relevant obedientiary in the same way as cash would have been, so rendering the question of carriage costs irrelevant to the priory (though it must surely have been a major consideration for the tenants in calculating how it would be most advantageous to pay their rents).

Occasionally additional carriage costs are mentioned in the accounts, and these would appear to have been for goods that were not covered by one of the above arrangements, but for which ad hoc arrangements had been made. For example, in 1470/1 the bursar made three purchases of salt. Two of these were as usual from the tenants of Cowpen Bewley with no mention made of carriage, whilst one was from the merchant Robert Bartram who was paid £3. os. od. for three weys of salt, and an additional 6s. od. for their carriage. This was presumably a top-up purchase; other one-off carriage charges might be for more unusual items, such as the payment of 14s. 0d. made to Roger Bunde and Peter Andrew for the carriage of seven seals from Farne to Durham in 1495/6.

There are also certain commodities for which transport costs are frequently specified individually in these accounts, such as many of the wine transactions. This evidence suggests firstly that most of the goods bought in bulk in market transactions by the priory's obedientiaries were bought at the home town of the merchants concerned, and that the priory was then responsible for arranging transport to Durham. Several of the entries in the few surviving sacrist's accounts, for example, record the purchase of wine which is described as 'from Newcastle, with carriage and rolling'.[41] Unfortunately, these entries do not separate out the various cost elements. However, the hostillar's accounts frequently give details of the carriage costs involved in his purchases of wine. These included two elements, carriage from Newcastle (which cost around 2s. 0d. for a tun of wine) and 8d. or so paid to the porters of Newcastle for carrying the wine over the Tyne bridge.[42] Less information is available for the transport of wine from places other than Newcastle. The main purchase of wine from York made in this period, the three tuns bought there in 1471/2, were bought with carriage, but the cost is not separated in the accounts from that of the wine itself, and cannot be estimated.[43] Interestingly, there are no details given for carriage costs from Hull. It is possible that the description of merchants as being 'of Hull' did not preclude their having sold wine to the bursar at Newcastle; however, one tun at least of the wine bought in 1484/5 was specifically described as 'bought at Hull'. Perhaps this wine was contracted for at Hull but actually handed over in Newcastle, or maybe it was brought to Durham by the agents of the priory who had purchased it at Hull.

Secondly, the existence of such carriage charges enables a rough calculation of the cost of transport of such goods in this region to be made. For wine, the figure of 2s. 0d. per tun, plus 8d. porterage over the Tyne, has been given from the hostillar's accounts. As has been

[41] DCM Sacrist's account rolls, 1483/4, 1486/7, 1487/8.
[42] DCM Hostillar's account rolls, e.g. 1486/7.
[43] The cost elements cannot be estimated since the wine cost was clearly not commensurate with the other purchases made that year. The York cost was £18. 10s. 8d. for three tuns with carriage, compared to around £4 per pipe or £7. 6s. 8d. per tun for the wine bought at Newcastle.

seen, the bursar's accounts tend to include wine in the general carriage charge for the year; in 1475/6, however, the bursar did account separately for the carriage of five tuns of wine from Newcastle, again at the rate of 2s. 0d. per tun, and this figure is also found in the rental of 1495/6, when it was accepted as a payment in kind for rent owed to the priory.[44] The household book for 1531/2 records that the carriage charges ruling then were 1s. 4d. per hogshead, or 2s. 4d. per tun. Two hogsheads of the wine brought to Durham that year came by boat, and the saving this represented was considerable—the total cost for the carriage of both hogsheads and the 20 quarters of barley that accompanied them was only 1s. 0d.[45] It is surprising, in the light of this difference, that more goods were not moved by water.

In calculating the cost per mile of carriage, modern distance estimates (that is, using modern routes) have been used, as the medieval equivalents are impossible to ascertain. Using a figure of fifteen miles as the distance between Newcastle and Durham, the cost of road transport (excluding porterage) for a tun of wine works out at 1.6d. per mile. The cost of water transport is unclear due to the inclusion of barley in the load, but was certainly much less than this. If the transport cost is divided between the load on the basis of weight, then the wine travelled from Newcastle to Durham for 1.7d., equivalent to 0.2d. per tun per mile.[46] This rough estimate of the relative costs of the two modes of transport is comparable with the assessment made by Edwards and Hindle that water transport was far cheaper than carriage by road, 'by a factor of up to 6'.[47]

Both road and water transport costs for the carriage of a tun of wine compare favourably with those estimated for the Midlands in 1452/3 by Dyer, at 3.2d. per tun per mile by road and 0.6d. by water.[48] In Suffolk in 1412/13, Alice de Bryene paid around 3s. 0d. per year to her usual wine supplier for delivery from Ipswich of her usual order, a total of four tuns annually. She also paid 1s. 6d. for the expenses of her agent going to Colchester with a cart and seven horses

[44] DCM Bursar's account 1474/5; Lomas and Piper (eds.), *Durham Cathedral Priory Rentals*, 136.

[45] Raine (ed.), *Durham Household Book*, 63.

[46] Two hogsheads of wine contain 126 gallons, or 572.796 litres, and thus weighed roughly 573 kg (excluding packaging). A quarter of wheat contained 384 lbs, or 174.182 kg, so 20 quarters weighed 3483.648 kg. The wine thus accounted for 14.12 per cent of the total cargo.

[47] Edwards and Hindle, 'Transportation System', 129.

[48] C. Dyer, *Everyday Life*, 262.

TABLE 5.3. Transport costs for livery cloth consignments,
1465–1505

Carriage to Durham from	Estimated distance (miles)	Cost (s. d.)	Cost (d. /mile)
York (1465)	64	5	0.9
York (1466)	64	6 8	1.3
York (1467–9)	64	10	1.9
York (1470–82)	64	8	1.5
Halifax (1484)	94	6 8	0.9
London (1486)	256	31	1.5
London (1487)	256	40	1.9
Leeds (1492–3)	77	13 4	2.1
Leeds (1494–1505)	77	12	1.6
AVERAGE			1.5

to collect a pipe of wine.[49] The distance from her home at Acton to
Ipswich was about thirty-two miles, and from Acton to Colchester
around twenty-six miles, so these carriage charges work out at
roughly 0.3*d.* and 2.7*d.* per tun per mile respectively, suggesting that
the carriage from Ipswich must have been largely by water, probably
along the coast to the Stour estuary and then via the Stour to Sudbury,
only three or four miles from Acton.

Carriage costs can also be examined for the livery cloths bought by
the bursar in each year, for which a transport charge was always
recorded except in the years when the cloth was bought in Durham
itself. These charges, and the equivalent cost per mile, calculated
using modern distances are shown in Table 5.3. It is notable that in
the case of cloth, variations in the amount of cloth involved in each
year did not lead to equivalent variations in carriage charges. This
is particularly noticeable in the case of the long series of identical carriage charges, 8*s.* 0*d.* from York in the twelve years from 1470 to
1482, and 12*s.* 0*d.* from Leeds in the eleven years from 1494 to 1505.
The quantity of cloth in these cases varied considerably over these
periods, between 285 and 441 yards, averaging 380 yards, in the first

[49] F. Swabey, *Medieval Gentlewoman: Life in a Widow's Household in the Later
Middle Ages* (Stroud, 1999), 87–8.

instance and between 150 and 489 yards, averaging 363 yards in the latter. In both cases there was great consistency of carrier as well as price, suggesting that some sort of fixed contract may have been behind the stable price: John Welbury undertook the carriage from York in all but one of these years and Thomas Richardson, who was the cloth merchant involved in all but the last two of the Leeds consignments, also handled the carriage in each year in which he dealt with the priory.

It is difficult to know how the carriage costs calculated in Table 5.3 compare with those charged elsewhere, since little work has been done on this question. These costs do seem to have been much higher than those calculated for grain in the fourteenth century by James Masschaele, based on the purchasing details given in the surviving sheriff's accounts for that period. His calculations produced an average land carriage charge of 1.5d. per ton per mile over the whole of England.[50] This is identical to the average 1.5d. per load per mile given by the bursar's accounts. However, these figures are not of course directly comparable due to the different units involved. It seems probable that the consistency in the bursar's carriage charges despite changes in the quantity carried implies that the charge was based on a cart's journey, so that a half-full cart incurred the same costs as a fully laden one. Masschaele does give some cart-load charges: these were usually 14d. (occasionally 18d.) per day, and a laden cart travelled around 15 to 20 miles per day.[51] An extremely rough and ready calculation based on these figures yields a cart cost of around 0.8d. per mile (14d. divided by 17.5 miles), suggesting that the carriage of a ton of grain needed two carts. The weight of the average load of cloth bought by the bursar in these years would have been well within the capabilities of a single cart.[52] The most comparable figures are thus the cart cost of 0.8d. per mile calculable from Masschaele's data, and the load (assumed also to be a cart) cost of

[50] J. Masschaele, 'Transport Costs in Medieval England', *Economic History Review*, 2nd ser., 46 (1993), 271.

[51] Ibid. 269–70.

[52] The individual cloths purchased by the priory probably contained around 84 lbs of wool, equivalent to a weight per ell of around 3.5 lbs (J. H. A. Munro, *Textiles, Towns and Trade: Essays in the Economic History of Late-Medieval England and the Low Countries* (Aldershot, 1994), 17). The average yearly purchase of 347 ells would thus have weighed 0.54 of a ton, sufficiently low to allow for the purchases of even the highest years to be carried on a single cart.

1.5*d*. per mile derived from the Durham figures. The time difference of over a century between these two makes any attempt at regional interpretation invalid.

Kowaleski calculates the carriage cost of a tun of wine in the Exeter region in the early fourteenth century as between 4*d*. and 5.2*d*. per mile, with distances calculated as the crow flies. This is much higher than the other costs noted here, but merchants from Taunton in 1381–91 were not deterred by these charges from purchasing a total of 189 tuns of wine at Exeter, twenty-eight miles away.[53] The high transport costs found here may be at least partially explained by the topology of the local area, since the area between Taunton and Exeter is covered by the Black Down Hills. These may well have presented difficulties which were reflected in a higher price for carrying services, and in addition would have increased the actual distance that it was necessary to travel so that the real cost per mile might well be lower than an estimate of distance as the crow flies would suggest.

Other transport cost data based on cart-loads is also available in the obedientiary accounts relating to the carriage of hay and building materials. These commodities are generally measured in these accounts in cart-loads, and journeys are often described by start and end point, enabling reasonable estimates of the cost per mile to be made. In the first place, it is clear that the distance involved did affect the price charged: in 1490/1, for example, the cellarer paid for hay to be carried from the field at Relley to Durham at 6*d*. per cart-load, from the field to the manor at Relley at 2*d*. per cart-load, and from Bellasis to Durham at 4*d*. per cart-load. Relley was around two miles from Durham, giving a cost per cart per mile of *c*.3*d*., although for small distances such as this the margin of error involved in using modern distances rather than the medieval road system is likely to be enhanced. The identification of Bellasis is not certain, as the priory had a manor of that name at Billingham, but the relative cost of transporting hay from there compared to that given for Relley suggests that the farm which lies immediately over the Wear from Durham Cathedral is referred to here, in which case the small distance involved makes cost per mile analysis redundant, as the time involved in loading and unloading the cart would be likely to outweigh the actual travel element.

---

[53] Kowaleski, *Local Markets and Regional Trade*, 268.

The point that more was involved in determining carriage costs than simply the distance to be travelled can also be seen in that the commodity involved played a part in determining the price charged for carriage. Whilst hay was regularly carted from Relley to Durham at a price of 6*d*. per cart-load throughout this period, other commodities transported between the same two places attracted different charges. In 1480/1, for example, the cellarer was carrying out various building and repair works in South Street in Durham, and paid for stone and timber to be carried there. The stone came from Broom, adjacent to Relley, and was carried at a cost of 3*d*. per cart-load; the timber was carried from Relley itself at a cost of 6*d*. per cart-load. Different carriers were used for these commodities, and it is possible that the different prices reflected this. It may have been the case that a relative difficulty in handling the two materials, or different cart requirements, were the underlying cause of the price difference; or even that the carts belonging to the respective carriers were of different sizes.

The question arises of who the carriers employed by the priory were, in other words whether they were specialist carriers by trade, general priory servants, or perhaps journeymen or small tradesmen who engaged in a wide variety of money-making pursuits. In an attempt to answer this question, a comparison has been made between the names that recur in the priory accounts as carriers and the names recorded in Christine Newman's database of those employed on the priory estates in the latter half of this period, information also derived from the Durham Cathedral Priory obedientiary accounts.[54] However, little overlap has been found. The name John Bailya occurs on one occasion, in 1492, acquiring rock salmon for priory feasts along with two other men, but none of the other carriers looked at here are to be found engaged in such activities. The names John Atkinson and John Walker do appear, but only in connection with building and general labouring work. This may imply that they were general labourers, but the names are common ones and may refer to different individuals. The other carriers found in this study, William Welbery, John Welbury, and Richard Clyff, do not occur anywhere in Newman's research. However, a family connection might be surmised in the case of Richard Clyff, since a William Clyff appears

[54] Newman's work on those employed by the priory in the period has been reported in Newman, 'Employment'.

forty-three times between 1492 and 1507 in Newman's database, always in connection with the carriage of various goods. The evidence is inconclusive, therefore, but it is noteworthy that none of the carriers mentioned are to be found in the pensions and stipends sections of the priory accounts, implying that whatever their relationship to the priory or their state of employment might have been, at least they were not 'salaried' priory employees, or retained by the priory on an annual basis. Finally, it should be noted that the merchant supplying the priory with the livery cloths was also paid for its carriage in a third of the bursar's accounts from this period, although whether this was indeed undertaken by the draper himself or was subcontracted by him is unknown.

As has already been noted, there was probably no physical bar to travel and the transport of goods to, from, and within the north-east in this period.[55] Unfortunately, it is not possible to calculate the precise impact of transport costs and practicalities upon the priory's purchasing decisions. On the one hand carriage costs are only rarely given, suggesting that at least non-bulky goods were frequently brought to the priory by someone making the journey for other reasons, and so they were not charged for separately, and on the other hand prices varied so much from year to year that total costs given for goods in different years, one of which included a carriage element, cannot be used with any certainty to assess the magnitude of the carriage element. A rare example of costs which are to some extent comparable comes in the bursar's purchases of Holland and Flemish cloths. Two such purchases were made at London, of 41 ells in 1468/9 at a total cost of £1. 17s. 8d. which was specified in the account to have included the cost of carriage, and of 54 ells in 1478/9 at 8d. per ell, a total cost of £1. 16s. 0d. (without a carriage element). These cloths almost always cost 8d. per ell, and if it is assumed that that bought in 1468/9 was no exception then the carriage element of the total cost can be calculated to have been 10s. 4d. No other locations are given for the purchase of such cloths except for one purchase of 5 ells in 1466/7, which was specified to have been made at Pipewellgate in Gateshead; it seems likely that the remaining cloth was purchased in Newcastle, particularly since many of the names that occur as suppliers (such as William Cornforth, William Shotton, and John Farne)

---

[55] See Ch. 1.

are those of well-known Newcastle merchants who appear many times in the accounts. That being so, there is no apparent reason for the Holland cloth bought in London in 1468/9 to have been bought in London; and the presence of a significant carriage charge does not appear to have been a disincentive to such a purchase. It is possible that no Newcastle supplier happened to be able to supply the priory with the quantity or quality of cloth that they required on that one occasion; certainly the London purchase was the only purchase of such cloth in 1468/9, but then it was by no means unusual for only a single purchase of this nature to be made in any one year.

However, the infrequency with which goods were sourced from outside the immediate region, even when price differentials clearly existed, suggests that powerful disincentives to such activity either were in place or were at least perceived to be in place. Although letters clearly show that individuals in London were on occasion asked to purchase goods and forward them to the priory, and occasional purchases in London did take place, these were very much the exception. It is not surprising that a bulky, common and relatively low-value commodity such as grain was purchased only outside the region when failure of local supply occurred and the pressure of price differentials made transporting the large quantities needed worthwhile. However, that even such luxury specialist goods as malmsey were generally purchased in Newcastle, and that such high-value goods as livery cloths were purchased in Durham by the end of this period, suggests that supply was the key to this pattern. In the absence of any pressing need to buy goods elsewhere, local suppliers were more likely to be used, providing they could supply the types, qualities, and volumes that were required. Sourcing locally must have presented a range of advantages, such as the ability more accurately to assess and sample the goods before purchase and quicker delivery; in addition, however, it seems probable that personal relationships with local suppliers would be an important factor.

CONCLUSION

Ultimately, the priory's purchasing strategy, whatever the method used for an individual purchase, was based on credit and trust. As such, knowledge of and relationships with suppliers would have been at a premium.[56] When it was necessary to make purchases remotely the priory overcame the lack of such personal knowledge by using trusted agents who themselves had such relationships or access to the necessary networks to acquire them. Local suppliers could be known directly, and relationships could be built up with them so that the quality of their goods and their reliability could be assessed on the basis of past experience or personal trust. This was undoubtedly one advantage of the tenurial system of purchasing; the suppliers were by definition known, the relationship was stable, and issues of credit and payment were avoided by the adoption of a largely cashless system. In a system in which personal relationships and the individual supplier were of such importance, the detail and high degree of survival of the priory accounts can shed a great deal of light both on some of the individuals concerned and on the prosopographical details of the cohort of priory suppliers as a whole. It is to a consideration of the suppliers themselves, therefore, that this discussion will now turn.

---

[56] C. Muldrew, *The Economy of Obligation* (London, 1998), 4–5; North, 'Transaction Costs in History', 560.

6

The Suppliers of the Priory

INTRODUCTION

The value of trust in relationships with suppliers has been recognized as an important but unquantifiable factor in medieval purchasing decisions and transaction costs.[1] Indeed, trust is still a valuable commodity in the modern marketplace, something the public relations and advertising industries continually strive to package and capitalize upon. When it comes to making purchasing decisions, particularly in the face of rapidly changing variables or when a great many such decisions have to be made, relying on trusted suppliers or on tried and tested ways of doing things is an effective and efficient coping strategy. Durham Cathedral Priory's use both of tenurial relationships and of agents in the supply process suggests that this was one of the monks' purchasing strategies. However, whilst it would be possible to construct a defence of traditionalism as rational choice on the basis of an economy of trust, the startling fact emerges that in fact the Priory was almost profligate in its use of thousands of different suppliers, only a few of whom were used repeatedly.

Very little is known about the merchants trading in the north-east in this period, and the evidence that does exist relates primarily to their involvement in overseas trading activities.[2] The information contained in the Durham Cathedral Priory obedientiary accounts is thus both rare and important, providing a detailed record of the priory's dealings with a wide variety of suppliers throughout the region. This analysis of the merchant community of the region looks in depth at the information contained within a single source.[3] A study

---

[1] Muldrew, *The Economy of Obligation*, 4–5; North, 'Transaction Costs in History', 60.

[2] See e.g. Wade (ed.), *Customs Accounts*, and Fraser, 'Early Hostmen'.

[3] The merchants who supplied Durham Cathedral Priory with imported goods in this period are discussed more fully, with some individual biographies, in Threlfall-Holmes, 'Import Merchants'.

of this nature cannot rival in detail or breadth of research the pro-sopographical studies that have been carried out elsewhere using a wider range of sources to shed light on the social composition and economic well-being of a single group of people or even a whole town.[4] However, the Durham obedientiary accounts do provide a unique opportunity for the study in depth of a 'slice' of medieval society, of a group of medieval men and women defined not by geography, or even by their cohesiveness as a class, but by their common involvement in supplying goods to a major consumer.

For the great majority of transactions recorded in the accounts the name of the merchant or merchants involved is given, and from an analysis of the information several interesting points emerge about the group of merchants who were supplying the priory at this time. The myriad concerns of the priory meant that a wide variety of commodities were purchased from an equally wide variety of suppliers, and by a variety of means. For some, the business of supplying the priory may have been a major element in their livelihoods while for others it was clearly tangential to their main concerns, and an element of randomness is thus inherent in this sample of the economically active population of the region. By studying the suppliers of the priory, therefore, it is possible to examine several aspects of the lives and livelihoods of a cross section of the producers, manufacturers, and traders active in the north-east of England in the late middle ages.

NUMBERS OF SUPPLIERS AND REPEAT SUPPLIERS

The main impression gained on a first examination of the merchants' names given in the obedientiary accounts is of the wide variety and sheer number of the suppliers from whom goods were bought in each year. A total of 264 suppliers were engaged in selling fish and 567 in selling livestock in the sample years for which the bursar/cellarer indentures have been analysed, whilst over the whole of the period 362 suppliers of cloth are named in the accounts alongside 123 suppliers

---

[4] The best examples of this in recent years include Kowaleski, *Local Markets and Regional Trade*, and (for Durham itself) Bonney, *Lordship and the Urban Community*. Other detailed studies include Thrupp, *Merchant Class*; M. J. Bennett, *Community, Class and Careerism: Cheshire and Lancashire Society in the Age of Sir Gawain and the Green Knight* (Cambridge, 1983); G. Rosser, *Medieval Westminster 1200–1540* (Oxford, 1989); and J. I. Kermode, *Medieval Merchants: York, Beverley and Hull in the Later Middle Ages* (Cambridge, 1998).

of iron, 96 suppliers of wine, 53 suppliers of miscellaneous foodstuffs, and 20 suppliers of spices to the priory. Although some of them were engaged in supplying more than one type of commodity to the priory (an issue which will be addressed below), the total number of suppliers to the priory which have been identified as active over this period was well over 1,200 even after taking such overlap into account.

The majority of the suppliers did not enter into anything approaching a long-term or exclusive marketing relationship with the priory. Many names appear only once in the accounts, and only a select few appear more than twice. Of the identifiable suppliers of the priory analysed 56 per cent appear only once in the accounts, whilst a further 19 per cent appear twice and 10 per cent three times. The number of suppliers associated with more than three transactions in the accounts is much smaller. A total of 10 per cent are associated with four, five, or six transactions, and only 5 per cent have seven or more. The highest number of transactions associated with one supplier occur in the case of the livery cloths and furs bought by the bursar. These goods stand out in the accounts as commodities which were bought from only a small number of merchants in total, and which were generally supplied to the priory by a single merchant for several years in succession.

Most of the merchants who did secure repeated orders still appear in the accounts only occasionally. This means that, whilst a substantial amount of statistical information about the whole body of merchants who supplied the priory can be derived from the data, details of the biographies of individual merchants can be given for only relatively few. It should also be noted that the large numbers of merchants who appear only once or twice in the accounts means that the evidence of the accounts cannot be brought to bear on such issues as the average length of a merchant's career.

These accounts reveal that the priory's tendency was to spread its business between several suppliers in each product category in each year. A clear distinction is visible between the pattern observed for imported and manufactured goods, purchased primarily via the market, and that for agricultural produce which was acquired largely via tenurial relationships. The average number of merchants from whom the bursar purchased wine in any one year was only 5, varying between 2 and 9. A similar pattern may be seen in the bursar's purchases of iron, where the average was again 5 named merchants, varying from 2 to 12. Cloth and furs were purchased from an average of 16 suppliers each year, although furs and livery cloths were purchased from only a single merchant each in each year. Spices, too, were bought from one principal merchant in each year, although supplementary purchases were generally also made from several others. Salmon, a fish which appears to have been frequently bought via market transactions, was purchased from an average of 10 suppliers per year, whilst other fish came from around twice as many; herring were purchased from an average of 20 suppliers per year, and dogdraves from 18. With the exception of sheep, which came from an average of 15 suppliers per year, livestock was acquired much more widely than these other goods. On average, poultry was supplied to the priory by 45 individuals each year, pigs by 48, and cattle by 56. Grain, meanwhile, was supplied to the priory by 127 individuals in 1495/6 alone, and there is no reason to suspect that this was by any means an exceptional year; indeed, the rentals for 1507–10 show a similar pattern.

WIDER RELATIONSHIPS BETWEEN THE PRIORY AND ITS SUPPLIERS

However, it is clear that the priory did have closer relationships with some merchants than would appear from a glance at the number of transactions entered into with each one. The names of several Newcastle merchants and other suppliers of the priory are to be found in the *Liber Vitae*, a book of names which was kept upon the altar in Durham Cathedral and added to throughout the medieval period.[5] The exact significance of inclusion in this book is not clear, but it certainly argues a more complex relationship with the priory than one based simply on trading relationships or the occasional transaction, and many of the names included appear to have been those of the families of monks. In an attempt to quantify the extent to which these social relationships penetrated the priory's supply networks, a comparison has been made between the supplier names collected in the course of this research and the names recorded in the *Liber Vitae* that have been dated by palaeographic means to the late fifteenth or early sixteenth century.[6]

---

[5] Thompson (ed.), *Liber Vitae*.

[6] I am indebted to Lynda Rollason for her assistance with this comparison in the course of her research into the composition and significance of the *Liber Vitae* (L. S. Rollason, 'The Liber Vitae of Durham (British Library Manuscript Cotton Domitian A. VII): A Discussion of its Possible Context and Use in the Later Middle Ages', Ph.D. thesis (University of Durham, 2003).

In all, 70 surnames are common to the two sources, and whilst the exact identification of individuals in one with those in the other is not possible, 71 individuals with exactly the same first name and surname combination are to be found. These represent 6 per cent of the cohort of suppliers identified here. In addition, the *Liber Vitae* contains a further 70 individuals (whose names are written in hands that have been dated to this period) who can be identified as monks of Durham and who have surnames matching those of suppliers to the priory. For many of these cases it is explicitly spelt out in the *Liber Vitae* that the lay individuals listed were the family of the monks concerned, and indeed a link is sometimes made with individuals of different surnames. For example, John Robinson of Newcastle (probably the merchant of the same name who supplied wine to the priory in this period) and his wife Maiona are listed with the monk Edward Hebburn who is explicitly described as their son.[7] Entire family groupings were also described on occasion, as was the case with the entry for William Lawe, a monk of Durham in the second half of the fifteenth century, who is listed in the *Liber Vitae* with his father Thomas, his mother Agnes, and nine other members of his family.[8] In other cases, a monk's name is given and his parents are mentioned, but their names are not given. For example Robert Spink, a monk of Durham who entered the monastery in the early sixteenth century, is listed 'with his parents' but no further details are included in the book.[9]

Whilst it is not possible to identify positively the names in the *Liber Vitae* with the suppliers' names found in the obedientiary accounts, it seems very likely that many of the names found in both sources denote the same individual or at least members of the same family. It is also worthy of note that several of the more prominent surnames in both sources are the same, suggesting the presence of families who were closely connected with the priory on a variety of levels. For example, the Willys were a prominent monastic family whose name appears several times in the *Liber Vitae*. Individuals of that name recorded there included a monk named Robert and his father Edward, and two other monks, Christopher Willy and Henry Willy, who were described as being the sons of Richard and Elizabeth Willy and the siblings of Roland, Thomas, Robert, William, Alice, Johanna,

---

[7] Threlfall-Holmes, 'Import Merchants', 85; Thompson (ed.), *Liber Vitae*, fo. 83^r.
[8] Ibid., fo. 66^v.   [9] Ibid., fo. 81^v.

William, and Alice.[10] A large group of Willys (John, Ralph, Richard, Robert, Thomas, and William) also supplied the priory with a range of livestock, poultry, and grain. These individuals were mainly described in the accounts as hailing from East (Kirk) Merrington and thus were almost certainly a family grouping. Other names that occur several times in each source include Coke, Duket, Forest, Lawson, Rakett, Richardson, and Robinson, although the latter is so common that it almost certainly denoted the members of more than one family.

Further evidence from a different source of such a family relationship between the monks and the suppliers of the priory comes in 1477, when a John Esyngton entered Durham College at Oxford, probably with the intention of later joining the monastery himself. This is known because his father entered into a bond with the prior which has survived in the Durham archive, in which he promised to pay a sum of money if his son misbehaved whilst at the college or left before taking his degree.[11] The boy is described specifically in the source as the son of the merchant of Newcastle upon Tyne of the same name. The merchant John Esyngton of Newcastle was a notable supplier of the priory, appearing at least ten times in the accounts between 1465/6 and 1485/6, selling a typical range of imported and processed goods; wine, Spanish iron, processed fish, and oil.[12] Without being able to quantify precisely the degree of integration between the social or familial networks of the members of the priory and the supply networks which they drew upon, it is nevertheless clear that there was a significant degree of intercourse between the two.

COMMODITY SPECIALISTS AND GENERALISTS

The figures for the number of suppliers of each commodity in each year give an impression of a rather larger total than the actual cohort of suppliers to the priory, since there was a degree of overlap between

---

[10] Ibid., fo. 80ʳ⁻ᵛ.   [11] DCM Reg. Parv. III, fo. 173ʳ.

[12] John Esyngton appears in the bursar's accounts selling wine in 1472/3 and 1482/3 and Spanish iron in 1467–9, 1470/1, and 1472–4 (Threlfall-Holmes, 'Provisioning' 75–6, 87–8). He is also mentioned three times in the bursar/cellarer indentures, supplying oil in 1465/6, a barrel of sturgeon in 1467/8, and an aughtendell of salt eels in 1485/6.

the suppliers of certain commodities. Here again a distinction between commodities may be observed, and the differentiation already noted between the agricultural products of the region and imported or manufactured products becomes especially marked when it is seen that the suppliers of each of these two groups of products overlapped very little, whereas there was a distinct tendency for suppliers to be generalists within one or other of these sectors. In addition, however, it can be seen that certain commodities in both classes tended to be supplied by specialists in that particular commodity.

For grain suppliers, a comparison has been made between the names occurring in the bursar's account for 1495/6 and the names of the individuals who supplied other goods to the priory. The pattern of specialism or generalism which this analysis reveals varied across the different places from which grain was acquired. That is to say, for some villages which supplied grain there was an exact correspondence between the names that appear in connection with grain and in connection with the supply of other goods, while at others there was little connection between the two. Overall, however, this analysis reveals a high degree of correlation, implying a striking lack of specialization in particular commodities by individual farmers, even those who were clearly farmers in a big way.

In all, 118 individually named tenant-suppliers from seventeen villages are listed as supplying grain to the bursar, with an additional nine individuals named separately (that is, not in a list of tenants from a village). For seven of the seventeen villages listed, all the suppliers named in the grain accounts also appear supplying other commodities. A further four places yield close matches. Of the remaining six villages that supplied grain to the priory, five (Cowpen Bewley, Newton Bewley, Wolviston, Billingham, and Aycliffe) each have around half of their grain suppliers also supplying other goods to the priory in the sample years looked at. Dalton is the exception, since whilst 'the vicar of Dalton' and 'the tenants of Dalton' are both mentioned in the accounts supplying various goods on occasion; no individually named suppliers are recorded as having been from there. It would seem highly probable, however, that many of the priory's named grain suppliers from Dalton would have been represented in 'the tenants of Dalton'. The other five places each have a mixture of grain suppliers who are identified by both name and place as supplying other goods in the sample years looked at, names which match but for which no place is given so that it is by no means certain that the two can be identified, and names which simply do not appear in the other accounts looked at for this study. In all, of the 49 grain suppliers from these five villages, 17 are definitely identified as supplying other goods, 10 are uncertain matches, and 22 are not mentioned in connection with other commodities in the years under consideration.

Finally, there are nine individuals named as supplying grain to the priory who are listed in their own right in the bursar's account, rather than as part of a village list. Six of these also appear supplying a variety of goods other than grain: Roger Morland of the manor of Pittington, John Henryson of South Pittington, Richard Wilkinson of the manor of Eden, William Brown of Hesleden, Richard Denom of Newhouse, and Richard Smith of Shadforth. The three who do not also appear are John Kape and John Matho, both of Southwick, and the widow of Thomas Strangeways of Newton Ketton, although her husband does appear.

Overall, therefore, 87 of the 127 individuals named in the grain supply sections of the bursar's account for 1495/6 also definitely appear supplying other goods. Of the remaining 40, 26 names do not appear elsewhere, whilst 11 are uncertain matches and 3 are widows whose husbands appear but who do not themselves. Somewhere between 69 and 80 per cent of grain suppliers were therefore also involved in supplying a variety of other goods to the priory in 1495/6. Given that most individuals named in the accounts studied here occur only once or twice, and that the study uses accounts from decade intervals, it is likely that a still higher degree of mixed farming activity would be revealed if the analysis were to be extended in scope to the years immediately preceding and subsequent to 1495/6.

Within the class of local agricultural produce other than grain, certain distinct patterns stand out. First, by looking at the various types of fish purchased by the priory it can be seen that, in terms of who was supplying these goods, fish was divided into sea and river fish. In the first place were sea fish, dogdraves and herring, between the suppliers of which there was a significant degree of overlap. A total of 108 suppliers of dogdraves and 117 of herring are named in the bursar/cellarer indentures used for this analysis, with an overlap of 29 per cent (175 suppliers in total). Conversely, the suppliers of salmon, the other staple fish eaten by the monks in considerable quantities, were almost entirely specialists who are seen in these accounts supplying only salmon to the priory. There is no overlap at all between the suppliers of salmon and of dogdraves, and only 1 per cent overlap between the suppliers of salmon and of both herring and miscellaneous other fish respectively. Moreover, the suppliers of miscellaneous fish also overlap very little with the suppliers of herring and of dogdraves, by 4 per cent and 3 per cent respectively. The category of miscellaneous fish includes both the more expensive freshwater fish such as perch and pike and products of the sea such as seals and shellfish. The lack of overlap between the suppliers of these goods and the suppliers of either the staple sea fish or freshwater fish indicates that all fish were to some extent 'specialist' commodities. It should be noted, however, that the suppliers of the luxury freshwater fish purchased by the priory are rarely named in the accounts. This may have been because they were bought at market by agents, but may also hide a greater degree of overlap between suppliers of these and other fish than can be seen here.[13]

All these fish suppliers were an almost entirely separate group from the suppliers of other commodities to the priory. There was only negligible overlap, less than 3 per cent, between the suppliers of fish on the one hand and of either cloth or livestock on the other. Unlike the fish suppliers, however, the suppliers of livestock were by no means specialists. Overall, there was 52 per cent overlap between the suppliers of poultry, cattle, pigs, and sheep: transactions involving these commodities were made with 567 distinct suppliers, of which 208 were involved in the supply of poultry, 314 of cattle, 248 of pigs, and 90 of sheep. Suppliers were most likely to combine the sale of poultry with the sale of pigs (32 per cent overlap), poultry with cattle (20 per cent overlap), or cattle with pigs (16 per cent overlap). Mixed farming was clearly very common, and there was 47 per cent overlap between the suppliers of all three commodities. The only type of livestock that stands out as being largely the preserve of the specialist farmer was sheep, perhaps because of the marginal land that could be used for this purpose. Certainly, sheep farmers were the least likely to be involved in raising other livestock: there was only 10 per cent overlap between the suppliers of sheep and pigs, 9 per cent for sheep and cattle, and 6 per cent for sheep and poultry.

There was also only a small degree of overlap between the suppliers of such agricultural produce and the suppliers of manufactured and imported goods to the priory. The greatest correspondence to be found here was between cloth suppliers and suppliers of fish (who

---

[13] For fish purchasing by agents, see Ch. 5.

overlapped by 3 per cent) and suppliers of livestock (who overlapped by 9 per cent); these overlaps were accounted for by small parcels of cheap cloths which may well have been of local manufacture. The suppliers of Spanish iron show a 2 per cent overlap with the suppliers of cloth and a 1 per cent overlap with the suppliers of fish, whilst the suppliers of wine show a 2 per cent overlap with the suppliers of fish. Evidently, therefore, the overlap between the suppliers of agricultural and manufactured goods was negligible. Even the suppliers of locally produced Weardale iron were an almost entirely separate group, overlapping only with the priory's livestock suppliers and even then by only 1 per cent.

The suppliers of imported goods (wine, spices, and Spanish iron) show a slightly greater degree of specialism than the suppliers of agricultural produce, but overlapped much more with each other than they did with the suppliers of local products. The greatest correspondence was between the suppliers of wine and of Spanish iron, who overlapped by 13 per cent. Spice suppliers were a more distinct group, overlapping with the suppliers of Spanish iron by 5 per cent and with the suppliers of wine by only 3 per cent. The priory's purchases of cloths specified to have been imported (in other words, of cloths designated as 'Flemish' or 'Holland' cloths in the accounts) do not show up in the statistics since only a small number of such purchases were recorded. However, it is worth noting that seven of the ten named suppliers of such cloths also appear in the priory accounts supplying other imported goods: two supplying Spanish iron only, one supplying wine only, one supplying spices only, and one each supplying a combination of spices and wine, spices and Spanish iron, and Spanish iron and wine.

The distinctiveness of the group of import merchants active in Newcastle at this period is also indicated by the fact that the dealers in Weardale iron were an almost entirely separate group, and did not overlap to any notable degree with the suppliers of imported iron. Only 2 of the 54 merchants who sold local iron to the priory also sold imported iron.[14] These were Robert Stroder, who supplied small amounts of both in 1514/15 only; and Richard Dixon, who supplied 40 stones of Spanish iron in 1478/9 and 20 and 40 stones of Weardale iron in the following two years respectively. None of the merchants who sold Weardale iron to the bursar supplied the priory with either

---

[14] Threlfall-Holmes, 'Late Medieval Iron Production', 119.

spices or wine.[15] In contrast, just under a quarter of the merchants who supplied imported iron are recorded in the bursar's and hostillar's accounts as selling wine to the priory in this period (with several others sharing a surname with other wine suppliers), and 3 of these 17 also supplied some dried fruit.[16] In addition, only one of the 54 names recorded here as dealing in local iron also appears in the Newcastle customs accounts, that of William Kirklay.[17] He sold Weardale iron to the priory on one occasion only, in 1496/7, along with several other merchants. The name may or may not refer to the same man, but it seems reasonably likely that it did, since the only transactions recorded for him in the customs accounts are two small exports of wool in 1471, and the import of 2,240 lbs of osmund iron (a high-quality iron from Sweden) in 1472. Apart from this, none of the suppliers of Weardale iron to the priory are recorded as having engaged in the import or export trades. This local industry was thus the preserve of a group of individuals who were largely separate both from the producers and suppliers of local agricultural produce and from the merchants active in the import and export trade of Newcastle, including those involved in the import and resale of iron produced elsewhere.

It is also notable that none of the major suppliers of spices to the priory appears in the surviving customs accounts for Newcastle, whilst the merchants who are recorded as having imported spices into Newcastle are the same men who appear in connection with the import of wine, iron, and all sorts of other commodities.[18] This implies that these merchants (people such as John Brandling, George Bird, Edward Baxter, and Christopher Brigham) were importers and wholesalers whose interests extended to a wide variety of commodities. Conversely, the merchants who sold spices to the priory appear to have been mainly retailers. It should be noted, however, that the merchants who specialized in the import trade certainly also engaged in direct sales to important consumers such as the priory, but that these sales were always of bulk quantities, so that the distinction is not so much between wholesalers and retailers as such, but between sellers of goods in bulk and in smaller quantities.[19] It is possible that

[15] Threlfall-Holmes, 'Provisioning', 94–6.
[16] Threlfall-Holmes, 'Import Merchants', 85–7.
[17] Wade (ed.), *Customs Accounts*, 113–14, 121.
[18] Threlfall-Holmes, 'Provisioning', 60.
[19] Thrupp, 'Grocers of London', 272–7.

the spice suppliers may have purchased for resale the spices that were imported into Newcastle, but the customs accounts record very few of these imports, implying that the majority of the spices that local grocers dealt in must have come via the London merchants.[20] Thrupp has argued that the country as a whole was almost entirely dependent on London for such commodities, and certainly the imports recorded for Newcastle were neither large, frequent, nor diverse enough to have satisfied local demand.[21]

FAMILIES AND LOCATIONS

The differentiation between the suppliers of local agricultural produce and the suppliers of high-value imported goods is maintained in the differing prosopographical profiles of the two groups. The clearest distinction to be seen here is that family name groupings were both larger and more common amongst the suppliers of local produce and Weardale iron than amongst the suppliers of wine or imported iron (the pattern for spices appears to have been similar to that for the latter goods, but there were too few spice suppliers for a comparison to be meaningful). Of the fifty-four merchants named as supplying the bursar with Weardale iron, thirty-two, or 59 per cent, share a surname with at least one other in the same list, whilst eighteen, 33 per cent of the total, form five groupings of three or more. The incidence of multiple suppliers with the same surname is even higher amongst the suppliers of meat, fish, and other miscellaneous foodstuffs recorded in the bursar/cellarer indentures, of whom 69 per cent shared a surname with at least one other and 48 per cent shared a surname with two or more other individuals. Whilst the sharing of a surname is by no means proof of kinship, it is clear from the accounts that many of the individuals in these family name groupings lived in the same area and were probably related. Relationships are sometimes implied in the accounts by use of the terms 'the younger', 'junior', or 'senior', although this generally occurs only when

[20] Wade (ed.), *Customs Accounts*: spice imports appear 13 times in the surviving Newcastle customs accounts, sugar on nine occasions (pp. 182, 189, 194, 226, 234, 269, 271 (twice), and 275); 'diverse spices' once (p. 121); ginger twice (pp. 133, 225); and liquorice once (p. 32).
[21] Thrupp, 'Grocers of London', 273.

purchases are made from two men of the same name in the same section of an account; in some cases, a clear family relationship is noted
in the rentals when a tenancy is taken over by a widow, son, or other
relation upon the original tenant's death.

    Although the exact proportion of family members implied by family
name groupings cannot be calculated, it can be seen that the high
occurrence of such groupings amongst the suppliers of local produce
contrasts with the much lower occurrence among the merchants who
sold imported goods to the priory. Only 30 per cent of the suppliers
of imported iron fall into surname groups, and only 10 per cent into
groupings of three or more. For the suppliers of wine the contrast is
even more marked, 25 per cent sharing surnames and only 4 per cent
doing so with more than one other individual. Furthermore, there
are three instances in these accounts of two merchants with the same
surname selling locally produced goods together, suggesting that
they may have been trading as an informal family partnership, a phenomenon which does not occur among the sellers of wine, spices, or
imported iron.[22]

    Whilst no detailed information about family structure or the
length of individual careers can be inferred from these accounts, the
occurrence of family name groupings can be used negatively to suggest the maximum size of family networks engaged in supplying the
priory. It is generally thought that medieval merchant families rarely
engaged in trade for more than two, or exceptionally three, generations.[23] This conclusion is certainly supported by the priory accounts,
since under 10 per cent of the Newcastle merchants recorded as supplying the priory share a surname with two or more other suppliers
of the priory over the period. However, it would appear not to have
been the case for some of the more prominent of the local tenant
families. The surnames shared by the highest number of individual
suppliers of the priory were probably so common as to relate to more
than one family: for example, the priory bought goods from at least
twenty-eight Robinsons, eighteen Johnsons, fifteen Pearsons, fourteen Thomsons, and twelve Atkinsons. Nevertheless, many of the

---

    [22] Richard and William Greneswerd jointly sold 149 stones of Weardale iron to the
bursar in 1475/6, and William and Robert Wren sold 40 stones in the same year. In
1504/5, George and Robert Burrell jointly sold six barrels of salmon to the cellarer.
    [23] Childs, Anglo-Castilian Trade, 189, and W. G. Hoskins, 'English Provincial
Towns in the Early Sixteenth Century', Transactions of the Royal Historical Society,
5th ser., 6 (1956), 9, both found this to have been the case.

recurring surnames indicate the presence of substantial family networks, although it is not clear how many generations they represent since many siblings and their spouses may well have traded concurrently. Examples of less common recurring surnames are Lax (nine individuals), Woodifield (eight), Willy and Rakett (seven individuals each), and Fuke (six).

In addition to such differences in family structure and the size of surname networks, the locations with which suppliers of local and other goods are associated in the accounts are also clearly differentiated. The overwhelming majority of import merchants came from, or at least had settled in and did most of their business at, Newcastle or other major regional centres, whereas local produce was sold predominantly by the producer from the place of production.[24] This applied not only to agricultural produce such as grain and livestock but also to local iron; all the purchases of local iron for which a place of purchase was specified in the accounts were made at Muggleswick, and although the 'address' of a merchant is only infrequently and erratically specified in the priory accounts, where such detail is given small local place names predominate in the records of local iron purchases.[25] It is notable that the vast majority of instances of a place being mentioned in the wine and imported iron accounts refer to Newcastle, which is not mentioned at all in the local iron purchases. Table 6.1 demonstrates this difference by listing the place names mentioned in connection with the bursar's purchases of wine and local and imported iron. As has been seen, agricultural produce was bought from a much wider range of local places; for example, grain was bought from twenty-three and cattle from sixty-six locations.

Moreover, in stark contrast to the merchants supplying imported goods to the priory (the majority of whom were from Newcastle), only four suppliers from Newcastle are to be found supplying what may have been local produce. These are George Bird (who supplied oil in 1485 and stockfish in 1495), John Brandling (who supplied eels in 1515), Edward Baxter (who supplied oil in 1504 and herring in 1515), and Robert Stokall (who supplied eels and herring in 1474). It is interesting to note that these men did not supply any of the farm produce that made up the vast majority of the foodstuffs bought by the priory, but only goods that were to some extent processed. The oil

---

[24] See Chs. 4 and 5.
[25] Threlfall-Holmes, 'Late Medieval Iron Production', 119.

TABLE 6.1. Place names mentioned in association with wine and iron merchants in the bursar's accounts, 1464–1520

Wine merchants	Spanish iron merchants	Weardale iron merchants
Newcastle	Newcastle	Muggleswick
Hull	Durham	Durham
York	Hull	Unthank
Durham	Nether Heworth	Knitsley
London	Gateshead	Lanchester
	Wallsend	Weardale
	Stockton	Whitehall
		Edmondbyers
		Espershields
		'Colpekyn' (?Coldpike Hall)

may have been imported, or may have been of local manufacture, for the type of oil is not specified; the herring, eels, and stockfish were probably all locally caught and processed (the herring and eels were sold in barrels, salted). All of these men were well-known Newcastle merchants, and also supplied imported goods to the priory.[26] George Bird supplied wine on eight occasions, Edward Baxter supplied wine twice and dried fruit once, Robert Stokall supplied wine twice and Spanish iron five times, whilst John Brandling supplied wine seven times and dried fruit and Spanish iron once each.[27]

In addition to these Newcastle merchants, seven names associated with Gateshead appear in the accounts. Little is known about most of them, who do not appear in any civic records or customs accounts, but it is notable that like the Newcastle merchants they were not selling basic foodstuffs to the priory but were supplying oil, salmon (probably salted), and cloth. The seven were the widow of Robert Rede, who sold salmon in 1504/5; Thomas Carr, who sold linen in 1501/2 and salmon in 1504/5; Thomas Robinson, who sold oil in 1495/6; John Robinson, who sold oil in 1504/5; John Laxton (described on one occasion as of Gateshead and on another, more specifically, as of Pipewellgate), who sold salmon in 1467/8 and 1504/5; John Pearson, who sold haircloth in 1505/6; and John

---

[26] Threlfall-Holmes, 'Provisioning', 67–8.   [27] Ibid. 94–6.

Brown of Pipewellgate, who sold Holland cloth in 1466/7 and salmon in 1467/8, and also supplied Spanish iron to the priory in the years 1475–7.

MALE AND FEMALE SUPPLIERS

The inclusion of first names for almost all suppliers named in the accounts has meant that it has been possible to look in some detail at what difference, if any, the gender of a supplier made to their supply relationship with the priory. Just enough transactions involved female suppliers for meaningful comparisons to be made between the cohorts of male and female suppliers on such issues as the number of transactions in which they participated and the average value of such transactions. Of the 3,346 transactions looked at here, the gender of the supplier is unknown in 335 cases (10 per cent). The remaining transactions comprise those in which the supplier is named, in which case their gender has been inferred from the Christian name or from the description 'widow', and those for which only the office of the supplier is given (for example, 'the vicar of Dalton') where the supplier has been presumed to be male. Of these 3,011 transactions, 180 involved female suppliers and 2,831 male. Females were thus active in 6 per cent of the transactions made by the priory for which the gender of the supplier is ascertainable. Men clearly predominated in supplying the priory; not only did they participate in 94 per cent of the transactions but the incidence of repeated involvement in supplying the priory was also higher amongst men. The average number of transactions per female supplier was 1.5, compared to 2.5 for male suppliers, and whilst most individuals participated in only one transaction whatever their gender, this was the case for a smaller proportion of men than of women. Of the priory's male suppliers 54 per cent appear only once in the accounts, compared to 68 per cent of female suppliers, whilst 28 per cent and 11 per cent respectively appear three or more times.

In addition, the average values of these transactions were significantly higher for male suppliers than for female suppliers, although the types of goods dealt with did not vary by gender to any marked degree. Overall, the average value of a transaction involving a female supplier was 11s. 8d., compared to 17s. 2d. for transactions involving a male supplier. The tendency for transactions involving men to be worth more on average was not simply a by-product of a few men being involved in some major transactions, but applied even when only the individuals who supplied goods on just one or two occasions are considered, although the gap was smaller among the suppliers who traded only once with the priory.[28]

One indication of the extent to which the women who appear in these accounts were economically active in their own right rather than simply administering their husbands' estates on their deaths is the way in which they are described in the accounts. The majority of women recorded here were described in terms of their husband, mainly as their widow. For example, the five women who supplied grain to the priory in 1495/6 were 'Robert Lawson's widow', 'Thomas Stoddert's widow', 'John Smith's widow', 'Richard Clifton's widow', and 'Thomas Strangeways' widow'. In all, sixty-nine of the 119 female suppliers of the priory (58 per cent) were described in this way in the accounts. A further three women (2.5 per cent) are described as their husbands' wives, not widows. The remaining forty-seven women (39.5 per cent) are described in their own right, that is, are given their own Christian name without reference being made to a husband. The two most prominent examples are Katherine Bywell and Agnes Brown, who each appeared four times in the accounts. Katherine supplied pullets, pigs, linen, and canvas in 1465/6, whilst Agnes supplied linen in 1492/3, hens in 1495/6, and hardyn in 1496/7 and 1497/8. The only woman named in her own right as supplying imported goods was Alice Bird, who supplied Spanish iron to the priory on three occasions over the period.[29] However, whilst these women were named and presumably trading in their own right, it would be misleading to assume that they had attained any very high degree of economic independence or equality. Whilst there is little difference between the number of transactions entered into by the women named in their own right and those defined in terms of their husband in these accounts, the average values of the transactions were significantly lower for the first group. Women described as widows had an average transaction value of 14s. 5d., similar to that for wives at 14s. 3d., whereas women named in their own right

---

[28] The average transaction value for those involved in only one transaction was 12s. 3d. for women and 15s. 7d. for men, whilst for those involved in two transactions the figures were 7s. 6d. and 16s. 11d. respectively.

[29] Threlfall-Holmes, 'Provisioning', 64.

had an average transaction value of only 7s. 6d., only just over half as much.

CASE STUDY: THE SUPPLIERS OF CLOTH

As can be seen from the above discussion, the number and variety of suppliers and transactions which are recorded in the Durham obedientiary accounts present in some ways an embarrassment of riches. Analysis of the information as a whole provides an overview of the broad sweep of individuals who were involved in supplying the priory over the period, and whilst this is valuable in its own right some detail is inevitably lost when suppliers of any amount of any commodity are looked at together. As a counterbalance, this section takes the form of an in-depth case study of the suppliers of a single commodity type. Cloth has been chosen for the case study because it is a category which includes both large and small transactions involving a range of locally and regionally produced and imported goods with a wide range of values (both monetary and symbolic). As such, it incorporates many of the features that have been identified as characteristic of the supply both of local agricultural produce and of manufactured or imported goods.

Of a total of 965 cloth supply transactions analysed here, 172 (18 per cent) give no information about the source or supplier of the cloth concerned. A further thirty-two transactions (3 per cent) involve suppliers who are not identified by personal names in the accounts. For example, on four occasions the cloth is simply described as having been purchased 'at London'. On three occasions multiple unnamed suppliers are specified: twice in the bursar's accounts no names are given but the cloth is noted to have been purchased 'from various [people]', and once the vendors are noted to have been 'the tenants of Aycliffe'. There remain 761 cloth supply transactions recorded in the accounts for which the individual or individuals concerned in the transaction are named. Of these transactions 684 (71 per cent of the total) can be allocated to 329 individually identifiable suppliers. The remaining seventy-seven transactions cannot be confidently assigned to individuals, and the figures used below are therefore subject to a margin of error of around 10 per cent.

A minimum of at least 329 individuals can thus be seen to have supplied cloth to the priory in this period. Only a few of these secured

TABLE 6.2. Number of cloth transactions per supplier, 1464–1520

No. of transactions per supplier	No. of suppliers	Suppliers (% of total)	Transactions (% of total)
1	229	69.6	33.5
2	47	14.3	13.7
3	22	6.7	9.6
4	13	4.0	7.6
5	6	1.8	4.4
6	4	1.2	3.5
7	2	0.6	2.0
10	2	0.6	2.9
15	1	0.3	2.2
19	1	0.3	2.8
41	1	0.3	6.0
81	1	0.3	11.7
TOTAL	329	100.0	99.9

the repeat trade of the priory, and those who did so to any great degree were almost entirely the merchants who supplied the expensive livery cloths to the bursar. As many as 229 of these suppliers (70 per cent) were involved in only a single transaction. A further 25 per cent each took part in two to four transactions, while the remaining 5 per cent were involved in 5 to 80 transactions each, together accounting for 36 per cent of the transactions entered into by the priory.[30] The exact distribution of transactions per supplier and the extent to which a few suppliers accounted for a disproportionate number of the priory's cloth transactions are shown in Table 6.2, which includes only the transactions associated with an individually identifiable supplier.

A similar pattern is to be seen in the distribution of the average value of the transactions undertaken by each individual. As can be seen from Fig. 6.1, 266 (80.9 per cent) of the priory's cloth suppliers had an average transaction value of under 10s. 0d., whilst over half (170, or 51.7 per cent) had an average transaction value of under

---

[30] A similar though not identical distribution was to be found among the drapers at Exeter, where five individuals supplied 36% of the cloth sold in the town (not to a single consumer, as here) (Kowaleski, *Local Markets and Regional Trade*, 147–8).

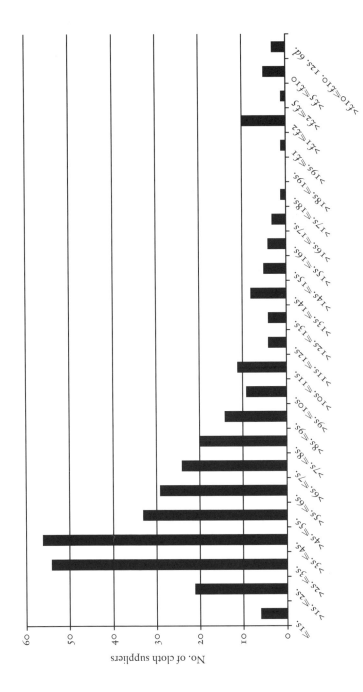

Fig. 6.1. Distribution of cloth suppliers by average transaction value, 1464–1520

TABLE 6.3. Average number of transactions per supplier for various types of cloth, 1464–1520

Commodity	No. of transactions	No. of suppliers	Average no. of transactions per supplier
Livery cloth	157	7	22.4
Hardyn	199	148	1.3
Linen	188	147	1.3
Sackcloth	86	71	1.2
Flemish/Holland cloth	17	9	1.9
Haircloth	13	10	1.3
Canvas	8	8	1.0

5s. od. Only 44 suppliers, 13.4 per cent of the total cohort, had an average transaction value of between 10s. od. and £1. os. od., whilst the average values associated with the 19 remaining suppliers ranged from exactly £1. os. od. to £10. 12s. 6d., these high values being the preserve of the livery cloth suppliers.

Different patterns for the suppliers of different types of cloth can be discerned. The first point to note is the clear distinction that existed between the major drapers, supplying the relatively valuable woollen cloths used for the various priory liveries, and the shifting mass of smaller cloth dealers supplying the much lower value cloths such as linen, hardyn, and sackcloth. A special case would appear to have existed for the more expensive imported linen cloths, although evidence for this is extremely limited since only a few such purchases were made by the priory. The drapers, variously described in these accounts also as clothmen or clothiers, tended to supply the priory's entire livery cloth order in any one year, and often remained the sole supplier of such cloths for several years at a time. These suppliers were primarily Yorkshiremen (although London and Durham are also represented). The suppliers of other cloths were much less likely to appear in the accounts more than once; as Table 6.3 shows, the average number of transactions per supplier was only just over one for each cloth type other than the livery cloths. Moreover, it should be remembered that in all cases the mode number of transactions per supplier was even lower, the majority of suppliers appearing only once and the averages being skewed by the few suppliers who did achieve multiple transactions.

The outstanding figure of an average of 22.4 transactions per supplier for the suppliers of the livery cloths emphasizes the difference between these men and the suppliers of the other cloths. In most years, the bursar's livery cloth accounts contained five cloth transactions (for cloth for the prior, obedientiaries, gentlemen servants, valets, and grooms respectively) all involving the same draper, and thus the average draper supplied these cloths to the priory for a period of four years. However, this average conceals some important variations. In fact, three main drapers had remarkably long-term relationships with the priory, whilst the other four appeared in the accounts for only a few years. The majority of these men were important mercers and substantial citizens of the major regional towns, in itself a major point of difference with the suppliers of the cheaper cloths, and as such it has been possible to piece together something of their individual biographies.

The most important of all the priory's cloth suppliers in this period, as well as chronologically the first, was John Marshall of York, draper, who supplied all the priory's livery cloths from at least 1449/50 up to 1480/1.[31] His identification is made slightly more complex by the fact that two distinct John Marshalls are recorded in the York records for this period, one described as a merchant and one more specifically as a draper. Indeed, in 1454 the two served together as chamberlains, making it explicit that the name referred to two separate individuals.[32] The draper, with whom we are concerned, entered the freedom of the city ten years previously in 1454, when he was described as a mercer, and died in July 1481.[33] In the intervening thirty-five years he was clearly a prominent member of the town community, and is frequently mentioned in the York Memorandum Book

[31] The bursar's accounts exist for all these years from 1462/3, except 1463/4 and 1477/8. John Marshall was also the only named supplier of livery cloths to the priory in the surviving bursar's accounts in the previous decade, those of 1453/4 and 1456/8, and is named in the last surviving account from the 1440s, that of 1449/50. No supplier is given in 1445/6, and the accounts from the intervening years have not survived.
[32] F. Collins (ed.), *Register of the Freemen of the City of York, from the City Records*, i: 1272–1558 (Surtees Society, 96, 1897), 174.
[33] Ibid. 163. The will for John Marshall, *pannarius*, was dated 2 July 1481 and granted probate on 26 July 1481 (F. Collins (ed.), *Index of Wills in the York Registry, 1389–1514* (Yorkshire Archaeological Society Record Ser., 6, 1889), 111.

in various civic capacities.[34] He had been supplying the livery cloths to the priory for at least thirty-two years when his association with the priory ended on his death.[35]

It is conceivable that William Chymnay, who appears as the livery cloth supplier in the bursar's accounts for 1481/2 and 1482/3, took over John Marshall's contract with the priory as his heir or as the purchaser of his business. He was certainly a York merchant of long standing, having been admitted to the freedom of the city in 1454 although little more is known of him.[36] It seems likely that it was the priory who made the decision to cease trading with him two years later, since he continued in business for over twenty-five years after he last sold cloth to the priory, dying only in 1508.[37] This suggests that the bursar's previous choice to trade with John Marshall until his death was a deliberate, active decision rather than the result of apathy, inertia, or a general policy of maintaining long trading relationships.

The 1480s appear to have been a time of upheaval in the priory's cloth supply, as in the kingdom at large. There is no evidence that the two phenomena were related, but in the absence of any other explanation it certainly remains a possibility. The accounts for 1483/4, 1485/6, and 1488–91 are missing and so the relationships seen in this decade may have been slightly longer-term than the remaining accounts suggest, but even so change was clearly the order of the decade. Richard Cliff, a draper of Halifax about whom nothing else is known, supplied the livery cloths in 1484/5. In 1486/7 the supplier of the livery cloths was not specified in the account, whilst in 1487/8 the cloths were described only as having been purchased 'at London'. This was particularly unusual and may indicate the temporary disruption of trade in the north-east.

---

[34] In a document of 1 Jan. 1458, John Marshall, sheriff, appears as a witness to a feoffment and gift relating to lands and goods in the City of York between two merchants. He was noted to have been present at the creation of the Ordinances of the Fletchers on 3 Apr. 1476, when he was described as an alderman, and he was also present at the creation of the Ordinances of the Ostlers on 20 Oct. 1477, described as 'of the Twelve' (J. W. Percy (ed.), *York Memorandum Book* (Surtees Society, 186, 1973), 190, 205, 243.

[35] The accounts from the three years prior to 1449/50 have been lost, and so it is possible that John Marshall's relationship with the priory was in fact in place for up to 35 years.

[36] Collins (ed.), *Register of the Freemen*, 174.

[37] Collins (ed.), *Index of Wills, 1389–1514*, 37.

For eleven years from 1492/3, the priory settled on another long-term supplier, Thomas Richardson, a draper of Leeds.[38] Thomas Richardson had substantial land-holdings in Leeds, and was clearly a manufacturer as well as a retailer of cloth, as he also rented a 'tenter', or cloth-stretching house, adjacent to the town fulling mill.[39] A will exists for him in the York Registry, dated 1 July 1502 but granted probate only on 9 July 1505.[40] In fact, two Thomas Richardsons of Leeds have wills listed in this period, the other being dated 1 June 1502 and granted probate on 6 July 1502, a year before the cessation of the trading relationship with Durham Cathedral Priory. It may well have been that the two men were brothers or other close relations, and the will dates suggest that both men were ill in June/July 1502, perhaps indicating a communicable disease. It is of course possible that after the death of one in 1502 the other took over the priory's supply, but it seems likely that were this to have been the case some distinction would have been made in the bursar's accounts: designations such as 'junior' and 'senior' were fairly commonly used, and their absence here suggests that the same man continued to be referred to.

Thirty-one years later, in 1536/7, a Thomas Richardson was still recorded as renting the tenter next to the fulling mill, so it would seem likely that the son of the first Thomas Richardson continued the family business.[41] However, the priory's ability and willingness to change supplier when they chose to do so was demonstrated on the death of Thomas Richardson as it had been on the death of John Marshall, and their custom was transferred to two other Leeds drapers, probably related: Alexander Burton in 1504/5 and Robert Burton in 1505/6. These men are virtually unknown in the surviving civic records, although a will exists in the York Registry for Alexander Burton of the borough of St Peter, Leeds, dated 21 October 1541 and granted probate the following February.[42] Finally, the priory forged

---

[38] Thomas Richardson appears in every bursar's account from 1492/3 to 1503/4; only the account for 1502/3 is missing from the series.

[39] J. W. Kirby (ed.), *The Manor and Borough of Leeds, 1425–1662: An Edition of Documents* (Thoresby Society, 57, 1989), 25, 30.

[40] Collins (ed.), *Index of Wills, 1389–1514*, 137.

[41] Kirby (ed.), *Manor and Borough of Leeds*, 36.

[42] F. Collins (ed.), *Index of Wills in the York Registry, A.D. 1514 to 1553* (Yorkshire Archaeological Society Record Ser., 11, 1891), 31. A great many Burtons are listed (pp. 28–31) including two Roberts who died in 1532 and 1539 respectively, although the only other Burton to be described as being of Leeds is a William who died in 1512.

TABLE 6.4. Distribution of hardyn transactions between identifiable suppliers, 1464–1520

No. of transactions	No. of suppliers	% of total transactions	% of total suppliers
1	117	59	79
2	22	22	15
3	6	9	4
4	1	2	0.5
5	1	2.5	0.5
11	1	5.5	0.5
TOTAL	148	100	99.5

the last of its three long-term cloth supply relationships in this period, with William Middley of Durham, again an obscure figure outside these accounts. The series of accounts begins to be broken up at this point so it is not possible to be clear as to exactly how long the relationship lasted, but it probably covered at least the nine years from 1506/7 to 1515/16, and quite possibly longer.[43]

In addition to the major drapers, the large number of transactions recorded in the accounts for hardyn and for linen allow an analysis to be made of the suppliers of these commodities. It must be noted, however, that the investigation into the suppliers of linen is rendered less reliable by the existence of a large proportion of unstated suppliers (the supplier is not given in 37 per cent of all the linen transactions in this period). This is a result of a similar proportion of the linen figures being derived from the accounts of obedientiaries other than the bursar, which do not tend to include supplier details. The profiles of supply of each of these commodities parallel, indeed shape, the picture we have for the entire cloth supply of the priory, with a majority selling to the priory on only a single occasion (Tables 6.4 and 6.5).

The rather different supplier profile for the expensive imported linens described in the accounts as Flemish and Holland cloths is,

---

[43] Accounts survive from 1506/7 to 1509/10, and from 1515/16, and in all of these William Middley is named. The pattern set in earlier years suggests that he would have been the supplier in the missing years, and he may have continued after 1515/16.

Table 6.5. Distribution of linen transactions between identifiable suppliers, 1464–1520

No. of transactions	No. of suppliers	% of total transactions	% of total suppliers
1	118	63	80
2	20	21	14
3	6	10	4
4	3	6	2
TOTAL	147	100	100

unfortunately, not statistically significant due to the small number of transactions involved. One merchant, William Cornforth, was responsible for nine transactions, 41 per cent of the total number of transactions. Another man, John Atkinson, made three sales to the priory, accounting for a further 14 per cent of transactions, whilst each of the remaining seven suppliers appears only once. The most significant aspect of this is not the distribution of these few transactions but the appearance of William Cornforth, who has already emerged from the accounts as a Newcastle merchant dealing in high-value imported goods.[44] William Cornforth appears in the cloth accounts only selling these imported and relatively expensive textiles, further evidence that the Newcastle import and export merchants dealt in a wide range of imported goods, and largely only in such goods.

In addition to the much smaller average number of transactions per supplier described above, a further way in which the profile of those selling the cheaper textiles to the priory is different from that of the drapers is in the degree of specialism exhibited in a particular type of cloth. As has already been noted, the drapers sold only the relatively expensive woollen livery cloths to the priory, whilst these cloths were rarely dealt in and then only on a very occasional and piecemeal basis by other, smaller dealers. Although some degree of specialism can be discerned among the suppliers of the cheaper cloths it is rarely very pronounced. Most of the cloth suppliers excluding the drapers, as has been seen, were involved in only one transaction, but of those involved in several transactions it was unusual for a single

---

[44] Threlfall-Holmes, 'Provisioning', 59, 95–6.

TABLE 6.6. Cloth-type specialism amongst suppliers of cloth to
Durham Cathedral Priory, 1464–1520

Name	No. of transactions	No. of cloth types dealt in	% of transactions accounted for by main cloth type
Richard Wren	15	3	73
John Robinson	12	2	75
William Cornforth	10	3 (all linen types)	60 (100)
Thomas Howe	8	2	50
John Cook	7	3	43
John Thomson	6	2	50
Robert Wilkinson	6	3	67
Thomas Ryhope	6	3	67
John Clerk	6	3	33
Robert Simson	6	2	83
John Bowet	6	2	67
John Anderson	5	2	80
Widow Alex. Rob.	5	4	40
William Robinson	5	1	100
William Jolybody	5	3	40
John Sourby	5	2	60
Jacob Green	5	3	40

Note: Table shows the number of different types of cloth dealt in by suppliers
involved in five or more cloth transactions with the priory in this period, excluding
the main livery drapers.

cloth type to account for more than two-thirds of these transactions.
In the analysis and tabulation of this data (Table 6.6) only the suppliers
involved in five or more cloth sale transactions have been looked at,
and the drapers have been excluded. As can be seen, in only one or
arguably two cases is specialism total, and on average commitment to
a main product accounts for only 60 per cent of a supplier's sales.

CONCLUSION

Both the case study of the priory's cloth suppliers and the overview of
the priory's suppliers as a whole show, firstly, that the monks bought
from a wide variety of merchants in each product category, and did

not tend to have long term or exclusive relationships with particular merchants. An important exception to this was in their purchases of certain types of cloth, although even here several names occur over the period. For the other commodities bought, around three-quarters of the suppliers named in the accounts looked at here appear only once or twice over the years. Secondly, it has emerged that (with some exceptions, such as livery cloths, furs, and sheep) the priory's suppliers did not tend to be specialists but to supply a range of goods within the bounds of the broadest possible commodity classifications.

It is also notable that the merchants from whom the monks bought imported and luxury goods—wine, spices, Spanish iron, and Holland and Flemish cloth—overlapped to a noticeable degree, whilst the suppliers of lower-value locally produced goods such as grain, meat, fish, Weardale iron, and utility cloths such as hardyn and sackcloth were an almost entirely separate group with again a significant degree of overlap occurring between the suppliers of the various commodities in this class. It can be seen that the distinction made in Chapters 4 and 5 between commodities acquired by the tenurial and by the market purchasing methodologies continued to be apparent in the individuals who supplied them. Further, the distinction between the two groups of suppliers is emphasized by several other features. Suppliers of imported goods tended to be associated with the larger towns, whilst suppliers of locally produced goods tended to be associated, as has been seen, with the countryside and villages that made up the priory's land-holdings. More and larger family name groupings are also to be seen amongst the suppliers of locally produced goods.

It is also worth noting both the wide-ranging area from which goods were purchased—from Berwick to London—and the strong regionality implicit in that on only very few occasions were goods bought from outside the north-east. Overall, the large number of people involved in supplying the priory, the fact that so few of these individuals supplied the priory regularly, and the apparent ease with which the priory switched between suppliers, even of specialist goods such as the livery cloths, suggests that a significant degree of choice was available to consumers in the north-east of England. In addition, that this choice is reflected in the accounts, in other words in the actual practice of the priory, implies both that the priory was informed about the choices and that tradition did not stand in the way of their ability to exercise them.

7

Conclusion

The quality of evidence available about Durham Cathedral Priory's economic activities in this period means that the findings presented here give a unique insight into the purchasing strategies practised by a major medieval consumer. It can be seen that the priory was in many ways a sophisticated consumer, able to make rational and informed choices and to deploy a number of different purchasing strategies where appropriate. Furthermore, the degree to which the economic activity of the priory can be seen to have been inextricably intertwined with its social, religious, and other activities is unprecedented. Lack of comparable research elsewhere means that it must remain an open question whether this was a feature of the organization of other great households. However, that a medieval monastery, so often assumed to have been a bastion of tradition, was exercising rational choice and a range of intelligent strategies implies that it is likely to have been more widely the case for medieval consumers as a whole. In addition, the evidence of the priory's purchasing sheds a rare shaft of light on the economic well-being and the nature of trade in the north-east region as a whole and in Newcastle upon Tyne in particular.

STANDARDS OF LIVING

Durham Cathedral Priory was a household of major importance in the north-east of England, both spiritually and economically. Comparisons with other major households in the region and in the country at large are hard to draw since for nowhere else has a comparable quantity and quality of evidence survived. In terms of wealth and influence, Durham could be compared only with a handful of other major monasteries and with the principal secular households of the time. However, it would appear from the evidence that is available that whilst Durham Priory was in many ways a typical large establishment, there were also striking exceptions to this picture.[1] The analysis of the diet of the priory in this period that has been made here demonstrates that the monks' standard of living was on an aristocratic scale in many ways, and yet their apparel was startlingly modest in comparison with that bought and used by equivalent households.

The priory's diet, a key indicator of the standard of living enjoyed by the monks, can be compared with that found by Harvey for this period at Westminster Abbey.[2] The comparison reveals a much higher level of spending on luxurious foodstuffs at Durham than at Westminster, as well as differences in the varieties bought which may well reflect regional differences in pastoral farming and in fishing, and thus represent different patterns of consumption to be found in the north and south of England at this time. Even after making all possible allowances for differences in the data, the Durham monks can be seen to have served four or five times as much meat and 50 per cent more fish than those at Westminster. Of the meats eaten at the two monasteries, beef was by far the most important meat served at Durham, accounting for 66.3 per cent by edible weight of the meat bought by the priory, whilst mutton took second place, accounting for 18 per cent. In contrast, mutton was the most common meat at Westminster, accounting for 46 per cent of the meat served there, and beef was relegated to second place at 35.5 per cent. Similarly, herring accounted for 50 per cent of the fish served at Durham but for only 8 per cent at Westminster, whilst cod was more common at Westminster, accounting for 49 per cent of the fish served there compared to 34.1 per cent at Durham.

Furthermore, both wine and spices, classic indicators of aristocratic diet, were bought in large quantities by Durham Priory. It can be estimated that the average consumption of wine per monk was just over a pint a day, much higher than that for Westminster which was just over a quarter of a pint. The Durham figure exceeds even the higher amounts calculated for other aristocratic households, where

---

[1] Kate Mertes has provided average income and expenditure summaries under various headings from a sample of 92 records relating to 35 households of over 50 inhabitants (and 71 households below that size). It can be seen from these that Durham's overall expenditure under the general headings was by no means untypical of the larger households, though at just over £1,877 p.a. its total expenditure was considerably larger than the average Mertes found of £1,102 (Mertes, *English Noble Household*, 218–19).

[2] B. Harvey, *Living and Dying*, 34–71.

the average consumption has been estimated by Dyer to have been around two-thirds of a pint.[3] Similarly, the priory spent significantly more on spices than Westminster Abbey, although the picture is less clear-cut when comparisons are made with large secular households. The household of the Earl of Northumberland spent rather more on spices than did the priory, whereas the household of the Duke of Buckingham spent somewhat less. It is clear, however, that the priory's purchases of wine, spices, and meats firmly placed the diet of the monks on a par with that of the higher nobility of the country.

In contrast, the cloth bought for the livery of the priory was relatively modest when compared with that bought by a range of other contemporary households. The highest-priced cloth bought by the priory was that purchased for the prior, costing 4s. 0d. per yard, whilst the other obedientiaries were provided with cloth costing around 3s. 0d. per yard. This places the monks' standard of dress on the level of the gentry rather than the aristocracy.

The food eaten and the clothing worn by an individual are generally indicative of a broader range of economic and social markers. The standard of living enjoyed by the priory is therefore revealed by this study to have been a complex mixture of the aristocratic and the merely genteel. This combination suggests both that the last days of the great monasteries were not as corrupt and luxurious as suggested by their post-reformation caricature, and that the whole question of medieval standards of living may be more nuanced than is sometimes thought.

THE PRIORY AS A CONSUMER

It is clear that the obedientiaries had a range of purchasing strategies available to them, and were able to make choices between a wide range of goods and suppliers. As has been seen, the factors influencing their decisions varied according to the particular commodity in question. For a staple need such as grain a certain amount had to be bought each year regardless of the prevailing price or other considerations, and Durham Priory bought a minimum of just under 1,300 quarters of grain in each year. For purchases over this minimum some correlation to changing prices can be seen, although the year's

[3] C. Dyer, 'English Diet in the Later Middle Ages', 194.

prevailing price was clearly not the only factor involved in the decision. In addition, changing prices did not affect all grains equally, and there is some evidence to suggest that the priory bought less wheat and more other grains in years of high prices.

Wine too seems to have been treated as a staple item of diet by the priory, being bought in large quantities every year regardless of price fluctuations. This was despite the fact that the priory was clearly conscious of price changes, there being some evidence to suggest that the bursar was prepared to shop around for his wine and source wine from outside the immediate area when the price was sufficiently different to justify the additional carriage charge incurred. The total amount of wine bought by the priory did increase over this period, and this correlates with a long-term drop in the average price of wine, but in the short term the priory seems to have purchased the required amount of wine despite fluctuations in price. With other luxury foodstuffs the pattern is different. For both dried fruits and sugar, a drop in price over the period correlates with a significant increase in the amount purchased by the priory.

A similar distinction can be seen for the cloth bought by the priory. This falls broadly into two categories: cloth that was bought for utilitarian purposes and cloth that was bought for display or with conscious social differentiation in mind. A case might also be made for a third category of cloths which fell between the two extremes, such as many of the linens and other middling quality materials such as serge, bought for purposes that were neither purely utilitarian nor strictly a matter of display—such as bedlinen and undergarments. The priory's purchases of the cheap cloths that were used for a variety of household purposes, such as hardyn and sackcloth, to some extent correlate with changing prices. This was particularly the case for hardyn, purchases of which more than doubled over this period as the price fell by 50 per cent.

The situation was very different for the cloths that were bought to be on display and to convey social and hierarchical messages. Vestments were not bought frequently enough for price responsiveness to be analysed, but when they were bought the prices paid were breathtakingly high (although price consciousness was still displayed). It is the livery cloths, however, that best demonstrate the priory's highly developed sense of social stratification, and its conscious use of different qualities and differentially priced goods to reinforce such divisions. Different qualities of cloth were bought for every level of the household, from the prior to the liveried grooms, and these purchases also make it clear that the priory was conscious of the relationship of price to perceptions of quality, referring to the different cloths only in terms of their prices and intended wearers.

When the priory came to the actual buying of the goods that had been chosen, two distinct purchasing strategies can be seen. Much of the local agricultural produce and other items of local manufacture or provenance which the priory acquired were bought via its network of tenurial relationships. Over 95 per cent of the grain that entered the priory was acquired in this way, as well as around half the meat and fish, and varying amounts of certain other goods such as honey, salt, oil, and locally produced cloth. These items were not 'bought' in the usual sense of the word but were given to the priory as payments in kind for the rents that their tenants owed, or occasionally for other payments due such as that for the purchase of a tithe. Such payments in kind were widespread at Durham, being used to some extent in 57 per cent of the rental payments made in 1495/6.[4] The use of items other than cash to make such payments does not appear to have been a response to currency shortages, and does not seem to have had any fixed pattern to it. In the absence of any evidence for an element of compulsion, the continuance of this system thus implies that it was mutually agreeable to both priory and tenants, and moreover that in general a good working relationship must have existed between both parties.

The market was not redundant, however, being used both for other goods—mainly manufactured, processed, or imported items— and for top-up purchases of the commodities that were bought mainly using the tenurial system. For example, grain was almost entirely acquired from tenants of the priory as payment in kind, but additional small amounts were bought on the open market in most years, and the market was resorted to on a large scale in years of dearth such as the early 1480s, when grain could be bought from outside the region at significantly lower prices. Around half the fish and livestock that entered the priory was also bought, often from the same individuals who also supplied some in the form of rental payments.

In making market purchases the priory used agents extensively, even when purchasing goods from the immediate region. These agents could be priory servants, officials, monks, or simply merchants or

---

[4] Lomas, 'Priory and its Tenants', 117–19.

individuals known to the priory who happened to be in the right place at the right time. They were used throughout the purchasing process, from collecting samples and transmitting them to the priory, to choosing goods, paying for them, and sometimes arranging for their carriage to Durham or bringing them back personally. Credit arrangements may well also have been one of the agents' responsibilities, and there must have been some element of credit involved in many transactions which were carried out at second- or third-hand, but the evidence for this is scanty since precise dates of transactions and payments are only rarely given in the priory records. Acting as an agent for the priory was one of the ways in which some of the suppliers of the priory were involved in more complex relationships with the priory than simply that of supplier and customer. As has been seen, many of the priory's suppliers were also its tenants; others were clearly kinsmen of the monks; and still others are listed in the *Liber Vitae* for no apparent reason, but may well have had some sort of confraternity relationship with the priory which went beyond the purely mercantile.

The existence of such wider and interlocking relationships between the priory and its suppliers, the priory's use of agents, and the unprecedented level of goods received in kind from tenants all strongly suggest that knowledge, trust, and personal relationships were the key unifying factors in the obedientiaries' purchasing strategies and decisions. The priory invested heavily in information, building up networks of informants and advisers at all levels in society. This can be seen partly in the sheer quantity of archival material that survives, but also from such things as their expenditure on food, drink, and liveries. Such 'luxury' goods did not function solely to feed and clothe, or even to send out hierarchical messages but also, as Douglas and Isherwood have convincingly argued, as 'mediating materials' to create and foster social interaction.[5] The social linkages of the priory were clearly a top priority, and were extremely well developed and maintained. This was in itself a highly successful strategy for the efficient sourcing and purchasing of the goods required by the priory, since it reduced transaction costs and increased the chances of transactions being satisfactorily completed.[6]

[5] M. Douglas and B. Isherwood, *The World of Goods: Towards an Anthropology of Consumption* (London, 1979), 4.
[6] North, 'Transaction Costs in History', 560.

THE STATE OF TRADE IN NEWCASTLE
AND THE NORTH-EAST

It is notable that the majority of the priory's needs could be and were supplied from the immediate Durham and Newcastle region. This was increasingly the case over the period, and Newcastle was increasingly the regional focus of the priory's purchasing. In particular, the subordinate place of London in the provisioning of the priory is notable, even for luxury items such as malmsey and spices. The majority of research into towns, trade, and urban hinterlands in this period has emphasized the gravitational pull of London; for example, Dyer has recently suggested that 'for luxury and semi-luxury goods the whole of England formed London's hinterland'.[7] However, the evidence from Durham Cathedral Priory reveals the north-east to have had a vigorous independent mercantile culture, comparable perhaps to that in the south-west.[8] This finding fits well with the results of recent research by Keene, using debt pleas to investigate the extent of London's economic hinterland in this period, although he suggests that economic integration with London may have been an important factor in Newcastle's success.[9]

The suppliers of the priory can be looked at as two main cohorts, on the one hand those who supplied the kind of local agricultural produce that was frequently bought via the tenurial system outlined above, and on the other hand those who supplied other goods primarily via the market system. Within each of these categories there was some overlap between the suppliers of different goods (although this was much more the case for the suppliers of local produce than for the suppliers of other goods), but there was virtually no overlap between the suppliers of these two categories of goods. The prosopographical profiles of the two groups of suppliers also differed significantly: suppliers of local produce were more likely to appear alongside others

[7] C. Dyer, 'Trade, Urban Hinterlands and Market Integration, 1300–1600: A Summing Up', in J. A. Galloway (ed.), *Trade, Urban Hinterlands and Market Integration, c.1300–1600* (Centre for Metropolitan History Working Papers Ser. 3, 2000), 106.

[8] Ibid. 108.

[9] Derek Keene, 'Changes in London's Economic Hinterland as Indicated by Debt Cases in the Court of Common Pleas', in Galloway (ed.), *Trade, Urban Hinterlands and Market Integration*, 79.

of the same surname and were associated with larger kinship groups involved in the provisioning of the priory than were the merchants and other suppliers of manufactured and imported goods. The locations with which the two groups are associated in the accounts also differ, small local place names predominating for the suppliers of local produce, and references to London and the major regional market centres (primarily Newcastle) being reserved for the suppliers of other goods.

Overall, however, the most notable feature of the priory's suppliers as a group was their number and variety. Well over 1,200 suppliers were involved in provisioning the priory over the period, and these individuals ranged from small tenants of the priory involved in a single transaction to major merchants supplying high-value items over a period of years. The majority of the suppliers appear only infrequently in the accounts; of the individuals identified here, over half appear only once and around two-thirds only once or twice. In each product category (with the sole exception of the livery cloths bought by the bursar) the priory tended to spread its business between multiple suppliers in each year, and this could involve as many as the 127 individuals who supplied grain in 1495/6. Even the priory's wine purchases were split between an average of five merchants in each year, and never fewer than two.

The large number of individuals whom these accounts reveal to have taken an active part in the provisioning of the priory implies that the north-east region was one in which competition flourished, and in which the state of trade was sufficiently healthy to enable the numbers involved to make a satisfactory living. This observation reopens the question of whether Newcastle escaped from the economic malaise that afflicted the trade and economic vitality of other east coast ports in the fifteenth century.[10] Several historians have argued that Newcastle stood out as a rare example of success and prosperity in this period; however, the chronic lack of evidence available for medieval Newcastle has made this a necessarily tendentious conclusion.[11] Indeed Dobson, whilst referring to Newcastle as the

---

[10] This point is also made in Threlfall-Holmes, 'Import Merchants', 82–4.

[11] Hoskins argued for the success of Newcastle despite the lack of evidence, concluding that 'there can be little doubt that *had Newcastle been taxed in 1523–7* she would have emerged as not lower than fourth among the provincial towns' (Hoskins, 'English Provincial Towns', 4; my emphasis).

most successful of the medieval new towns, points out that 'the sparsity of evidence makes it almost pointless to put the question' of how it fared in the fifteenth century.[12]

The view of Newcastle as an exception to late medieval decline has been challenged, however, especially by Butcher's analysis of the rental income from Newcastle properties belonging to University College, Oxford. From the evidence that these afforded of declining rents and growing arrears, he concluded that 'most probably Newcastle experienced the same kind of decline, and for the same reasons, as most other provincial towns'.[13] Those reasons, at least for the other east coast ports with which Newcastle might be compared, are generally agreed upon. The crucial factor was declining overseas trade, which is blamed on the increasing share being channelled through London, and on the closure of the Baltic to English ships for much of this period. Declining populations, the result of recurrent epidemics, are also thought to have played a part in economic decline. It is generally agreed that in York, and concurrently in its outlet port, Hull, decline was exacerbated by the loss of the cloth-making trade as it relocated to new centres.[14] However, the evidence from Durham Cathedral Priory suggests that more than the cloth trade was at stake for towns like York, and that the increasing dominance of London cannot be wholly blamed for their declining share of overseas trade.[15]

The evidence contained in the obedientiary accounts of Durham Cathedral Priory for the imported goods purchased by the priory cannot directly address the question of whether overseas trading activity through Newcastle declined.[16] However, as Kowaleski points

[12] Dobson, 'Urban Decline', 19.
[13] Butcher, 'Rent, Population and Economic Change', 75.
[14] D. M. Palliser, 'A Crisis in English Towns? The Case of York, 1460–1640', *Northern History*, 14 (1978), 115; Kermode, 'Merchants, Overseas Trade and Urban Decline', 52.
[15] A comparison might be drawn with Chester in the west, where competition from Liverpool was at least as significant as the magnet of London in its declining importance in the 16th cent. (J. I. Kermode, 'The Trade of Late Medieval Chester, 1500–1550', in R. H. Britnell and J. Hatcher (eds.), *Progress and Problems in Medieval England* (Cambridge, 1996), 286–307).
[16] Some evidence for the volume of such trade can be found in the enrolled customs accounts, such as those edited by H. L. Gray, 'Tables of Enrolled Customs', in Power and Postan (eds.), *Studies in English Trade in the Fifteenth Century*, for the years 1398 to 1482. These suggest that Newcastle may indeed have survived the 15th cent. with its overseas trade largely intact; e.g. tunnage was paid on an average of 69 tuns of wine per year in the period 1410–29, 74 tuns in 1430–49, and 124 tuns in 1450–79.

out for Exeter, local trade was likely to have been much more important in the town's economy than the better documented and more glamorous imports on which attention tends to be concentrated.[17] What this study illuminates is the extent to which a substantial local consumer, willing and able to source goods from elsewhere in the country when it wished to do so, chose to buy from Newcastle. Not only did Durham Cathedral Priory continue to obtain luxury imported goods from Newcastle rather than London, but from the second half of the fifteenth century the priory came to rely almost exclusively upon Newcastle as a supply centre for all goods except those bought directly from the priory's own tenantry. This suggests that at least the range and availability of goods in Newcastle was unlikely to have decreased in the period. Indeed, a surprising range of the more expensive imported goods were to be found in Newcastle, including malmsey and other sweet wines, the trade of which was generally centred on London. In addition, the large number of Newcastle merchants who were to a greater or lesser extent involved in supplying the priory points to the economic health of Newcastle in the late fifteenth and early sixteenth centuries.

CONCLUDING REMARKS

Ultimately, the purchases recorded in the Durham Cathedral Priory obedientiary accounts emphasize the extent to which the economic activity of the priory was inextricably entwined with its other activities as landlord, church, and great household. Marketing, purchasing, renting, and even selling were not carried out as economically discrete activities, but were undertaken within a structural and administrative framework which bound all such transactions together. The priory's choice of suppliers was based on unquantifiable factors such as personal knowledge, history, family, and land tenure as well as on clearer-cut issues such as the availability of goods and the prices being charged, just as choices about which commodities to purchase could be based as much on considerations of display, social stratification, rank, and position as on more narrowly economic matters. At the same time such choices and relationships were not fossilized, that is, they were not based on tradition and expectation to the exclusion

---

[17] Kowaleski, *Local Markets and Regional Trade*, 4.

of flexibility, and surprisingly were based on long-term relationships with suppliers in only a few exceptional cases.

The priory was extremely price conscious, whether this meant seeking out the best bargain for a particular commodity, adapting the amount bought to the prevailing price, or simply being conscious of and making use of price differentials for their own purposes, such as in establishing and maintaining the differentiation between ranks with the livery cloths. It is impossible not to conclude that the priory was a sophisticated consumer, situated in a region in which competition thrived.

Appendix

In the following table, the year denotes the year in which the account was commenced, that is, 1460 refers to the 1460/1 accounting year. A solid block of colour denotes that an account is extant in the archive for that year, in usable form, whilst a grey area denotes a year in which an account exists but for which the sections relevant to this study are badly damaged or missing.

TABLE A.1 The surviving obedientiary accounts, 1460–1520

Account/indenture
Bursar's accounts
Hostillar's accounts
Chamberlain's accounts
Sacrist's accounts
Communar's accounts
Almoner's accounts
Terrar's accounts
Feretrar's accounts
Infirmarer's accounts
Granator's accounts
Bursar/granator indentures
Cellarer's accounts
Bursar/cellarer indentures

Bibliography

MANUSCRIPT SOURCES

All manuscripts referred to here are to be found in the Durham Cathedral Muniments (DCM) collection, held at No. 5 The College, Durham. The relevant obedientiary accounts are shown in the Appendix.
DCM B. Bk. G
DCM B. Bk. H
DCM B. Bk. J
DCM Reg. Parv. II
DCM Reg. Parv. III

PRINTED WORKS

ABEL, W., *Agricultural Fluctuations in Europe*, trans. O. Ordish (London, 1980).

ADMAN, P., BASKERVILLE, S. W., and BEEDHAM, K. F., 'Computer-Assisted Record Linkage: or How Best to Optimise Links without Generating Errors', *History and Computing*, 4 (1992).

ARMITAGE, P. L., 'British Cattle Husbandry', *Ark*, 9 (1982).

ASHTOR, E., *Levant Trade in the Later Middle Ages* (Princeton, 1983).

AUSTIN, T. (ed.), *Two Fifteenth Century Cookery Books* (Early English Text Society, OS 91, 1888).

BALDWIN, F. E., *Sumptuary Legislation and Personal Regulation in England* (Baltimore, 1926).

BENNETT, H. S., *The Pastons and their England* (3rd edn., Cambridge, 1990).

BENNETT, M. J., *Community, Class and Careerism: Cheshire and Lancashire Society in the Age of Sir Gawain and the Green Knight* (Cambridge, 1983).

BEVERIDGE, W. H., *Prices and Wages in England from the Twelfth to the Nineteenth Century* (London, 1939).

—— 'The Yield and Price of Corn in the Middle Ages', *Economic History*, 2 (1927), repr. in E. M. Carus-Wilson (ed.), *Essays in Economic History: Reprints Edited for the Economic History Society*, i (London, 1954).

BIDDICK, K., *The Other Economy: Pastoral Husbandry on a Medieval Estate* (Berkeley, 1989).

BLANCHARD, I. S. W., 'Commercial Crisis and Change: Trade and the Industrial Economy of the North-East, 1509–1532', *Northern History*, 8 (1973).

—— 'Seigneurial Entrepreneurship: The Bishops of Durham and the Weardale Lead Industry 1406–1529', *Business History*, 15 (1973).

BOND, C. J., 'Monastic Fisheries', in M. Aston (ed.), *Medieval Fish, Fisheries and Fishponds in England* (British Archaeological Reports, British Ser., 182; Oxford, 1988).

BONNEY, M., *Lordship and the Urban Community: Durham and its Overlords, 1250–1540* (Cambridge, 1990).

BOORDE, A., *The Fyrst Boke of the Introduction of the Knowledge made by Andrew Borde, of Physycke Doctor* (1542), ed. F. J. Furnivall (Early English Text Society, extra ser., 10, 1870).

BOWDEN, P., 'Agricultural Prices, Farm Profits and Rents', in J. Thirsk (ed.), *The Agrarian History of England and Wales*, iv: *1500–1640* (Cambridge, 1967), 593–695.

BRENNER, Y. S., 'The Inflation of Prices in Early Sixteenth Century England', *Economic History Review*, 2nd ser., 14 (1961).

BRIDBURY, A. R., *Medieval English Clothmaking: An Economic Survey* (London, 1982).

BRITNELL, R. H., 'Avantagium Mercatoris: A Custom in Medieval English Trade', *Nottingham Medieval Studies*, 24 (1980).

—— *Growth and Decline in Colchester, 1300–1525* (Cambridge, 1986).

BUTCHER, A. F., 'Rent, Population and Economic Change in Late-Medieval Newcastle', *Northern History*, 14 (1978).

BUTLIN, R. A., 'The Late Middle Ages, *c.*1350–1500', in R. A. Dodgshon and R. A. Butlin (eds.), *An Historical Geography of England and Wales* (London, 1978).

CAMBRIDGE, E., 'The Masons and Building Works of Durham Priory 1339–1539', Ph.D. thesis (University of Durham, 1992).

CARUS-WILSON, E. M., *Medieval Merchant Venturers* (London, 1954).

CHENEY, C. R., *Handbook of Dates for Students of English History* (London, 1961).

CHILDS, W. R., *Anglo-Castilian Trade in the Later Middle Ages* (Manchester, 1978).

—— (ed.), *The Customs Accounts of Hull 1453–1490* (Yorkshire Archaeological Society Record Ser., 144, 1986).

CLARKE, E. G., 'Medieval Debt Litigation: Essex and Norfolk, 1270–1490', Ph.D. thesis (University of Michigan, 1977).

CLAY, C. (ed.), *Early Yorkshire Families* (Yorkshire Archaeological Society Record Ser., 135, 1973).

CLAYTON, D. J., DAVIES, R. G., and McNIVEN, P., *Trade, Devotion and Governance: Papers in Later Medieval English History* (Stroud, 1994).

COBBAN, A. B., *The King's Hall within the University of Cambridge in the Later Middle Ages* (Cambridge, 1969).

COLEMAN, D. C., *The Economy of England, 1450–1750* (Oxford, 1977).

COLLIER, J. P. (ed.), *The Household Books of John, Duke of Norfolk and Thomas, Earl of Surrey, 1481–1490* (London, 1844).

COLLINS, F. (ed.), *Index of Wills in the York Registry, 1389–1514* (Yorkshire Archaeological Society Record Ser., 6, 1889).

—— (ed.), *Index of Wills in the York Registry A.D. 1514 to 1553* (Yorkshire Archaeological Society Record Ser., 11, 1891).

—— (ed.), *Register of the Freemen of the City of York, from the city records*, i: *1272–1558* (Surtees Society, 96, 1897).

CONWAY DAVIES, J., 'Shipping and Trade in Newcastle upon Tyne, 1294–1296', *Archaeologia Aeliana*, 4th ser., 31 (1953).

—— 'The Wool Customs Accounts of Newcastle upon Tyne for the reign of Edward I', *Archaeologia Aeliana*, 4th ser., 32 (1954).

CRAWFORD, A., *The Household Books of John Howard, Duke of Norfolk, 1462–1471, 1481–1483* (Stroud, 1992).

CROSS, C., *Church and People, 1450–1660* (London, 1976).

CROWFOOT, E., PRITCHARD, F., and STANILAND, K., *Textiles and Clothing c.1150–c.1450: Medieval Finds from Excavations in London* (London, 1992).

DENDY, F. W., 'The Struggle between the Merchant and Craft Gilds of Newcastle in 1515', *Archaeologia Aeliana*, 3rd ser., 7 (1911).

—— (ed.), *Extracts from the Records of the Merchant Adventurers of Newcastle-upon-Tyne*, i (Surtees Society, 93, 1895).

DENLEY, P., and HOPKIN, D., *History and Computing* (Manchester, 1987).

DOBSON, R. B., *Church and Society in the Medieval North of England* (London, 1996).

—— *Durham Cathedral Priory, 1400–1450* (Cambridge, 1973).

—— 'Mynistres of Saynt Cuthbert', Durham Cathedral Lecture 1972 (Durham, 1974).

—— 'Urban Decline in Medieval England', *Transactions of the Royal Historical Society*, 5th ser., 27 (1977).

DOUGLAS, M., and ISHERWOOD, B., *The World of Goods: Towards an Anthropology of Consumption* (London, 1979).

DUFFERWELL, M., *Durham: A Thousand Years of History and Legend* (Edinburgh, 1996).

DUNSFORD, H. M., and HARRIS, S. J., 'Colonization of the Wasteland in County Durham, 1100–1400', *Economic History Review*, 56 (2003).

DYER, A., 'Urban Decline in England, 1377–1525', in T. R. Slater (ed.), *Towns in Decline, A.D. 100–1600* (Aldershot, 2000).

DYER, C., 'The Consumer and the Market in the Later Middle Ages', *Economic History Review*, 2nd ser., 42 (1989).

DYER, C., 'The Consumption of Fresh-water Fish in Medieval England', in M. Aston (ed.), *Medieval Fish, Fisheries and Fishponds* (British Archaeological Reports, British Ser., 182; Oxford, 1988).

—— 'English Diet in the Later Middle Ages', in T. H. Aston *et al.* (eds.), *Social Relations and Ideas* (Cambridge, 1983).

—— *Everyday Life in Medieval England* (London, 1996).

—— *Standards of Living in the Later Middle Ages: Social Change in England c.1200–1520* (Cambridge, 1989).

—— 'Trade, Towns and the Church: Ecclesiastical Consumers and the Urban Economy of the West Midlands, 1290–1540', in T. Slater and G. Rosser (eds.), *The Church in the Medieval Town* (Aldershot, 1998).

—— 'Trade, Urban Hinterlands and Market Integration, 1300–1600: A Summing Up', in J. A. Galloway (ed.), *Trade, Urban Hinterlands and Market Integration, c.1300–1600* (Centre for Metropolitan History Working Papers Ser., 3, 2000).

EDWARDS, J. F., and HINDLE, B. P., 'The Transportation System of Medieval England and Wales', *Journal of Historical Geography*, 17 (1991).

EVANS, N., *The East Anglian Linen Industry: Rural Industry and Local Economy, 1500–1850* (Pasold Studies in Textile History, 5, 1985).

FARMER, D. L., 'Prices and Wages 1350–1500', in E. Miller (ed.), *The Agrarian History of England and Wales*, iii: *1348–1500* (Cambridge, 1991).

FERNIE, E. C., and WHITTINGHAM, A. B., *The Early Communar and Pittancer Rolls of Norwich Cathedral Priory with an Account of the Building of the Cloister* (Norfolk Record Society, 41, 1972).

FITZHERBERT, J., *The Boke of Husbondrye*, ed. W. W. Skeat (English Dialect Society, 1882).

FOSTER, M. R., 'Durham Cathedral Priory 1229–1333: Aspects of the Ecclesiastical History and Interests of the Monastic Community', Ph.D. thesis (University of Cambridge, 1979).

FOWLER, J. T. (ed.), *Extracts from the Account Rolls of the Abbey of Durham, from the original MSS*, 3 vols. (Surtees Society, 99 (1898), 100 (1898), 103 (1900)).

—— (ed.), *The Rites of Durham* (Surtees Society, 107, 1903).

FRASER, C. M., 'The Early Hostmen of Newcastle-upon-Tyne', *Archaeologia Aeliana*, 5th ser., 12 (1984).

—— 'The Pattern of Trade in the North-East of England, 1265–1350', *Northern History*, 4 (1969).

—— (ed.), *Accounts of the Chamberlains of Newcastle-upon-Tyne, 1508–1511* (The Society of Antiquaries of Newcastle-upon-Tyne, Record Ser., 3, 1987).

FRY, T. (ed.), *The Rule of St. Benedict* (Collegeville, Minn., 1981).

GEMMILL, E., and MAYHEW, N., *Changing Values in Medieval Scotland: A Study of Prices, Money and Weights and Measures* (Cambridge, 1995).

GRAS, N. S. B., *The Evolution of the English Corn Market from the Twelfth to the Eighteenth Century* (New York, 1915; reissued 1967).

GRAY, H. L., 'English Foreign Trade from 1446 to 1482' and 'Tables of Enrolled Customs', in E. Power and M. M. Postan (eds.), *Studies in English Trade in the Fifteenth Century* (London, 1966).

GREATREX, J. (ed.), *Account Rolls of the Obedientiaries of Peterborough* (Northamptonshire Record Society, 33, 1984).

GREENSTEIN, D. I., *A Historian's Guide to Computing* (Oxford, 1994).

GUNN, S. J., *Early Tudor Government, 1485–1558* (London, 1995).

GUY, J., *Tudor England* (Oxford, 1988).

HALE, J. R., *Renaissance Europe 1480–1520* (London, 1971).

HAMMOND, J. C., and WILBRAHAM, A., *The Englishman's Food* (London, 1957).

HANHAM, A. (ed.), *The Cely Letters 1472–1488* (Early English Text Society, 273, 1975).

HARDING, V. A., 'Some Documentary Sources for the Import and Distribution of Foreign Textiles in Later Medieval England', *Textile History*, 18 (1987).

HARTE, N. B., 'State Control of Dress and Social Change in Pre-Industrial England', in D. C. Coleman and A. H. John (eds.), *Trade, Government and Economy in Pre-Industrial England: Essays Presented to F. J. Fisher* (London, 1976).

—— and PONTING, K. G. (eds.), *Cloth and Clothing in Medieval Europe: Essays in Memory of Professor E. M. Carus-Wilson* (London, 1983).

HARVEY, B., 'The Aristocratic Consumer in England in the Long Thirteenth Century', in M. Prestwich, R. H. Britnell, and R. Frame (eds.), *Thirteenth Century England 6: Proceedings of the Durham Conference* (Woodbridge, 1997).

—— *Living and Dying in England 1100–1540: The Monastic Experience* (Oxford, 1993).

—— *Monastic Dress in the Middle Ages: Precept and Practice* (The William Urry Memorial Trust, 3, 1988).

—— *The Obedientiaries of Westminster Abbey and their Financial Records, c.1275–1540* (Woodbridge, 2002).

—— *Westminster Abbey and its Estates in the Middle Ages* (Oxford, 1977).

—— and OEPPEN, J., 'Patterns of Morbidity in Late Medieval England: A Sample from Westminster Abbey', *Economic History Review*, 54 (2001).

HARVEY, C., GREEN, E. M., and CORNFIELD, P., 'Record Linkage Theory and Practice: An Experiment in the Application of Multiple Pass Linkage Algorithms', *History and Computing*, 8 (1996).

—— and PRESS, J., *Databases in Historical Research* (London, 1996).

HARVEY, J. H., *Early Nurserymen: With Reprints of Documents and Lists* (London, 1974).

HATCHER, J., *Rural Economy and Society in the Duchy of Cornwall, 1300–1500* (Cambridge, 1970).

HAY, D., *Europe in the Fourteenth and Fifteenth Centuries* (London, 1966).

HEATH, P., *Medieval Clerical Accounts* (Borthwick Institute of Historical Research, St. Anthony's Hall Publications, 26, 1964).

HEATON, H., *The Yorkshire Woollen and Worsted Industries, from the Earliest Times up to the Industrial Revolution* (2nd edn., Oxford, 1965).

HECTOR, L. C., *The Handwriting of English Documents* (2nd edn., London, 1966).

HIEATT, C. B., and BUTLER, S. (eds.), *Curye on Inglysch: English Culinary Manuscripts of the Fourteenth Century (including the Forme of Cury)* (Early English Text Society, supplementary ser., 8, 1985).

HINDLE, B. P., 'The Road Network of Medieval England and Wales', *Journal of Historical Geography*, 2 (1976).

—— 'Roads and Tracks', in L. Cantor (ed.), *The English Medieval Landscape* (Croom Helm Historical Geography Ser., 1982).

—— 'Seasonal Variations in Travel in Medieval England', *Journal of Transport History*, NS 4 (1978).

HOCKEY, S. F. (ed.), *The Account Book of Beaulieu Abbey* (Camden Society, 4th ser., 16, 1975).

HOOPER, W., 'The Tudor Sumptuary Laws', *Economic History Review*, 30 (1915).

HOPKINS, S. V., and PHELPS-BROWN, E. H., 'Seven Centuries of the Prices of Consumables', *Economica*, NS 23 (1956).

HORROX, R. (ed.), *Selected Rentals and Accounts of Medieval Hull, 1293–1528* (Yorkshire Archaeological Society Record Ser., 141, 1983).

HOSKINS, W. G., 'English Provincial Towns in the Early Sixteenth Century', *Transactions of the Royal Historical Society*, 5th ser., 6 (1956).

—— 'Harvest Fluctuations and English Economic History, 1480–1619', *Agricultural History Review*, 12 (1964).

HUNT, R. W., PANTIN, W. A., and SOUTHERN, R. W. (eds.), *Studies in Medieval History Presented to Frederick Maurice Powicke* (Oxford, 1948).

HUNTLEY, J. P., and STALLIBRASS, S., *Plant and Vertebrae Remains from Archaeological Sites in Northern England: Data Reviews and Future Directions* (Architectural and Archaeological Society of Durham and Northumberland Research Report, 4, 1995).

JAMES, M. K., *Studies in the Medieval Wine Trade*, ed. E. M. Veale (Oxford, 1971).

KAYE, J., *Economy and Nature in the Fourteenth Century: Money, Market Exchange and the Emergence of Scientific Thought* (Cambridge, 1998).

KEENE, Derek, 'Changes in London's Economic Hinterland as Indicated by Debt Cases in the Court of Common Pleas', in J. A. Galloway (ed.), *Trade,*

Urban Hinterlands and Market Integration, c.1300–1600 (Centre for Metropolitan History Working Papers Ser., 3, 2000).

KERMODE, J. I., *Medieval Merchants: York, Beverley and Hull in the Later Middle Ages* (Cambridge, 1998).

—— 'Merchants, Overseas Trade and Urban Decline: York, Beverley and Hull, *c.*1380–1500', *Northern History*, 23 (1987).

—— 'The Trade of Late Medieval Chester, 1500–1550', in R. H. Britnell and J. Hatcher (eds.), *Progress and Problems in Medieval England* (Cambridge, 1996).

KERSHAW, I. (ed.), *Bolton Priory Rentals and Ministers' Accounts, 1473–1539* (Yorkshire Archaeological Society Record Ser., 132, 1970).

KING, S., 'Historical Demography, Life-Cycle Reconstruction and Family Reconstitution: New Perspectives', *History and Computing*, 8 (1996).

KINGSFORD, C. L. (ed.), *The Stonor Letters and Papers, 1290–1483*, 2 vols. (Camden Society, 3rd ser., 29 and 30, 1919).

KIRBY, J. W. (ed.), *The Manor and Borough of Leeds, 1425–1662: An Edition of Documents* (Thoresby Society, 57, 1889).

KIRK, R. E. G. (ed.), *Accounts of the Obedientiars of Abingdon Abbey* (Camden Society, NS 51, 1892).

KITCHEN, G. W., *Compotus Rolls of the Obedientiaries of St. Swithun's Priory, Winchester* (London, 1892).

KNEISEL, E., 'The Evolution of the English Corn Market', *Journal of Economic History*, 14 (1954).

KOWALESKI, M., *Local Markets and Regional Trade in Medieval Exeter* (Cambridge, 1995).

LANCASTER, J. C., 'Coventry', in M. D. Lobel (ed.), *The Atlas of Historic Towns*, ii (London, 1975).

LANDER, J. R., *Conflict and Stability in Fifteenth-Century England* (3rd edn., London, 1977).

LEE, J. S., 'Feeding the Colleges: Cambridge's Food and Fuel Supplies, 1450–1560', *Economic History Review*, 56 (2003).

LOMAS, R. A., 'Durham Cathedral Priory as a Landowner and a Landlord, 1290–1540', Ph.D. thesis (University of Durham, 1973).

—— 'A Northern Farm at the End of the Middle Ages: Elvethall Manor, Durham, 1443/4–1513/4', *Northern History*, 18 (1982).

—— 'A Priory and its Tenants', in Britnell (ed.), *Daily Life in the Late Middle Ages* (Stroud, 1998).

—— 'The Priory of Durham and its Demesnes in the Fourteenth and Fifteenth Centuries', *Economic History Review*, 2nd ser., 31 (1978).

—— and PIPER, A. J. (eds.), *Durham Cathedral Priory Rentals*, i: *Bursars Rentals* (Surtees Society, 198, 1989).

LUTZ, H. L., 'Inaccuracies in Rogers' History of Prices', *Quarterly Journal of Economics*, 23 (1909).

MARTIN, G. H., 'Road Travel in the Middle Ages: Some Journeys by the Warden and Fellows of Merton College, Oxford, 1315–1470', *Journal of Transport History*, NS 3 (1975/6).

MASSCHAELE, J., 'Transport Costs in Medieval England', *Economic History Review*, 2nd ser., 46 (1993).

MATE, M., 'Medieval Agrarian Practices: The Determining Factors', *Agricultural History Review*, 33 (1985).

MAUWDSLEY, E., MORGAN, N., RICHMOND, L., and TRAIR, R. (eds.), *History and Computing III: Historians, Computers and Data—Applications in Research and Teaching* (Manchester, 1990).

MAYHEW, N. J., 'Population, Money Supply and the Velocity of Circulation in England, 1300–1700', *Economic History Review*, 2nd ser., 48 (1995).

MENNELL, S., *All Manners of Food* (Oxford, 1985).

MERTES, K., *The English Noble Household, 1250–1600* (Oxford, 1988).

MITCHELL, D. M., ' "By your Leave my Masters": British Taste in Table Linen in the Fifteenth and Sixteenth Centuries', *Textile History*, 20 (1989).

MORIMOTO, N., 'The Demand and Purchases of Wine of Durham Cathedral Priory in the First Half of the Fifteenth Century', *Nagoya Gakuin Daigaku Ronshu*, 20 (1983).

MULDREW, C., *The Economy of Obligation* (London, 1998).

MUNRO, J. H. A., *Bullion Flows and Monetary Policies in England and the Low Countries, 1350–1500* (Aldershot, 1992).

—— *Textiles, Towns and Trade: Essays in the Economic History of Late-Medieval England and the Low Countries* (Aldershot, 1994).

MYERS, A. R., *Crown, Household and Parliament in Fifteenth Century England* (London, 1985).

NEWMAN, C. M., 'Employment on the Priory of Durham Estates, 1494–1519: The Priory as an Employer', *Northern History*, 26 (2000).

NICOLAS, N. H., *Privy Purse Expenses of Elizabeth of York: Wardrobe Accounts of Edward the Fourth. With a Memoir of Elizabeth of York, and Notes* (London, 1830).

NIGHTINGALE, P., *A Medieval Mercantile Community* (London, 1995).

NIJENHUIS, W. F. (ed.), *The Vision of Edmund Leversedge* (Nijmegen, 1991).

NOBLE, C., *Farming and Gardening in Late Medieval Norfolk: Norwich Cathedral Priory Gardeners' Accounts, 1329–1530* (Norfolk Record Society, 61, 1997).

NORTH, D. C., 'Transaction Costs in History', *Journal of European Economic History*, 14 (1985).

The Oxford English Dictionary (2nd edn., Oxford, 1989).

PALLISER, D. M., 'A Crisis in English Towns? The Case of York, 1460–1640', *Northern History*, 14 (1978).

PANTIN, W. A. (ed.), *Documents Illustrating the Activities of the General and Provincial Chapters of the English Black Monks, 1215–1540* (Camden Society, 3rd ser., 45, 47, and 54, 1931–7).

PELHAM, R. A., 'Medieval Foreign Trade: Eastern Ports', in H. C. Darby (ed.), *An Historical Geography of England before A.D. 1800* (Cambridge, 1951).

PERCY, J. W. (ed.), *York Memorandum Book* (Surtees Society, 186, 1973).

PERCY, T. (ed.), *The Regulations and Establishment of the Household of Henry Algernon Percy the Fifth Earl of Northumberland at his Castles of Wressle and Leckonfield in Yorkshire, begun A.D. 1512* (2nd edn., London, 1905).

PHELPS-BROWN, E. H., and HOPKINS, S. V., 'Seven Centuries of the Prices of Consumables, compared with Builders' Wage-Rates', *Economica* (1956), repr. in E. M. Carus-Wilson (ed.), *Essays in Economic History: Reprints Edited for the Economic History Society*, ii (London, 1962).

PIPER, A., 'The Size and Shape of Durham's Monastic Community, 1274–1539' (forthcoming).

POLLARD, A. J., *North-Eastern England during the Wars of the Roses* (Oxford, 1990).

PROTHERO, R. E., *English Farming Past and Present* (London, 1912).

PYTHIAN-ADAMS, C., *Desolation of a City: Coventry and the Urban Crisis of the Late Middle Ages* (Cambridge, 1979).

—— and SLACK, P., *The Traditional Community under Stress* (Milton Keynes, 1977).

RAINE, J. (ed.), *The Durham Household Book: or, The Accounts of the Bursar of the Monastery of Durham, from Pentecost 1530 to Pentecost 1534* (Surtees Society, 18, 1844).

—— (ed.), *The Inventories and Account Rolls of the Benedictine Houses or Cells of Jarrow and Monk-Wearmouth in the County of Durham* (Surtees Society, 29, 1854).

—— (ed.), *The Priory of Finchale* (Surtees Society, 6, 1837).

REYERSON, K. L., 'Commercial Fraud in the Middle Ages: The Case of the Dissembling Pepperer', *Journal of Medieval History*, 8 (1982).

ROGERS, J. E. T., *A History of Agriculture and Prices in England, From the Year after the Oxford Parliament (1259) to the Commencement of the Continental War (1793), Compiled Entirely from Original and Contemporaneous Records*, 7 vols. (Oxford, 1882).

ROLLASON, L. S., 'The Liber Vitae of Durham (British Library Manuscript Cotton Domitian A. VII): A Discussion of its Possible Context and Use in the Later Middle Ages', Ph.D. thesis (University of Durham, 2003).

ROSSER, G., *Medieval Westminster 1200–1540* (Oxford, 1989).

RYDER, M. L., 'Livestock Remains from Four Medieval Sites in Yorkshire', *Agricultural History Review*, 9 (1961).

—— 'Medieval Sheep and Wool Types', *Agricultural History Review*, 32 (1984).

SAUNDERS, H. W., *An Introduction to the Obedientiary and Manor Rolls of Norwich Cathedral Priory* (Norwich, 1930).

SAVINE, A., 'English Monasteries on the Eve of the Dissolution', in P. Vinogradoff (ed.), *Oxford Studies in Social and Legal History*, i (Oxford, 1909).

SCOTT, J., 'Rational Choice Theory', in G. Browning, A. Halcli, and F. Webster (eds.), *Understanding Contemporary Society: Theories of the Present* (London, 2000).

SCULLY, T., *The Art of Cookery in the Middle Ages* (Woodbridge, 1995).

SEARLE, E., *Lordship and Community: Battle Abbey and its Banlieu, 1060–1538* (Toronto, 1974).

—— and ROSS, B. (eds.), *Accounts of the Cellarers of Battle Abbey, 1275–1513* (Sydney, 1967).

SIMON, A. L., *The History of the Wine Trade in England*, 2 vols. (London, 1906–7).

SLICHER VON BATH, B. H., *Yield Ratios, 810–1810* (Wageningen, 1963).

SMITH, R. A. L., *Collected Papers* (London, 1947).

SNAPE, R. H., *English Monastic Finances in the Later Middle Ages* (Cambridge, 1926).

SPUFFORD, P., *Handbook of Medieval Exchange* (London, 1986).

—— *Money and its Use in Medieval Europe* (Cambridge, 1988).

STANILAND, K., 'Clothing Provision and the Great Wardrobe in the Mid-Thirteenth Century', *Textile History*, 22 (1991).

—— 'The Great Wardrobe Accounts as a Source for Historians of Fourteenth-Century Clothing and Textiles', *Textile History*, 20 (1989).

STONE, D., 'Medieval Farm Management and Technological Mentalities: Hinderclay before the Black Death', *Economic History Review*, 54 (2001).

STRATTON, J. M., and BROWN, J. H., *Agricultural Records, A.D. 220–1977*, ed. R. Whitlock (2nd edn., London, 1978).

SUTTON, A. F., 'Order and Fashion in Clothes: The King, his Household and the City of London at the End of the Fifteenth Century', *Textile History*, 22 (1991).

SWABEY, F., *Medieval Gentlewoman: Life in a Widow's Household in the Later Middle Ages* (Stroud, 1999).

THIRSK, J., *England's Agricultural Regions and Agrarian History, 1500–1750* (London, 1987).

—— (ed.), *Land, Church and People: Essays Presented to Professor H. P. R. Finberg* (Agricultural History Review Supplement, 18, 1970).

THOMPSON, A. H. (ed.), *Liber Vitae Ecclesiae Dunelmensis. A Collotype Facsimile of the Original Manuscript, with Introductory Essays and Notes*, i: *Facsimile and General Introduction* (Surtees Society, 136, 1923).

THRELFALL-HOLMES, M., 'Durham Cathedral Priory's Consumption of Imported Goods: Wines and Spices, 1464–1520', in Michael Hicks (ed.), *Revolution and Consumption in Late Medieval England* (Woodbridge, 2001).

—— 'The Import Merchants of Newcastle upon Tyne, 1464–1520: Some Evidence from Durham Cathedral Priory', *Northern History*, 40 (2003).

—— 'Late Medieval Iron Production and Trade in the North East', *Archaeologia Aeliana*, 5th ser., 27 (1999).

—— 'Provisioning a Medieval Monastery: Durham Cathedral Priory's Purchases of Imported Goods, 1464–1520', MA thesis (University of Durham, 1997).

THRUPP, S. L., 'The Grocers of London', in E. Power and M. M. Postan (eds.), *Studies in English Trade in the Fifteenth Century* (London, 1966).

—— *The Merchant Class of Medieval London (1300–1500)* (Chicago, 1948).

TILLOTSON, J. H., *Monastery and Society in the Late Middle Ages: Selected Account Rolls from Selby Abbey, Yorkshire, 1398–1537* (Woodbridge, 1988).

TITOW, J. Z., *Winchester Yields: A Study in Medieval Agricultural Productivity* (Cambridge, 1972).

TROW-SMITH, R., *A History of British Livestock Husbandry to 1700* (London, 1957).

TURNER, J. H., *The Structure of Sociological Theory* (Homewood, Ill., 1991).

VAN DER WEE, H., *The Growth of the Antwerp Market*, 3 vols. (The Hague, 1963).

VAN HOUTTE, J. A., *An Economic History of the Low Countries* (London, 1977).

VEALE, E. M., *The English Fur Trade in the Later Middle Ages* (Oxford, 1966).

VERLINDEN, C. (ed.), *Documents pour l'histoire des prix et des salaires en Flandres et en Brabant* (Bruges, 1959).

VILLON, F., *Poems*, ed. J. Fox (London, 1984).

WADE, J. F., 'The Overseas Trade of Newcastle upon Tyne in the Late Middle Ages', *Northern History*, 30 (1994).

—— (ed.), *The Customs Accounts of Newcastle-upon-Tyne 1454–1500* (Surtees Society, 202, 1995).

WAKE, C. H. H., 'The Changing Pattern of Europe's Pepper and Spice Imports, c.1400–1700', *Journal of European Economic History*, 8 (1979).

WEINER, A. B., and SCHNEIDER, J. (eds.), *Cloth and Human Experience* (Washington, 1989).

WILLIAMS, C. H. (ed.), *English Historical Documents*, v: *1485–1558* (London, 1967).

WILLIAMSON, J., 'One Use of the Computer in Historical Studies: Demographic, Social and Economic History from Medieval English Manor Court Rolls', in A. Gilmour-Bryson (ed.), *Computer Applications to Medieval Studies* (Studies in Medieval Culture, 17, 1984).

WOOD-LEGH, K. L. (ed.), *A Small Household of the XVth Century: Being the Account Book of Munden's Chantry, Bridport* (Manchester, 1956).

WOOLGAR, C. M., *The Great Household in Late Medieval England* (New Haven, 1999).

—— (ed.), *Household Accounts from Medieval England*, 2 vols. (Oxford, 1992, 1993).

Index

abbot 17, 49, 51, 131
Abingdon Abbey 55, 119
accounting system 17, 22–33, 137, 229
Acton 185
Acts of Apparell 128–9
    see also sumptuary legislation
administration 17–33
Advent 53, 67, 72
agents 13, 136, 147, 162, 175–80, 182,
    184, 191, 192, 200, 224, 225
Agnes Brown 208
Agnes Lawe 196
Alan Harding 164
albs 112, 117
alcohol 66–8
Aldin Grange 148
ale 39–41, 43–4, 67–8
Alexander Burton 215
Alexander Robinson:
    widow of 218
Alexandria 62
Alice Bird 208
Alice de Bryene 184
allowances 28, 30, 38
almonds 72
almoner 11, 20, 29, 32, 54
altar cloths 104, 116
amices 112, 117
Andrew Boorde 60, 70, 100
animal feed 38, 40, 41
aniseed 59, 60, 93, 99, 100, 101
Antony Elison 182
apples 55, 56
Atkinson family 204
auditing 30–2
Aycliffe 141, 147, 150, 152–5, 198, 209

Bailey 11
Baltic 9, 228
barley 8, 21, 38, 39, 40, 41, 43, 44, 77,
    78, 133, 138, 139, 140, 141, 163,
    164, 165, 167, 184
bastard 65, 66
Battle Abbey 18, 55, 69, 103, 132, 166

Bay salt, see salt
Beadnell 157, 159
beadnell fish 72
beans 41, 55
Bearpark 36
Beaulieu Abbey 67
Beaurepaire 159
bedlinen 21, 103, 112, 113, 132, 223
beef 36, 51, 73, 221
    see also cattle
Bellasis 187
Benwell 182
Berwick 158, 219
Bewley 140, 147
Billingham 40, 52, 140, 147, 150,
    152–5, 158, 187, 198
Bishop of Hereford 126
Bishop's Borough 11
blanketing 102–4
boars 47, 148
Boke of Husbondry 56
bolting-cloths 103, 113
Bordeaux 69, 93
Boston 9, 172, 175
brandy 65
bread 28, 38–45, 73
bream 47
Bristol 10, 166
broadcloth 123, 131
    see also woollen cloth
brocade 116, 117
Broom 188
budge 128
building 28, 30, 188
building materials 103, 187
bullocks 47
Burdon 146
bursar 14–25, 28–31, 36, 138–40
butter 20, 58, 72, 151

cabbages 56
Calais 10, 104
Caldronley 159
calendar adjustment 45–6

calves 45, 72, 148
Cambridge 4, 30
candles 58
Canterbury Cathedral Priory 18
canvas 102, 103, 104, 208, 212
capons 47, 72, 146, 148
caraway 65
carriage, see transport
carriers 181, 188, 189
carrots 56
cart-loads 186, 187, 188
cash:
    payments to monks 113, 120, 122,
    126; use of 29, 141, 145, 180, 224
    shortage of 144-5
Castle Eden 153, 199
caterer 20
cattle 8, 36, 45, 51, 53, 57, 72, 151, 152,
    154, 156, 160, 195, 200, 205
cellarer 17-22, 28, 34
chamberlain 21, 28-9, 69, 104, 113,
    118-19
cheese 52, 53
cheese fleke 53
cherries 55, 56
Chester 6
Chester-le-Street 158
Chilton 146, 153
choice 1, 3, 75, 144, 161, 214, 219, 229
Christmas 45, 47, 71
Christopher Brigham 202
Christopher Willy 196
cinnamon 59, 60, 65
City of London 126
claret 65, 66
climate 6
cloth 9, 15, 21, 30, 32, 74, 76, 102-33,
    137, 149, 150-2, 173, 174, 175,
    177, 222-4, 228
    carriage of 181, 185-6, 189
    colours of 121-6
    suppliers of 193, 200, 201, 206, 207,
    209-19
cloth of gold 116, 117, 130, 178
clothing 21, 28, 76, 102, 105, 118, 119,
    128-32, 222
cloves 59, 60, 65
coal 8, 9, 10
Coatsay Moor 148, 153
cockles 47, 72, 147, 158, 160
cod 47, 52, 73, 156, 159, 221
Coke family 197
Colchester 6, 173, 184

Coldingham 13, 14
colewart 55
Colpekyn (possibly Coldpike Hall) 206
comfits 59, 60, 62, 98
communar 21, 29, 31, 32, 61
competition 3, 97, 227, 230
Consett 159
consumers 1-5, 7, 10, 134, 202, 219,
    220, 222, 229, 230
consumption 2, 3, 5, 17, 28, 35, 36, 37,
    38, 39, 41, 43, 45, 49, 51, 52, 53,
    59, 62, 67, 68, 69, 70, 73, 90, 101,
    148, 221
copes 116
coriander 65
corn 8, 21
Cornhill 158
Corpus Christi 117
corrodians 71
Countess of Warwick 69
Courtladies salt 57
Cowpen Bewley 52, 141, 142, 144, 147,
    153, 158, 182, 198
cows 36, 45, 147, 148
cranes 47
credit 162, 177, 179-81, 190, 191, 225
cress 56
crimson 130
Crossgate 11
crozier 116
customs accounts 9, 104, 109, 176, 202,
    203, 206
cygnets 47, 71

dace 47
dairy products 28, 35
Dalton 152-3, 198
damask 130
Darlington 10, 172
dearth 168, 169, 171, 224
Derwent 8
Derwentdale 152
diet 34-74, 81, 85, 156, 157, 221-3
    seasonal variations 72
dogdraves 47, 48, 72, 73, 151, 152, 156,
    157, 159, 160, 195, 199, 200
dolphins, see seals
Doncaster 12
double-entry accounting 29
Dover 12
drapers 30, 189, 213, 214, 215
dried fruit 36, 59-64, 93-7, 133, 202,
    206, 223

currants 61
figs 9, 60, 61, 64
prunes 61
raisins 9, 60, 61, 64
dripping 22, 58
Duke of Buckingham, *see* Edward
   Stafford
Duke of Norfolk 130
Duket family 197
Durham 8–11, 13, 206
   marketplace 11, 76, 155
Durham Cathedral Priory 1–33
   archives 3, 16
   cells 13, 15
   income 14, 22
   landholdings 16, 137
   political importance 14
   population 14–16, 43, 44, 49
Dyetary 60, 70

Earl of Northumberland 64, 113, 222
Easington 149, 154
East Anglia 109, 167
East Merrington 147, 152–3, 197
East Rainton 148, 149, 152–3
Easter 45
edible weight 49, 221
Edmondbyers 206
Edmondsley 159
Edward Baxter 164, 202, 205, 206
Edward Dawson 143
Edward Hebburn 196
Edward IV 13, 145
Edward Stafford, Duke of Buckingham
   52, 64, 222
Edward Willy 196
eels 47, 52, 151, 159, 182, 205, 206
eggs 52–4, 72
elasticity of demand 75, 76, 81, 85, 90,
   93, 95, 97, 98, 101, 102, 107, 114,
   132, 134, 223
electuary 60
Elizabeth Willy 196
Elvet 11, 77
embroidery 116
employment 17, 188, 189
entrepreneurial activity 6
Esh 150, 155
Espershields 206
Essex 166
estates 2, 15–17, 18, 29, 188
ewes 47, 147, 148
exchequer 30, 103, 107, 113, 182

Exeter 6, 10, 167, 187, 229
Exmouth 8
exports 3, 9, 128, 202

fairs 171, 172
farming 2, 8, 29, 51, 73, 138–60, 167,
   199, 200, 221
Farne 13, 146, 149, 157, 158, 159, 183
fashion 3, 74, 75, 90, 93, 101, 102, 128,
   129, 130
fats 35, 53, 58, 151
Feat of Gardening 56
femoralia, *see* shirts
feretrar 21, 28, 30, 116
Ferryhill 147, 150, 152–3, 155
filberts 55
Finchale 13
fish 8, 9, 12, 28, 29, 35–8, 45–52, 71–3,
   145–8, 150–2, 156–9, 160, 177,
   193, 195, 197, 199, 200, 201, 203,
   219, 221, 224
fish-days 50
fish-house 36
fishing 12, 160, 221
fish-ponds 55
fish-weirs 158
Flanders 95
flax 9, 105, 110
Flemish cloth 109, 110, 112, 174, 189,
   201, 212
flour 39
fluke 47
Follingsby 159
Forest family 197
frails 61
François Villon 71
fruit 54, 55, 56, 57, 60, 61, 73, 206
fuel 8, 28
Fuke family 205
Fulwell 140, 158
furs 102, 120–2, 124, 126–7, 128, 129,
   194, 219

galingale 65
game 71, 73
gardener 54, 55, 56, 57
gardening manuals 56
gardens 54–7
garlic 55, 56, 59
garments 15, 102, 118–31
Gateshead 147, 158, 160, 189, 206
geese 47, 148, 154
George Bird 202, 205, 206

George Popley 141
George Williamson 147
gifts 23, 28, 29, 67
ginger 59, 60, 65, 93, 97, 98, 133
girths 103
gloves 102
goosehouse 53
gowns 102, 119, 121, 130
grain 17, 20, 22, 28, 29, 35, 36, 37,
  38–46, 75, 76–89, 133, 134,
  137–45, 146, 151–3, 160, 162–71,
  177, 180, 182, 186, 190, 195, 197,
  198, 199, 205, 208, 219, 222–4,
  227
grains of paradise 65
granary 36–7, 39, 40, 44, 83–9
granator 19, 20, 28, 34, 36–45, 138
guests 21, 28, 51, 67

habits 105, 112, 118, 119
haircloth 102, 103, 104, 105, 206,
  212
Halifax 150, 173, 185, 214
Hardwick 165, 180
hardyn 102–7, 133, 134, 208, 212, 216,
  219, 223
Hartlepool 10, 12, 150, 156, 157, 165,
  172
Harton 147, 157
harvests 3, 75, 81, 89, 167, 168, 169
  qualities 78, 167–70
  regionality of 163, 168–70
havermaltum 40
hay 32, 187, 188
hazelnuts 55
Hebburn 159
Heighington 141, 148, 154
Helton 116
hemp 54, 105
hemp seed 54
henhouse 53
Henry Percy 113
Henry VI 11
Henry VII 93
Henry Willy 196
hens 47, 53, 72, 147, 148, 208
herbs 54, 55, 57, 59
herring 9, 47, 49, 52, 72, 73, 151, 152,
  157, 159, 182, 195, 199, 200, 205,
  206, 221
herring-sprats 47
Hesilden 199
hides 22

hierarchies 10, 11, 70, 76, 102, 114,
  121, 124, 126, 128, 132
hogshead 89
Holland cloth 109, 110, 112, 174, 189,
  190, 201, 212, 216
Holmeside 159
Holy Island 13, 146, 156, 157, 158
honey 8, 36, 55, 58, 59, 65, 146, 147,
  159, 224
hoods 102
horsecloths 103
horsehides 103
hospitality 16, 67
hostiller 18, 21, 28, 54, 60, 67
household books 21
Hull 8, 9, 12, 92, 159, 160, 172, 175,
  176, 183, 206, 228
Hutton Henry 141

Impgarth 54
imports 3, 9, 63, 69, 75, 93, 101, 104,
  109, 128, 137, 149, 151, 160, 162,
  165, 171, 174, 176, 194, 197, 198,
  200–9, 212, 216, 217, 219, 224,
  227, 228, 229
  in foro 141, 155, 156
  in patria 156, 159, 163, 164
  in villa 163, 164
industries 8–9, 12
infirmarer 20, 23, 32, 54, 55
Ipswich 184, 185
iron 8–9, 32, 137, 149, 176, 182, 194,
  197, 201–8, 219

Jacob Green 218
Jarrow 12, 13, 147, 149, 150, 156, 157,
  158, 159, 160
John Anderson 218
John Atkinson 140, 188, 217
John Bailya 188
John Bowet 218
John Brandling 164, 202, 205, 206
John Brown 207
John Bukley 177
John Clerk 218
John Cook 218
John de Hyndley 177
John Denom 148
John Eland 100
John Esyngton 197
John Farne 100, 189
  widow of 100
John Fitzherbert 56

John Henryson 199
John Kape 199
John Laxton 206
John Marshall 213, 214, 215
John Matho 140, 199
John Pearson 206
John Robinson 196, 206, 218
John Saunderson 181
John Smith:
    widow of 208
John Sourby 218
John Tailor 164
John Thomson 218
John Walker 188
John Welbury 186, 188
John Youle 182
John, prior of Durham 176
Johnson family 204

Katherine Bywell 208
kelyng 47
Kirk Merrington, see East Merrington
kirtils 122
kitchen garden 54, 55
kitchener 17, 35, 49, 55, 56, 57
Knitsley 206

lambs 47, 72, 147, 148
lambskins 127–8
lampreys 72
Lancashire 13, 109
Lanchester 206
lard 58
larder 36
Lawson family 197
Lax family 205
Le menagier de Paris 56
lead 8, 9, 185
leather 22
Leeds 132, 149, 150, 173, 185, 186,
    215
leeks 55, 56
Lent 21, 45, 53, 61, 67, 72, 104
Levant 63, 232
Liber Vitae 15, 195, 196, 225
Lincoln 167, 175
Lindisfarne 13
linen 21, 102, 105, 109–15, 117, 118,
    132, 174, 206, 208, 212, 216–17,
    223
linen industry 109
ling 47
liquorice 59, 60, 93, 99, 100, 101

livery 15, 38, 102–3, 119, 120, 121–34,
    149, 173, 181, 185, 189, 190, 194,
    210, 212–17, 219, 222, 223, 225,
    229
livestock 137, 145, 147, 148, 151, 154,
    156, 182, 193, 195, 197, 200, 201,
    205, 224
loaves 44
London 9, 10, 12, 97, 110, 116, 150, 167,
    171, 172, 173, 174, 175, 177, 178,
    185, 189, 190, 203, 206, 209, 212,
    214, 219, 226, 227, 228, 229, 232
Low Countries 9, 95, 109
Ludworth 159
Lytham 13

mace 59, 60, 65
magnates 4
Maiona Robinson, wife of John 196
malmsey 65, 66, 173, 177, 190, 226,
    229
malt 41, 44
malt-kiln 105
Malton 10
manufactured goods 137, 151, 162,
    171, 194, 201
manure 54
Marescalia 76, 77
Margaret Paston 131
margin of error 35, 38, 124, 187, 209
markets 4, 10, 77, 92, 136–7, 141–2,
    146–7, 156–61, 162–91, 205–6,
    224, 226–9
Marom 158
Master Lawson 177
Master Swynburne 179
Matthew Paris 12
meat 28, 29, 34, 35–7, 45–52, 57, 72,
    73, 138, 145–8, 154–6, 203, 219,
    221, 224
merchant companies 2, 3, 232
merchants 10, 171–5, 192–219, 224–5,
    227
Merringtons 149, 150, 152, 154, 155, 156
Mid Merrington, see Middlestone
Middlestone 153–4
Midlands 184
milk 52, 53, 54
mining 8
misericord 49, 50, 51
mitre 116
mode price (of grain) 76–8, 81–5, 87,
    163–71

Monk Hesleden 141, 147, 152–3
Monk Wearmouth 13, 112, 158
moor 8
Moorsley 153
Morpeth 158
mortality 101
mudfish 47
Muggleswick 159, 205–6
muscatel 65, 66
mussels 47, 72, 147, 158, 160
mustard seed 56
mutton 51, 72, 73, 221

Nether Heworth 147, 160, 206
Neville family 13
Newcastle 6–7, 9–10, 12, 92, 104, 109,
    157–60, 164, 171–7, 182–4,
    189–90, 201–6, 226–9
Newhouse (Newton Aycliffe) 139, 153,
    199
Newton Bewley 141, 152–3, 159, 198
Newton Ketton 147, 150, 153, 155,
    199
Nicholas Newsham 178
Norham 158
Norman Maynerd 146
Normandy canvas 104
Northallerton 10, 12
North Pittington 153
north-east England 6, 7, 8, 10, 11, 95,
    171, 173, 174, 189, 192, 193, 214,
    220, 226
Norwich 10, 55, 167
Nunstainton 141
nutmeg 59, 60, 65
nuts 9, 56, 59, 60, 62

oats 8, 21, 38, 39, 40, 41, 43, 77, 78,
    138, 139, 141, 167
obedientiary system 17–32, 232
oil 9, 36, 58, 146, 159, 160, 197, 205,
    206, 224
onion seed 54, 55
onions 55, 56, 58, 59, 60, 72
orchards 55
orphreys 116, 117
Ovingham 182
oxen 45, 148
Oxford:
    Durham College 13, 197
    Merton College 12
    New College 126
    University College 228

parsley 55
Paston family 131
pasture 8
payments in kind 29, 78, 137–47, 184,
    224–5
pears 55, 56
Pearson family 204
peas and beans 38, 40, 41, 55–6, 77, 78,
    151, 165
pensions 15, 21, 28, 189
Pentecost 30, 45
pepper 59, 60, 62, 63, 65, 93, 98, 99,
    100, 133
pepperers 63
perch 200
Percy family 13
Peter Andrew 183
Peterborough Abbey 123, 126, 127,
    131, 132
pickerel 47
Picquigney, Treaty of 93
piglets 47, 72, 147, 148
pigs 8, 37, 47, 72, 147, 151, 152, 154,
    156, 160, 162, 195, 200, 208
pig-sty 55
pike 47, 71, 182, 200
pipe 89
Pipewellgate 189, 206, 207
pittances 21
Pittington 139, 152, 154, 199
plaice 47
plums 56
porpoises, see seals
porrets 55
porters 182, 183
ports 7–10, 12, 176, 227–8
pottage 40
poultry 8, 28, 47, 72, 151–5, 160, 195,
    197, 200
preference 3, 74, 75, 89, 102
price regionality 166
price stratification 124, 223, 229
prior 17, 20
prior's chaplain 20
pullets 47, 208
purchasing 1, 3, 4, 5, 7, 17, 35, 74, 75,
    76, 81, 85, 89, 92, 98, 99, 100, 101,
    105, 107, 114, 132, 134, 136, 137,
    160, 162, 165, 173, 174, 175, 176,
    177, 186, 187, 189, 192, 219, 223,
    224, 225, 226, 229
accounts 3
locations 148

strategies 1, 5, 34, 85, 133, 137, 162, 190, 192, 220, 222, 224, 225
purveyors 20, 147

Raintons 149, 150, 154, 155, 156
Rakett family 197, 205
rational choice 192, 220
recession 172
recipes 40, 52, 60, 61, 62, 63, 65, 95, 100, 101
refectory 49, 50
regions 6, 81, 163, 166
Relley 36, 187, 188
remainders (in accounts) 36
rentals 22, 29, 138–47, 157–61, 195
rents 11, 18–19, 21, 24–30, 137–61
repairs 28, 54, 188
rice 36
Richard Billingham 13
Richard Cliff 214
Richard Clifton:
    widow of 140, 208
Richard Clyff 188
Richard Denom 139, 199
Richard Dixon 201
Richard Simpson 176
Richard Smith 199
Richard Wilkinson 199
Richard Willy 196
Richard Wren 175, 218
Richardson family 197
Richmond 10
Ripon 10
Rites of Durham 19, 20, 21
river corridors 167
rivers 7, 12
roach 47, 182
roads 11
Robert Bartram 182
Robert Blake 182
Robert Burton 215
Robert Chepman 92
Robert Clyfton 144–5
Robert Lawson:
    widow of 208
Robert Rede:
    widow of 206
Robert Rock 178
Robert Rodes 116, 178
Robert Shoroton 143
Robert Simson 218
Robert Spink 196
Robert Stokall 205, 206

Robert Stroder 201
Robert Whitehead 176
Robert Wilkinson 218
Robert Willy 196
Robinson family 197, 204
Roger Bunde 183
Roger Morland 139, 199
Rome 13, 178
romney 65, 66
Rule of St Benedict 17, 33, 68
rye 39, 41, 81, 164
Ryton 158, 182

sackcloth 102–3, 107–8, 133, 212, 219, 223
sacrist 19, 21, 23–32, 54, 67, 117
saffron 55, 56, 59, 60
St Cuthbert:
    feast of 71, 182
    fraternity of 13
    shrine 11
St Swithun's Priory 53
St Benedict:
    altar of 117
    rule of, see Rule of St Benedict
St Mary Magdalene 11
salaries 15, 21, 28
salmon 47, 52, 72, 73, 151, 152, 157, 158, 182, 188, 195, 199, 200, 206, 207
salt 47, 57, 59, 149, 158, 179, 182, 224
satin 130
scaccarium 30
Scarborough 10
Scotland 13, 109
seals 47, 151, 158, 159, 183, 200
second-hand garments 22
seeds 54, 55, 56, 62
Selby Abbey 21, 56, 103, 104, 105, 113, 127
serge 102, 113, 118, 119, 132, 223
servants 15–20, 28–32, 44, 49, 51, 71, 102, 119–27, 129, 131, 132, 177, 188, 213, 224
Severn 166
Shadforth 153, 199
shallots 55, 56
sheep 8, 36, 47, 72, 151–2, 156, 195, 200
sheepfells 22
shellfish 47, 73, 151, 158, 200
Sheraton 141
shirting 102

shirts 118
Shoreswood 158
sieves 103
silver 144
Simonside 158
Sion Abbey 126
Sir Humphrey Stafford 64
slaughterhouse 36
socks 119
South Pittington 153, 199
South Shields 12, 147, 149, 150, 156, 157, 172, 182
South Street 11, 188
Southwick 140, 150, 153, 156, 157, 199
sparling 47, 147
spices 17, 21, 24–8, 36, 57, 59–64, 65, 93–102, 133–4, 194, 201–4, 219, 221–2
sprats 47
squirrel 128
stables 28
Staindrop 77
Stamford 13
staminum, see shirts
standards of living 4, 128, 220, 221, 222
steers 45
stipends 15, 28, 189
stockfish 38, 47, 49, 72, 159, 205, 206
stockpiling 85–9, 107
Stockton 206
Stonor family 131
Stour 185
stragulati 123
sturgeon 47, 159
subtleties 60
Sudbury 185
Suffolk 184
sugar 59, 60, 62, 95–7, 133–4, 223
sumptuary legislation 119, 128, 129
Sunderland 12, 150, 156, 157, 158, 182
suppliers 109, 150, 162–5, 172–6, 192–219, 225
surnames 196, 204, 205
sweating sickness 101
sweet wines 65–6, 71, 90, 101

table linen 102, 110–13
tallow 22, 58
Taunton 187
Tees 137, 152
Teesmouth 8
tenants 136–61, 182, 198–204, 224–5
tench 47, 182

tenurial purchasing 136–61, 219, 224–6
terrar 21, 23, 28, 31, 54
textiles, see cloth
Thomas Ayer 110, 174
Thomas Carr 206
Thomas Denom 148
Thomas Foster 141
Thomas Hergyll 141
Thomas Hilton 140, 147, 160
Thomas Howe 218
Thomas Kay 146, 147
Thomas Lawe 196
Thomas Lax 147
Thomas Potts 177
Thomas Richardson 186, 215
Thomas Robinson 206
Thomas Ryhope 218
Thomas Stoddert:
    widow of 208
Thomas Strangeways:
    widow of 199, 208
Thomas Swan 92
Thomas Young 182
Thomson family 204
timber 188
tithes 22, 89, 138, 140–2, 181
toppets 61
torts 60
towels 112–13
towns 6, 10–12, 149–51, 171–5, 226–9
transaction costs 4, 192, 225
transfers 28, 29, 178
transport 11–13, 181–90
    costs 12, 97, 132, 165, 167, 173, 181–9, 223
    ease of 11–13, 189–90
    infrastructure 11
treasurer, see bursar
trust 190, 192, 225
tun 89
Tyne 9, 10, 14, 137, 152, 182, 183
Tyne bridge 183
Tynemouth 8

undergarments 102, 113, 223
Unthank 206
urban crisis 6

veal 51
vegetables 35, 54–7, 73
velvet 116, 130
vestis 118

vestments 102, 112, 114, 116–17, 131–2, 177, 223
Vision of Edmund Leversedge 129, 130
visitation 54, 68, 69

Wallsend 206
walnuts 55
Walworth 141
Wardley 140, 147, 159, 160
wardrobe 120, 122
watering cans 55
waterways 11
wax 58
Wear 8, 12, 137, 152, 158
Weardale 137, 149, 152, 201, 202, 203, 206, 219
Wearmouth 157, 159
Wessington, Prior of Durham 14, 19
West Merrington 147, 149, 150, 153–4
West Midlands 2, 232
West Rainton 149, 152–3, 159
West Riding 174, 175
Westerton, see West Merrington
Westminster Abbey 4, 34, 39, 44, 49, 50, 51, 52, 57, 61, 64, 67, 69, 73, 221, 222
Westoe 157, 158
Weymouth 8
wheat 8, 38, 39, 40, 41, 43, 44, 45, 77, 78, 81, 83, 87, 138, 139, 140, 144, 163, 164, 165, 167, 168, 223
Whitby 10
white meats 52
Whitehall 206
whiting 52, 72, 73
widows 100, 140, 199, 204, 206, 207, 208
William Bird 178
William Brown 199
William Chymnay 214

William Cliff 148
William Clyff 188
William Clyfton 143–4
William Cornforth 100, 109, 189, 217–18
William Falker 182
William Hoton 165, 180
William Jolybody 218
William Kirklay 202
William Lawe 143, 196
William Maltby 146, 147
William Middley 174, 216
William Robinson 218
William Shotton 189
William Tailor 141
William Welbery 188
William White 143
William Wright 175, 176
William, prior of Durham 177, 178
Willy family 196, 197, 205
Winchester 166, 167
wine 9, 17, 24–9, 34, 35, 64, 65–71, 73, 89–93, 101, 133–4, 172–3, 175–7, 206, 221–3, 227, 229, 232
   carriage of 183–7
   suppliers of 194, 196, 197, 201–6, 219
Wolviston 140, 152–3, 198
Woodifield family 205
wool 9, 10, 22, 202
woollen cloth 118, 119, 121, 123, 131, 132, 174

Yarm 10
York 8, 10, 11, 12, 132, 149, 150, 159, 167, 172, 173, 174, 175, 182, 183, 185, 206, 213, 214, 215, 228
Yorkshire 8, 109, 150

zintar 60